Step In, Step Up

EMPOWERING WOMEN *for the* **School Leadership Journey**

JANE A. G. KISE   BARBARA K. WATTERSTON

Solution Tree | Press
a division of
Solution Tree

555 North Morton Street
Bloomington, IN 47404
800.733.6786 (toll free) / 812.336.7700
FAX: 812.336.7790

email: info@SolutionTree.com
SolutionTree.com

Visit **go.SolutionTree.com/leadership** to download the free reproducibles in this book.

Printed in the United States of America

Library of Congress Cataloging-in-Publication Data

Names: Kise, Jane A. G., author. | Watterston, Barbara K., 1960- author.
Title: Step in, step up : empowering women for the school leadership journey
   / Jane A.G. Kise and Barbara K. Watterston.
Description: Bloomington, IN : Solution Tree Press, 2019. | Includes
   bibliographical references and index.
Identifiers: LCCN 2018042850 | ISBN 9781943874309 (perfect bound)
Subjects: LCSH: Women school administrators. | Women in education. |
   Educational leadership.
Classification: LCC LB2831.8 .K57 2019 | DDC 370.82--dc23 LC record available at https://lccn.loc.
gov/2018042850

Solution Tree
Jeffrey C. Jones, CEO
Edmund M. Ackerman, President

Solution Tree Press
President and Publisher: Douglas M. Rife
Associate Publisher: Sarah Payne-Mills
Art Director: Rian Anderson
Managing Production Editor: Kendra Slayton
Senior Production Editor: Christine Hood
Senior Editor: Amy Rubenstein
Copy Editor: Jessi Finn
Proofreader: Evie Madsen
Text and Cover Designer: Laura Cox
Compositor: Abigail Bowen
Editorial Assistant: Sarah Ludwig

ACKNOWLEDGMENTS

For two very special younger women leaders in Jane's life, Mari and Lynn. And for two significant women in Barbara's life, her mother Grace and her daughter Emma.

Working together on this project while based in two far-flung countries means that our understanding of women in leadership benefitted from a wide network of voices from around the world.

First and foremost, we thank all the women who have attended conference sessions and programs on women in school leadership for sharing their thoughts, experiences, concerns, and suggestions for these pages. The other faculty members at the first Australian conference on this topic deserve special acknowledgment for helping to shape our thinking: Tonia Flanagan, Janelle Wills, and Dr. Lyn Sharratt.

We also want to thank the women who shared their stories of leadership with us for this book: Jennifer Abrams, Linda Douglas, Cassandra Erkens, Karen Gayle, Stacie Hansel, Joellen Killion, Annette Rome, Beth Russell, Dr. Lyn Sharratt, Lucy West, and Josephine Wise. Special thanks to our Hawaiian aunties, Trinidad Hunt and Lynne Truair, for their guidance on developing a leadership philosophy.

Gavin Grift of Solution Tree Australia originally introduced us to each other and encouraged this writing project, a clear example of how men and women can work together to encourage more women to step in and step up.

Solution Tree Press would like to thank the following reviewers:

Lorrie Hulbert
Principal
Floyd L. Bell Elementary
Windsor, New York

Lyn Turnell
Assistant Principal
Etowah High School
Woodstock, Georgia

Melani Mouse
Assistant Superintendent
  of Academic Services
Putnam City Schools
Oklahoma City, Oklahoma

Visit **go.SolutionTree.com/leadership** to download the free reproducibles in this book.

TABLE OF CONTENTS

Reproducible pages are in italics.

ABOUT THE AUTHORS

J<!-- -->**ane A. G. Kise, EdD,** is the author of more than twenty-five books and an organizational consultant with extensive experience in leadership development and executive coaching, instructional coaching, and differentiated instruction. She is considered a worldwide expert in Jungian type and its impact on leadership and education. She works with schools and businesses, facilitating the creation of environments where everyone—leaders, teachers, and students—is able to flourish.

Jane trains educators around the world on coaching, collaborative practices, effective change processes, and differentiated instruction, especially in mathematics. A frequent conference keynote speaker, she has spoken at education conferences and type conferences across the United States and in Europe, Saudi Arabia, Australia, and New Zealand. Jane has also written articles for several magazines and has received awards for her differentiated coaching research.

Jane teaches doctoral courses in educational leadership at the University of St. Thomas and is a past faculty member of the Center for Applications of Psychological Type. She also served as president of the Association for Psychological Type International.

Jane holds a master of business administration from the Carlson School of Management and a doctorate in educational leadership from the University of St. Thomas. She is certified in neuroscience and Jungian personality; is qualified to use Myers–Briggs Type Indicator (MBTI®) Steps I, II, and III as an MBTI Master Practitioner; and is certified in emotional intelligence instruments, Hogan assessments, and leadership 360 tools.

To learn more about Jane's work, visit www.janekise.com.

Barbara K. Watterston, EdD, has extensive experience in education and has held a number of school and executive leadership positions across Australia within the education and not-for-profit community sectors. She specializes in facilitation and research focused on the design and delivery of professional learning programs to develop, enhance, and promote the work of the education profession—in particular school and system leadership to ensure learning for all.

Barbara's Australian and international research, consultancy, coaching, and speaking engagements center on leadership development that emphasizes the impact of high-quality leadership on student learning. Her research report, *Insights: Environmental Scan—Principal Preparation Programs,* contributed to five major Australian recommendations for preparing future school leaders.

Barbara's advocacy for women in leadership was fueled by the lack of representation of women in leadership roles. Together with the importance of enriching a more inclusive perspective of leadership, she saw this as missing out on the incredible potential of women to influence and positively impact reforms and outcomes. She also found that a significant component to enabling greater diversity meant women letting go of some of their own self-imposed barriers. Barbara's doctoral thesis focused on gender, leadership, and learning, which informed her contribution as co-editor of the book *Women in School Leadership: Journeys to Success.*

Barbara has been recognized for her contributions to leadership and professional learning. She was the inaugural recipient of the Women of Achievement Award (Western Australia, 2005), is an Honorary Fellow of the Melbourne Graduate School of Education, and is a National Fellow of the Australian Council for Educational Leaders. Her expertise is regularly sought out to contribute in an advisory capacity as a member of numerous university, departmental, school, and professional boards.

Her Australian and international projects include emerging, executive, and system leadership programs. She has a special interest in the links between leadership sustainability, well-being, and impact on performance.

To connect with Barbara, follow @BarbKW on Twitter.

To book Jane A. G. Kise or Barbara K. Watterston for professional development, contact pd@SolutionTree.com.

THE *WHY* AND *HOW* OF WOMEN'S LEADERSHIP JOURNEY

Women in educational leadership—What does that mean to you? Women have incredible potential to bring about change in the world of education if they step up to lead at all levels. Yet, grasping how to make the valuable contributions they envision—by influencing others, empowering others, and commanding attention with self-assurance and presence—challenges many women globally, and with whom we have had the privilege to work.

Perhaps you're reading this because you're ready to step up. Or, perhaps you have someone telling you, "You'd make a great teacher leader [. . . principal . . . curriculum director . . .]." Or, perhaps you've already stepped into school leadership and you're wondering how other women navigate this terrain that men once exclusively navigated—and that still often seems colored with overtones from that era. At all these stages, we find women asking, "Do I truly wish to lead?"

If you hesitate to lead because you find the responsibilities of leadership rather daunting, take heart that women we have spoken with who are already on that journey unanimously tell us that they find the rewards worth it, especially the positive impact they have on students. If you hesitate because you wonder if you're cut out to become a leader, know that we'll guide you through creating a plan for your own development as a leader.

If, however, you hesitate to lead because you worry that others might see you as too ambitious, eager for control, or some other negative definition or view of power, we'd like to help you reframe that thinking right now.

Leadership and Power

We became acutely aware of women's uneasiness with power at the 2016 Women in Education Leadership conference in Australia. To most people, leadership and power are intertwined. As we facilitated sessions at the conference, we clearly saw that many attendees connected power with abuse of power, or with ego and self-aggrandizement. Women saw having power as a negative. We heard the following comments and the same sentiments at other similar events.

- "I don't tell anyone I'm a school principal. I don't want to put on airs that I'm more important than others at the school."

- "I keep my voice soft and my comments in a questioning mode. I don't want to be seen as aggressive."

- "No one likes a female who speaks her mind."

Can you imagine a man saying, "No one likes a man who speaks his mind," or "I never tell anyone I'm the school head"? We can't, but we've certainly seen women regularly criticized for leading "like a man."

With these concerns, it shouldn't come as a surprise that women are underrepresented in positions of power. However, how can you influence people so they view women who engage in high-impact leadership behaviors—sharing ideas, adding to collective wisdom, guiding a vision, and encouraging a shared purpose—as competent, rather than . . . well, you've heard the labels! These leadership behaviors aren't wrong; rather, people have inadequate and incomplete definitions of *power*.

Mary Beard (2017), professor of classics at Cambridge University, captures the problematic big picture of why women struggle to lead: "We have no template for what a powerful woman looks like, except that she looks rather like a man" (p. 54). And, she offers a solution: "If women are not perceived to be fully within the structures of power, surely it is power that we need to redefine rather than women?" (Beard, 2017, p. 83). She suggests separating power and prestige and including the collaborative power of followers in the definition. Not *power over* but *power with* sums up her message.

> Power . . . is not an end in itself, but is an instrument that must be used toward an end.
>
> —Jeane Kirkpatrick (1926–2006), first female U.S. ambassador to the United Nations

We agree that *power with* resonates with archetypal feminine values, such as behaving cooperatively and having empathy—those values and characteristics that, through millennia and across cultures, people have connected more with women than with men. However, striving for *power with* ignores the upside of positional power—the *power to* influence what will be done, when, in what ways, and by whom—that it can provide. Leaders, and especially women leaders, need to identify the impact they wish to have and where they might make it happen. And for women in education, this is the moral imperative of their *why*—for students to learn and flourish. To have an impact requires clarity of vision and courage.

What would you like to have the *power to* accomplish in education?

 WORDS FROM A LEADER

Women have learned to turn *power* into *empowerment*. They get the urgent work done. Women know the power of collective leadership through experience and do not find power over others a satisfactory way of working. Women have learned to listen carefully, critique options, and meaningfully integrate a variety of options as they lead change—often in small, subtle, and not-so-overt ways. When women use *power with* and not *power over*, new directions emerge. Often other voices from the margins feel empowered to make decisions alongside their women leaders. The strength is that women leaders see power as multidirectional and multidimensional. They embrace *co-* in collaborative leadership. *Co-learning*, *co-leading*, and *co-laboring* are three words for us all to live by. (Dr. Lyn Sharratt, Canadian teacher, principal, superintendent, and researcher, personal communication, April 12, 2018)

The *Why* of This Book

Why does this book focus on women? Don't men need to know these things too? Yes, they do. The path to effective leadership shouldn't create a male-female dichotomy, but in many ways, the masculine path to effective leadership differs from the feminine path, with men generally taking a more direct and intentional approach to the journey. As you explore our research, theory, and practice, you will see that women face more barriers and different challenges than men. The existing gaps in gendered paths to leadership mean that talent falls through the cracks. And education needs that talent—both because it needs great leadership and because research confirms that women lead in a different way that positively influences organizational success. In this book, we'll apply that research to what might blossom in education if it has more female leaders.

We need the best women and the best men in leadership because the impact that school leadership has on student outcomes is second only to that of teaching

(Leithwood, Louis, Anderson, & Wahlstrom, 2004). Schools don't become high performing in the absence of great leadership. Thus, schools need all the great leaders they can get—yet, in a female-dominated workforce, women remain underrepresented in senior educational leadership positions.

At the heart of our *why* for writing this book, we dream that the gender of those embarking on the school leadership journey will someday no longer influence their willingness or success—ultimately, a world where gender has no influence on whether students aspire to become educators, education leaders, or leaders in any other field. But we simply aren't there yet. Unconscious bias and the demands of balancing career with other commitments still prevent many women from achieving their leadership potential. In this book, we will delve into the barriers women face in the leadership journey through the ways in which they position themselves as leaders, how limiting notions of gender affect ambition and expectations, how others see women, and how women see themselves.

We need women in educational leadership with *power to* bring what people have historically seen as feminine wisdom to the world of education, where policies and practices have long stayed within the domain of men. We do not mean to suggest that the masculine approach is somehow wrong, but rather, that it remains incomplete without feminine wisdom contributing to more complex, nuanced, and holistic definitions of *power* and *leadership*.

We have both personally experienced gender bias. However, as we've listened to other women, gathered stories, and facilitated discussions around barriers that affect women who aspire to influence and lead others toward needed change, we've realized that we as white women face challenges that are the final, not the first, hurdle for many.

Imagine being an attorney of African American heritage who also holds a doctorate. You walk up to a registration table at a continuing education event for lawyers. The registrar barely glances at your business attire and says, "This is where the attendees check in, not the service staff, honey." This happened to one of Jane's colleagues, who told her, "I don't ever get to the sexism barrier, because the racism barrier still looms too large."

If you move in diverse circles, you've no doubt heard too many of these stories. We wish to acknowledge that other women face multiple barriers besides gender: racial prejudices, sexual orientation prejudices, religious prejudices, and mental health stigmas, to name just a few. We also want to acknowledge that these barriers cause pain and problems beyond those that women generally face on the path to impactful leadership.

The scope of this book simply cannot do justice to describing and supporting women in overcoming all these other barriers. As societies struggle to acknowledge—let alone confront and remedy—these prejudices, we hope that you can gain some wisdom from the school leadership journey as we describe it from a gender perspective.

The *How* of This Book

So, what do we want for you? As you read this book and interact with the suggested exercises and reflection activities, we want you to unleash *your* potential. We have included stories from our experiences and from other women—vivid accounts of their lived experiences and lessons, which they willingly shared with us with the hope of inspiring you to step into leadership. These stories, together with quotes from other successful women outside education, highlight the interconnectedness of our challenges and experiences as women and how we tacitly support, motivate, and empower each other no matter where we are. For this, we give them our heartfelt thanks.

We hope that through our research and observations on leadership, gender, and education, you'll find guidance for reflecting on your leadership identity—and, as a result, acknowledge and energize your strengths, gifts, and talents to step up as the leader you want to be.

We also hope this book will help you embrace pursuing leadership as a way to gain *power to*. No doubt women are more than their gender, but gender affects the way many women view leadership opportunities (Wise, 2018). Through the generous contributions of courageous, brilliant, wise, wonderful, and capable women who have successfully transitioned to leadership, you will see that while the road is paved with highs and lows, these ups and downs are part of life. You can make your identity as a leader all-encompassing, not separate from but aligned with who you are as a woman, how you live, what you find important, and the way you engage in opportunities to grow, learn, and lead.

Chapter Overview

Each chapter begins with guiding questions. We hope that you will take a moment to reflect on these questions before delving into the content. What do you already know about the topic? What messages have you heard? What thoughts do the questions bring to mind? Think of these guiding questions as a way to frame the ideas in each chapter. For example, consider the following questions to guide your thinking about these introductory pages.

GUIDING QUESTIONS

- Why focus on women in leadership?
- How might you benefit from leadership programs designed specifically for women?
- How do perceptions of power and position affect women as they contemplate becoming school leaders?

In chapters 1 and 2, we will explore what we know about women in leadership and what keeps them from becoming leaders with *power to*. These chapters provide context for the heart of our *why*—the research, statistics, and moral imperatives that point to why we need more women in educational leadership. In the chapters that follow, perhaps you'll find inspiration for stepping into leadership. And, you might find the answers you need when others ask, "Can't we set gender aside and just seek the best leaders?"

Chapter 3 guides you in finding time to undertake this important leadership journey, and in chapter 4, you'll realize why the leadership journey could have value for you. In chapters 5–8, you will examine your strengths, skills, and beliefs, identifying how to use them to become the leader you wish to be. Chapters 9–11 provide grounding in communicating as a female leader, having hard conversations, proactively seeking out opportunities for inspiration and support, and helping other women develop these crucial ways of leading. Finally, in chapter 12, you'll pull it all together in a plan for continuing this journey. The end of every chapter offers a Step in for Further Reflection section. You may use these activities to reflect on the ideas, strategies, and concepts presented in each chapter.

This isn't a book on instructional leadership skills, although working with the practical tools in these chapters may improve your capacity to foster teachers' professional growth. It also isn't a book on improving visioning or strategizing or using data to inform decisions—although you may gain new understandings of your strengths and challenges and what to do about them regarding these leadership responsibilities. Instead, these pages are about your own development into the wisest leader you can be, embracing the unique contributions that the feminine brings to personal leadership development and to education as a whole.

How to Get the Most From These Pages

As kindred spirits and passionate educators from Minneapolis, Minnesota, and Melbourne, Australia, we formed our partnership for this book after sharing the stage as keynote speakers at a Women in Education Leadership conference in Australia. We trust that our collaboration has produced a practical guide to engaging, encouraging, and supporting women on their leadership journey.

This journey includes the following.

- Finding your *why*—your motivation for the long haul of educational leadership

- Equipping yourself to navigate the gender-specific barriers women still face and ones that women, more than men, create for themselves

- Understanding your most effective leadership style and where you might need to adjust or develop key leadership skills (such as helping a team productively use emotions or finding your voice so you can speak up effectively when necessary)

Preparing as a leader involves an ongoing, organic process—a journey—not a one-time course or credential program. We hope this book will not just help you get started but also serve as a resource in the years ahead. Before you read on, we have a few suggestions for making the most of this book.

- **Commit to a twelve-week journey:** While we would find it flattering if you stayed up late reading our book, we envision readers setting aside some time each week for twelve weeks to read a chapter and respond to the chapter's various questions and exercises.

- **Find a partner, or two or three, for the journey:** Consider inviting other women who already aspire to leadership as well as those who haven't determined if it's the right path for them. Meet virtually or in person every week or two to discuss your responses to the questions and activities at the end of each chapter.

- **Keep a journal so you can revisit your thoughts:** In chapter 12 (page 203), we ask that you use your reflections to identify a few ideas for your next steps. A journal of written responses will come in handy. Don't underestimate the cognitive, creative, and emotional benefits of writing by hand—literally, the power of the pen. If you are pressed for time, use the audio memo app on your phone to record your responses.

As you begin, ponder: What does power mean to you? How does your definition help or hinder your leadership aspirations? Know that at every step in preparing these pages, we've strived to ensure that you will like who you become as you exercise that power.

CHAPTER 1

ENGAGING WOMEN IN SCHOOL LEADERSHIP

GUIDING QUESTIONS

- Does the gender of a leader make a difference in how he or she leads? If so, does the gender difference matter? Why or why not?

- Can you think of ways that gender has influenced your approach to leadership?

Teaching is arguably one of the world's most important professions, as it influences students' future. High-quality leadership comes second only to teaching in improving student learning (Louis, Leithwood, Wahlstrom, & Anderson, 2010). After all, you'd have a hard time finding a single school where student achievement improved in the absence of talented leadership. Australia and the United States, like many countries, face the major challenge of identifying, attracting, and developing the next generation of school leaders. While yes, these countries have the separate issue of encouraging more men to embrace the teaching profession, they need to ensure that women embrace leadership as a desirable future.

Take a moment to envision school leadership. Draw a picture or diagram if you wish. Who appears in the picture? What are they doing? How might you describe your visualization? What might you categorize as more masculine or feminine? Does the picture depict effective school leadership regardless of gender? Does gender matter to the picture?

What messages do you receive subtly and not so subtly? Do the images depict equity in school leadership? Let's turn to one of society's go-to information sources—Google—to see how people view school leadership.

In 2018, we did an online image search for *teacher*. The top sixteen images that this search generated featured 70 percent female teachers and exceedingly traditional teaching methods grounded in the "chalk and talk" era of 20th century education. On the same day, an image search for *principal* showed the reverse of the teacher images, with 70 percent of the principals being male. Try it yourself. What images pop up? Most disturbing to us were the depictions of *angry* female principals in the few images the search revealed.

In this chapter, we will examine the existing gender gap in educational leadership, what gender means in leadership, masculine and feminine archetypes, and the practical and the prophetic reasons why we need new leaders, especially female leaders. As you read our case for increasing the percentage of women leaders in education, think not only about how the gender imbalances affect you but also how the image of a leader as male affects the thoughts of girls and boys, parents and community leaders, professors, and everyone else who has a stake in what happens in schools.

If you're already convinced that more women need to step up to educational leadership, then consider this chapter a resource for facts you might need to convince others of the importance of engaging more women in the practical leadership development journey.

Gender Archetypes, Stereotypes, and Women in Leadership

Our discussions of masculinity and femininity focus not on individual men and women but on the *archetypes* that have evolved in Western cultures. Think of masculinity and femininity as interdependent sets of values that, over time, need each other.

The masculine lock on how people define leadership goes back centuries. Beard (2017) eloquently describes how deep-seated definitions of proper male and female roles date to at least ancient Greece. She quotes Telemachus in Homer's *The Odyssey*, who tells off his mother Penelope (Odysseus's wife) when she simply asks for a visiting bard to play a different tune for him:

> *Mother, go back up into your quarters, and take up your own work, the loom and the distaff . . . speech will be the business of men, all men, and of me most of all; for mine is the power in the household. (as quoted in Beard, 2017, p. 17)*

Beard (2017) then goes on to describe how speaking in public and the words that define *power* also define *masculinity*:

> *We are dealing with a much more active and loaded exclusion of women from public speech—and one with a much greater impact than we usually acknowledge on our own traditions, conventions and assumptions about the voice of women. What I mean is that public speaking and oratory were not merely things that ancient women didn't do: they were exclusive practices and skills that defined masculinity as a gender. As we saw with Telemachus, to become a man (or at least an elite man) was to claim the right to speak. Public speaking was a—if not the—defining attribute of maleness. Or, to quote a well-known Roman slogan, the elite male citizen could be summed up as vir bonus dicendi peritus, 'a good man, skilled in speaking'. A woman speaking in public was, in most circumstances, by definition not a woman. (p. 17)*

No wonder women who consider stepping up into leadership are often seen as challenging or threatening male archetypes of leadership even today!

Advice abounds on how women can gain leadership credibility by fitting into the masculine culture—how to dress; how to assume the proper postures; how to speak with a deeper, more resonant tone; and so on. However, leadership doesn't need more of the masculine.

Research actually backs up our collective desire to add the feminine to how we lead. John Gerzema and Michael D'Antonio (2013) first asked sixteen thousand people from thirteen countries around the world to classify a list of behavior traits as masculine, feminine, or neither. They then asked a different sixteen thousand people to rate how important they found the same traits to leadership. Across ages, genders, and cultures, people associated feminine traits with their image of an ideal modern leader. None of the identified masculine traits made the top ten, although two gender-neutral ones—collaboration and candidness—did (Gerzema & D'Antonio, 2013). The rest of the top ten featured traits associated with the feminine: humility, patience, empathy, trustworthiness, openness, flexibility, vulnerability, and balance.

Perhaps even more telling, the same research shows that 66 percent of adults, including 66 percent of the men polled, agree with the statement, "The world would be a better place if men thought more like women" (Gerzema & D'Antonio, 2013).

Thus, archetypes arise out of what cultures value. With this explanation, can you see how education systems seem to rely more on masculine values? For example, they over-emphasize standardized, objective testing and don't pay as much attention, especially in accountability measures, to more subjective but equally crucial data such as each student's developmental, social, and emotional needs. Accountability systems need both, don't they? This illustrates the essence of how we use the masculine and feminine archetypes, which we support with research, in these pages.

Leaders need to ensure that they add the feminine to the school leadership world—using *both-and* thinking rather than assuming that either set of values is more important than the other.

However, each person is an individual, so assuming that all people of a given gender have the same traits is *stereotyping*. In chapter 6 (page 99), you will have a chance to consider whether the male or female archetype is more your natural style and what that may mean for leadership development.

THINK ABOUT IT

- Offer some examples of ways people hold school leaders accountable for behaving in humble, patient, empathetic, trustworthy, open, flexible, vulnerable, and balanced ways.

- Offer some examples of opposite traits being the standard (for example, being results driven rather than flexible).

- Because what systems choose to measure often drives behavior and norms, what do your examples say about the current archetype for school leadership?

The Gender Gap in Educational Leadership

Women hold more school administrative positions than they did in the 1980s, so some might question whether schools need to pay attention to gender. Let's look at the facts.

Consider the following snapshot of statistics across the United States, Australia, and the United Kingdom.

- In the United States, in the 1980s, only about 25 percent of school principals were female (National Center for Education Statistics, 2016). In 2017, while about 75 percent of teachers were female, a little over half of principals were male, and the percentage of male principals was higher at the secondary level (National Center for Education Statistics, 2017).

- Also in the United States, as of 2015, only about 27 percent of school superintendents were female, up from 7 percent in 1992 (American Association of School Administrators, 2015). Also, female superintendents have higher mean and median ages than male superintendents. And, they appear to make more sacrifices in their personal lives. Significantly fewer female superintendents report being married or partnered, and female superintendents also report a higher divorce rate. The data suggest the price women might pay for their career choices:

  > Female respondents report slightly lower satisfac-
  > tion with their career choice; more than two percent
  > more female than male respondents say they would
  > not choose the superintendency again. (American
  > Association of School Administrators, 2015)

- In Australia, across the three schooling sectors—(1) government, (2) Catholic, and (3) independent schools—some notable changes have occurred, from increasing to stalling and decreasing representation, from 2006 to 2018 (McKenzie, Weldon, Rowley, Murphy, & McMillan, 2014).

  ○ Overall, while 57 percent of upper-secondary teachers are women, only 39 percent of principals are women. In the primary sector, 81 percent of teachers are women, while 57.5 percent of principals are women.

  ○ Independent schools have the lowest proportion of women in leadership roles. In government and Catholic schools, the percentage of women in leadership, including the principalship, continues to increase.

  ○ Note that while males still outnumber females in the principalship, the gap widens when you look just at leaders over age 55 and narrows for younger age cohorts—a heartening trend.

  ○ In 2013, less than 10 percent of primary and secondary teachers intended to apply for a principal, deputy, or vice principal position in the next three years. Even within this small percentage, women still had lower leadership aspirations than men—the percentage comprised 24 percent men and 6 percent women at the primary level, versus 10 percent men and 6 percent women at the secondary level.

  ○ Women in assistant or deputy principal roles still show less interest than men in principalships.

○ Also, 73 percent of male teachers report having an uninterrupted career (for example, not taking unpaid leave or relinquishing positions) in schools, compared with 46 percent of female teachers.

- In the United Kingdom, 90 percent of primary school teachers are female, compared with 70 percent of principals. In secondary schools, 63 percent of teachers are female, compared with 39 percent of principals—figures that have changed very little since these data were collected for the first time in 2010. An even wider gender gap, though, exists for many cultural minorities. Further, while the gender pay gap widens with seniority, women have lower median salaries than men at all levels (Department for Education, 2017).

Across Organisation for Economic Co-operation and Development (OECD) countries, females compose 70 percent or more of the teaching staff—though the gender distribution of school leadership staff does not reflect the gender mix among teachers. For example:

> While the proportion of male teachers in primary schools is relatively small in many countries, there is an over-representation of male principals. This suggests that male teachers tend to be promoted to principal positions more often than female teachers, although most of them are recruited from the ranks of teachers who are mostly women. (OECD, 2018, p. 402)

Web searches reveal similar statistics in many other countries. The leadership gender gap exists in education, as it does in so many other fields.

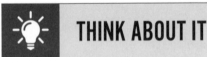

THINK ABOUT IT

Does anything surprise you about these statistics? If you were in charge of your education system, what would you wish to see change the next time such statistics are generated? What actions might you take to foster progress toward those changes?

This imbalance replicates in higher education, too. In higher education, men remain four times more likely than women to serve in the most powerful positions (Robinson, Shakeshaft, Newcomb, & Grogan, 2017). Researchers Katherine Cumings Mansfield,

Anjalé Welton, Pei-Ling Lee, and Michelle D. Young (2010), who have explored the lived experiences of female educational leadership doctoral students, describe progress for gender equity as glacial. In the United States, female professors continue to earn less, obtain promotions more slowly, and struggle with heavier teaching and service loads than male professors (Mansfield et al., 2010).

In political positions worldwide—where most education policy is formed—women hold less than one-third of the seats in the lower houses of national legislature (OECD, 2017). In 2018, the U.S. Senate had an all-time high of twenty-two female senators of one hundred total senators (Abramson, 2018). And, while a record number of women were elected to the U.S. House of Representatives in 2018, they still make up less than a quarter of the House (Jordan, 2018).

> When I'm sometimes asked when will there be enough [women on the Supreme Court], and I say when there are nine, people are shocked. But there'd been nine men, and nobody's ever raised a question about that.
>
> **—Ruth Bader Ginsburg,**
> U.S. Supreme Court justice

In summary, every way you look at it, women have plenty of room to increase their influence regarding what happens in schools.

Trends in Gender and Leadership

Does gender really matter in good leadership, or do the qualities of good leaders transcend gender? Do we need more women in educational leadership? After all, whatever a woman's motivations for pursuing a leadership position, neither the path nor the work is easy.

Gender does matter. Greatly. In this section, we will explore why closing this gender gap in school leadership is absolutely vital. What does gender have to do with leadership? A whole lot if you consider trends in pop culture, research, and statistics. Trending topics and issues include the following.

- Gender equality
- Sexism
- Pay parity
- The Me Too movement, which has prompted a long-overdue focus on sexual harassment
- The social and economic impacts of girls' access to education worldwide

- Stereotypes about women leaders and the discrimination they face—not just from men but also from other women
- How to sort biological and brain-based gender differences from the gender differences that culture produces

Not paying attention to gender's impact on leadership has perpetuated many of these issues, the consequences of which we have only begun to comprehend and remedy. Further, it has become increasingly clear that the barriers women face actually hurt all genders. Instead of creating a binary distinction between female and male leaders, we hope to create understanding of how this distinction influences choices and how effective leadership requires drawing on the best of both.

 THINK ABOUT IT

While the #MeToo hashtag may seem like a phenomenon that arose in 2017 from high-profile abuse cases, Tarana Burke founded the Me Too movement in 2006 to empower women, especially young and vulnerable women, through empathy. Burke (2018) states that the #MeToo conversation has expanded to focus on determining the best ways to hold perpetrators of abuse responsible and stop cycles of abuse. The Me Too movement's growth shows that needed conversations may take a decade or more to finally grow and bear fruit.

It's easy to be both encouraged and discouraged, given the relatively short time we have been discussing the issue compared to how long it has been an issue; time and persistent focus are required. What changes have you observed as a result of the Me Too movement in the media, in marketing, and in your workplace? What impact has the message of the movement had on your conversations with women? With men? How does it inform discussions about gender and expectations with your students?

Gender is not the same as sex, which describes biological and physical male and female differences. Gender, a nonbinary social construct, relates to the social and cultural behaviors we attach to people; as we discuss further in chapter 9 (page 153), it is widely acknowledged that greater variation occurs within the genders than between them. For the context of this book, we view the feminine and masculine constructions as widely as possible.

Our interest in influencing more women to take on leadership roles took root in our first work experiences, with Jane starting out in the archetypal male world of finance and Barbara delving into research on how women's lives differ from men's from the start of her broad career in education and leadership.

A Word From Barbara

Through the lens of my Portapak (a 1978 version of a GoPro camera), I learned some visceral lessons about gender, equity, and power. During my first year in university, my eighteen-year-old self wanted to investigate and share the stories of women and children who stayed in what were called women's refuge homes. These homes gave women and children a safe haven from domestic violence—then a concept that people talked about in hushed tones—if acknowledged at all.

The camera lens created a space for me to observe and engage in others' lived experiences. I aimed to put the spotlight on a significant social issue that needed attention and whose powerless victims needed greater access to quality support. Finally, I presented what I filmed to my class. Viewing the heart-wrenching and challenging experiences of the women, who articulated their vulnerability with dignity and generosity, we were rendered silent in our inner turmoil—first, at the injustice, and second, at our own dilemma of what we could or should do.

One challenging insight was that people seem to blame the victim for being in a situation of violence, and that domestic abuse was somehow lesser than similar abuses that occur outside the home. Perpetrators were not held to account and certainly saw their power over their partners as a right in their domestic partnership.

In the 21st century, topics around gender equity, pay equality, violence against women, and the motherhood penalty trend in the media. Daily commentary and research illuminate stereotyping and unconscious bias as significant barriers to recognizing female talent that undermine career advancement.

Do women have to make hard choices to get ahead, meaning does being a woman set you back and having a family stunt your career? Limiting notions of gender can devalue, obstruct, and confine women and men. In a wide variety of job-specific and cultural contexts, we observe male leadership identified as the norm. My own reflection was not to doubt myself, and to challenge limiting notions of gender, as a woman and a potential leader.

Practical and Prophetic Reasons to Have More Women Leaders

Education needs female leaders for four reasons, both practical and prophetic. The first two reasons are practical, revolving around tapping into all the available talent pool and balancing the many unbalanced education policies. The other two reasons are prophetic—in the sense of a key definition of that term. While your mind might skip to visions of the future, consider the more useful definition of *prophesying* as projecting what will happen based on what is happening. Thus, prophesying answers the following two prompts.

1.   If things continue as they have gone in education, this is what will come to be . . .

2.   If things change, and more women step up as school leaders, these are the possibilities that will come to be . . .

The four reasons we need more women in education are as follows.

1.   Practically, we need to remove gender-specific leadership barriers and consider all the available talent pool.

2.   Practically, we need a better balance in the mix of values that drive education decisions.

3.   Prophetically, we need a new vision of school leadership.

4.   Prophetically, girls, and the women we might mentor, need to see themselves as future leaders.

In the next four sections, we'll look at research-based reasons that have prevented women from entering school leadership and illustrate the previous four reasons why education needs more female leaders. And, we'll look at the impact that more female leaders might have on the next generation, when hopefully a Google search for leadership images will produce very different results than we described at the beginning of this chapter (page 9). The value and importance of the feminist perspective embraces equity for all, irrespective of gender, sexual orientation, race, economic status, and nationality. We still have a long way to go to reach that.

> I don't know why people are so reluctant to say they're feminists. Maybe some women just don't care. But how could it be any more obvious that we still live in a patriarchal world when feminism is a bad word?
>
> —Ellen Page,
> Canadian actor

An Unbiased View of Women, Who Make Up Half the Talent Pool

Why do public and private leadership globally have such a dearth of female representation? Understanding the answers to this question is crucial to ensuring we are finding qualified candidates of all genders.

In their work in schools and systems across Australia, Barbara and her partner continue to observe that women take a more circumstantial than intentional path to school leadership than men (Watterston & Watterston, 2010). Men begin to map a path toward a principalship earlier in their careers and then intentionally pursue that path. Many factors might influence these differences, from the need to balance work and family demands, devotion to classroom teaching or lack of confidence to fulfill the role, to unconscious biases in expectations of male and female leaders, workplace flexibility, or recruitment practices. Whether these are personal or systemic barriers or biases, they contribute to the percentage of women who aspire to take formal leadership roles.

In our work with women who choose to pursue educational leadership, they consistently share how they experience a far different reality than men who travel the same path. Developing as a leader is about choices. Do women have to make harder choices to unleash their leadership potential and nurture their talents and skills? Do we attempt to force female life cycles into a male career model, which will not work now nor in the future (Broderick, 2009)? Are organizations examining the policies that limit the choices women have? Are they looking for the unconscious biases that render leadership potential invisible based on gender?

These biases aren't really disappearing. *The Pursuit of Gender Equality: An Uphill Battle* (OECD, 2017) highlights that OECD countries have made little progress since the 2012 OECD report *Closing the Gender Gap: Act Now*. Not only have women faced these same issues for decades, but progress has stagnated. Here, Maisie Holder (2017) summarizes seven key findings from the 2017 OECD report:

1. *Women in OECD countries leave school with better qualifications than young men, but they are less likely to study in the higher earning STEM-related fields.*

2. *In every OECD country, women are still less likely than men to engage in paid work. When women do work, they are more likely to do it on a part-time basis.*

3. *Women continue to earn less than men. The median female worker earns almost 15% less than her male counterpart—a rate that has barely changed since 2010.*

4. *Gender gaps tend to increase with age, reflecting the crucial role that parenthood plays in gender equality. Much more than fatherhood, motherhood typically has sizable negative effects on workforce participation, pay and career advancement.*

5. *Women are underrepresented in political office, holding less than one-third of seats in lower houses of national legislatures, on average, in the OECD.*

6. *Countries need to invest in female leadership opportunities through for example mentoring opportunities and network supports.*

7. *Male role models in senior management need to drive the change in gender stereotypes and norms that continue to hamper women's access to leadership.*

Thus, practices and policies keep women from considering the leadership path. However, when women manage to reach higher and higher levels of leadership responsibility, whether in education or in other sectors, very real biases make it difficult for them to find equal footing with the men around them.

Let's look closely at just one of the biggest dilemmas most women face (that men simply do not): the double bind. Leaders are expected to be tough, and so are men. Thus, they cannot face the double bind. Women, on the other hand, often face criticism for being too tough or too soft. The Catalyst (2007) report *The Double-Bind Dilemma for Women in Leadership: Damned If You Do, Doomed If You Don't* explores gender stereotypes that create predicaments for female leaders. Sponsored by IBM, it involved surveys and in-depth interviews with working women and women leaders. People evaluate female leaders against a masculine leadership style, creating perception barriers regardless of how women behave or perform. This dilemma has the potential to undermine women's leadership. The double bind includes the following three predicaments (Catalyst, 2007).

1. **Extreme perceptions:** People perceive women leaders as too soft or too tough but never just right.

2. **A high competence threshold:** Women leaders face higher standards and lower rewards than men leaders.

3. **A tendency to be seen as competent or likable:** People perceive women leaders as competent or liked, but rarely both.

Almost everywhere you look, the workplace is skewed in favor of men. Women remain underrepresented in venture capital firms; music executive positions; movies, both on screen and in behind-the-scenes roles, such as director; high-profile professional athletics; and, as mentioned previously, politics. And even if successful, the lack of support and challenges founded in sexism can range from an irritation to the extreme.

> **Women belong in all places where decisions are being made. . . . It shouldn't be that women are the exception.**
>
> **—Ruth Bader Ginsburg,**
> U.S. Supreme Court justice

In 2012, when Australia's first female prime minister Julia Gillard made her now famous misogyny speech in the House of Representatives, she shared a fifteen-minute riposte to the misogyny to which she had been subjected by the opposition and the press since taking over as prime minister in 2010 (Gordon, 2018). With more than three million views on YouTube, the speech had a significant impact, resonating with women and men around the world.

Politics continues to provide stark examples of the lack of progess on gender inclusivity and engaging the perspectives of women. For example, on March 23, 2017, in the White House, members of the House Freedom Caucus—all men—decided the fate of maternity coverage in health care plans (Terkel, 2017). The picture that Vice President Mike Pence tweeted of men sitting at a table discussing women's health care was heavily shared online and became a meme.

At the same time, examples of positive progress for the voices of women in positions of power and influence are present as well. When it comes to female political power, the Queensland government in Australia is smashing the glass barriers. On February 13, 2017, the re-elected government was sworn in with fifty-fifty female-to-male representation and a significant number of women in senior ministerial roles (Caldwell, 2018). A news photo of the labor caucus stood out because of the even ratio and the inclusion of lawmakers of both genders holding their infants.

Reflect on these examples and how they create messages around power and voice. As educators, what messages will our students receive?

How many talented leaders do workplaces stymie because these biases and barriers continue to determine who "looks like" a leader? Our first reason for having more women in leadership focuses on recognizing and calling out these biases and barriers, because shining a light on hidden talent in all its diversity will find leaders who far more represent the world in which they live.

A Better Balance of What People Value in Education

Another practical reason that education needs more women in leadership involves an overemphasis in schools on certain priorities to the detriment of equally important priorities traditionally more connected with the feminine. Since the late 1990s, schools have emphasized academic achievement and standardized testing in reading and mathematics, leading to less emphasis on the arts, social studies, and physical education. Teacher accountability and evaluation systems have become commonplace. While these measures are meant to close achievement gaps among different student groups, U.S. schools saw no significant improvement for twelfth-grade high school students as a result of these measures between 2005 and 2015 (The Nation's Report Card, 2018). And levels of teacher and student engagement and satisfaction decreased.

Students who report that they feel engaged at school will more likely do well and pursue postsecondary education. The Gallup (2016) Student Poll reports that about 74 percent of fifth graders in the United States find school engaging. However, 34 percent of twelfth graders feel engaged at school, compared with 40 percent in 2011. Further, 32 percent of twelfth graders are actively disengaged, meaning they are ten times more likely to get poor grades and have less hope about their future. Similar figures are noted in Australia, where engagement levels decrease as students become older (Subban, 2016). This has implications not only for progress but also for graduation rates and, ultimately, quality of life.

Unsurprisingly, disengagement remedies involve high levels of teacher efficacy together with high expectations for student progress, with a personalized, purposeful, whole-person approach to learning—all of which relate to whole-child initiatives such as social and emotional learning, working on adult team dynamics, and so on. These adhere more strongly to the traditionally feminine emphasis on relationships and soft skills rather than only academic outcomes.

Similarly, the growing masculine overemphasis on teacher accountability since 2005 or so correlates with a decrease in teacher engagement—and teachers cannot be at their best if they are not engaged in their work. The 2012 *MetLife Survey of the American Teacher* (Markow & Pieters, 2012) shows that the percentage of teachers satisfied with their jobs dropped from 59 percent in 2009 to 44 percent in 2011. The percentage of teachers planning to leave the profession increased from 17 percent to 29 percent. Further, only about 45 percent felt optimistic that student achievement levels would improve over five years. The results from the Nation's Report Card (2018) bear out the teachers' pessimism.

Estimates of attrition vary widely in Australia (Australian Institute for Teaching and School Leadership [AITSL], 2016). According to the *Staff in Australia's Schools 2013* survey (McKenzie et al., 2014):

5% of primary and 8% of secondary teachers indicated they intended to leave teaching permanently prior to retirement. These figures were slightly higher (7% and 11%) for early career teachers. . . . The two most important reasons for intended early departures were "workload too heavy" and "insufficient recognition and reward."

While we will discuss this in depth in chapter 6 (page 99), the accountability measures that have dominated education policy since the late 1990s reflect the values associated with the masculine archetype—values such as being analytical, objective, and logical. These are strong, worthwhile values, but education remains incomplete without the equally worthwhile values that the feminine archetype encompasses, such as being empathetic, creative, and passionate.

Look at the following quotes from female leaders and educators, and consider how more women in power might bring more balance to how we are currently educating children.

The joy of learning is as indispensable in study as breathing is in running. Where it is lacking there are no real students, but only poor caricatures of apprentices who, at the end of their apprenticeship will not even have a trade (as cited in Weekes, 2007, p. 101).

—*Simone Weil (1909–1943), French social philosopher and activist*

It's not what is poured into a student, but what is planted (as cited in Weekes, 2007, p. 101).

—*Linda Conway, American media scholar*

It has always seemed strange to me that in our endless discussions about education so little stress is laid on the pleasure of becoming an educated person, the enormous interest it adds to life. To be able to be caught up into the world of thought—that is to be educated (as cited in Weekes, 2007, p. 99).

—*Edith Hamilton (1867–1963), American educator,*
translator, and classics scholar

The world is talking about girls' education and there is an impetus for change. . . . The shooting of Malala, the kidnapping of girls by Boko Haram, and the increased evidence of how transformative girls education is . . . Education is about a far more localized service. . . . It's got to be sensitive to culture and context (as cited in Isaac, 2016).

—*Julia Gillard, Australia's first (and only) female prime minister*

You might find equally inspiring quotes about educating the whole child from male individuals. We chose these to describe the essence of what more female voices might add, even though individuals of either gender might hold different values.

Thus, the critical points about how women might influence what is valued in education include the following.

- Education values are out of balance, putting at risk whether both teachers and students can engage wholeheartedly as learners.

- A focus on certain kinds of student achievement and testing correlates with a decline in student and teacher engagement, with no appreciable improvement in student achievement.

- This imbalance and the consequences came about while society emphasized traditionally masculine values of objectivity and measurability, perhaps in part because men were disproportionately represented in governmental and educational leadership positions while decisions that resulted in our current testing and accountability environment were being made.

If women's voices increase, might education begin to shift toward a more balanced approach? Similar shifts happened when women gained increased representation in other fields. Might schools pay more attention to gender issues and holistic considerations if more women enter educational leadership, as has happened in science and medicine when more women enter practice at the highest levels? For example, training doctors in whole-patient care—and measuring how well they do it through surveys and other tools—is becoming commonplace. Only one female need take part on a scientific study team for it to likely include analysis of sex and gender differences (Foley, 2017). Since 2016, in the United States, researchers seeking funding from the National Institute of Health must test new drugs on female as well as male animals before they go to human physical trials (Bischel, 2016). And examinations of gender and racial biases in how and when doctors provide care and manage pain have at last taken place (Foley, 2017).

How many potential solutions to the dilemmas we face in education remain hidden because the women who could formulate them haven't been nurtured to become the leaders they are meant to become? To summarize, to get that better balance of education values, education needs diverse voices and interdependent sets of values that embody the masculine and feminine archetypes.

WORDS FROM A LEADER

One of the barriers I had to navigate as a woman leader was understanding the dynamics of male networks that have dominated decision making in my profession and that indirectly wanted to discredit my voice due to my gender. I did this by finding my voice through being clear about what my vision was and how I would address getting to it, which often was quite different than how a man went about it.

I found that being transparent and honest in my communications, dealing with the emotional content of a message as well as the factual content, was not a negative but allowed a different type of connection. I feel I was able to stand up and have an opinion, but the dynamic of "men knowing best" perpetuated due to the fact that there were so many men in positions of authority of decision making. My self-awareness and self-knowledge allowed me to stand up to bullies and bully behavior in a professional way, and not to be diminished by them. (Beth Russell, retired U.S. middle school principal, personal communication, April 17, 2018)

A New Vision of School Leadership

Prophetically, we need more women as leaders to change what people expect from leaders. We both joined the workforce in the 1980s, and we can't forget the distinguishing fashion of the day: working women wore the "uniform" of power suits with enormous shoulder pads and rather ridiculous variations of the male tie to imitate the powerful male image of leadership and success. Yet in the 21st century, women still receive advice about acting like men at work, from how we dress to how we speak.

As mentioned in the introduction (page 1), Mary Beard (2017) points out, "We have no template for what a powerful woman looks like, except that she looks rather like a man" (p. 54). Let's start creating that template with seven key themes that emphasize how women might help reshape educational leadership.

1. Organizations with a higher percentage of female leaders deliver better financial results, as do those with more diverse teams (Krivkovich, Robinson, Starikova, Valentino, & Yee, 2017). While schools have different metrics, we might see similar results with student outcomes.

2. Women possess certain qualities that will become crucial as the world's pace of change increases. In her book *Own It: The Power of Women at Work*, Sallie Krawcheck (2017) lists these as risk awareness, relationship focus, holistic view of problems, long-term thinking, value of lifelong learning, and focus on meaning and purpose. Consider how school strategic plans might change if these qualities were truly valued.

3. Women's career histories are characteristically relational. They constitute a normal part of a larger and intricate web of interconnected people, in which women tend to make career decisions in relation to their impact on others, most notably family. This weblike way of living may also explain the different way that women's attention activates. As Sally Helgesen and Julie Johnson (2010) discuss in *The Female Vision: Women's Real Power at Work*, attention incorporates what you notice, what you value, and how you connect the dots. They describe women's attention as tending to operate like a radar, scanning the environment, picking up clues, and noticing many different things at once. Men tend to have more laserlike attention, focusing deeply on the matter at hand. Holistic leadership in schools requires using radar, not a laser, to see the impact of policies on multiple facets of the community, not just academics or discipline or other single focuses.

4. Female leaders display more characteristics associated with the *transformational* leadership model; through inspiration and empowerment, they act as positive role models, encouraging initiative and creativity. This would help school environments move away from carrot-and-stick approaches to motivation which have been shown ineffective (Pink, 2010).

5. Some feminine characteristics that make women more effective at stock-market trading than men may also serve schools. Peter Swan (2017) found that over a seventeen-year period, women's more pervasive buy-low and sell-high behavior indicated that they stayed more informed than male traders. They behaved more selectively, had a calmer approach, and took more time to evaluate trades. He surmises, "A female invasion of Wall Street might not only see far more stable markets, but also a far lower likelihood of the next global financial crisis" (Swan, 2017).

6. Having more women in educational leadership may reset the leadership norm and encourage a wider variety of leadership styles. Korn Ferry (2016) has explored how varied leadership styles affect employee engagement and effectiveness perceptions. While it remains true that each person needs to develop a comfortable leadership approach that honors her or his strengths, the most effective style for any leader—male or female—is a function of the people he or she leads and the situation. High-performing leaders have access to a repertoire of leadership styles and adeptly use the right style at the right time. The Korn Ferry Institute (2016) study also finds that women create better performance-driven climates than their male counterparts, using more visionary, affiliative, participative, and coaching leadership styles.

7. Educators should consider what might happen if more women rise to the top positions in educational leadership, given what they already know about female superintendents. In researching the leadership practices of Texas female superintendents, Jessica Garrett-Staib and Amy Burkman (2015) find that female superintendents seem to have strong self-concepts in two leadership areas that have the highest effect on positive institutional leadership outcomes; they "encourage the heart" and "inspire and share vision" (p. 164). In other words, they gain buy-in for organizational vision and motivate others to join in the effort via values and inspiring purpose rather than through positional power or rewards and consequences.

Setting aside for a moment the double-bind problem women face, it is absurd to desire women to act more like men in order to become school leaders. Instead, schools need women—and men—to actively engage in redefining leadership so it includes, as research supports, both masculine *and* feminine values.

Throughout this book, we'll use infinity loop diagrams, such as the one in figure 1.1 (page 28), when we emphasize *both-and*, not *either-or*, thinking about a concept or an issue. Before each value set named (for example, *masculine leadership* and *feminine leadership* in figure 1.1) is a summary of the upside of focusing on those values. And following each is the downside if we only focus on those values, neglecting the others. The infinity loop emphasizes the systems nature of interconnectedness. An ongoing tension exists between each side, requiring conscious thought and management to stay on the upside of both.

THINK ABOUT IT

This is Jane's favorite quote regarding the advice women often receive to act more like men in order to gain leadership access. What parallels does it have to education?

> *The thrust of The Confidence Gap's [Kay & Shipman, 2014] self-help prescription was "Be more like guys who may not know what the hell they're doing but just act like they do." This directive bypassed over a crucial complicating factor: almost every problem in current American economics was caused by arrogant, overconfident attitudes like those the authors were encouraging. (Zeisler, 2016, p. 210)*

Consider for a moment what you gain from the archetypal masculine and feminine ways of leading and what you lose when you set one aside.

Archetypal male leadership provides:
- Accountability
- A results-driven culture

Archetypal female leadership provides:
- Collaboration and coaching
- A relationship-driven culture

Masculine Leadership **and** Feminine Leadership

But overuse of the masculine style might lead to:
- An emphasis on *power over* at the expense of collaborative leadership
- Schools that value results more than students and teachers

But overuse of the feminine style might lead to:
- An emphasis on *power with* at the expense of accountability
- Schools that value relationship maintenance more than academic and professional growth

Figure 1.1: Infinity loop diagram representing masculine and feminine leadership styles.

In summary, to help get that new vision of school leadership that this third reason for more women leaders requires, education policies and practices need to shift to a better balance of values, not substitute feminine for masculine styles. This way, students benefit from the values and best ideas of both.

Girls' Visions of Themselves as Future Leaders

The fourth reason that women need to step in and step up to school leadership is to inspire the next generation of women to lead. Prophetically, consider how today's boys and girls might begin to envision leadership if women begin to swell the ranks at all levels of educational leadership. Gender inequities exist in all areas of life across all countries. So what does this mean for the next generation of school leaders?

Plan International (2017) has investigated girls' experiences of inequality, their ambitions to lead, and their views on gender stereotypes as they grow into adolescence and young adulthood. Its 2017 report *The Dream Gap: Australian Girls' Views on Gender Equality* highlights that the lack of visibility of girls' experiences lies at the heart of the agonizingly slow change toward gender parity (Plan International, 2017). This organization works around the world to make girls truly visible, acknowledge girls' power and potential, and not turn away when people exploit, discriminate against, and silence them.

Pakistani activist Malala Yousafzai was shot in the head in 2012 when she dared to suggest that girls go to school. We find it more than ironic that we are focusing on women in school leadership while, globally, girls' and women's lack of access to education not only forms a key barrier to creating self-actualized, contributing human beings, but also perpetuates a cycle of poverty and subjugation. Economic prosperity, education, and gender equality are intrinsically linked.

> There's a moment when you have to decide whether to be silent or stand up.
>
> —Malala Yousafzai,
> Pakistani activist and the youngest Nobel Prize laureate

According to Gayle Smith (as cited in Suliman, 2017), president of the ONE Campaign, "Over 130 million girls are still out of school—that's over 130 million potential engineers, entrepreneurs, teachers and politicians whose leadership the world is missing out on. . . . Girls are least likely to be in school in South Sudan, with nearly three-quarters of school-age girls out of the classroom." Without an education, young women are "locked away from a better future" (Suliman, 2017).

Education can help society transform toward gender equity (Unterhalter, 2007). Educators play a key role in nurturing students' self-worth as they explore their identities; they can enhance students' well-being and foster equity both within and beyond the classroom. The messaging that students receive from educators at a very young age can help debunk outdated and constricting gender stereotypes and create a more inclusive future in which gender is not limiting. If girls and boys see more women in leadership positions, they will begin to see it as the norm.

THINK ABOUT IT

An important part of this process is recognizing and challenging your own gender biases. Search YouTube (www.youtube.com) for the short video *Always #LikeAGirl* (Always, 2014). Watch it with at least one other woman. What feelings surface as you watch it? What actions might you take to change what the film depicts? What gender biases of your own does the video help you recognize? What actions might you take to challenge these biases and change the stereotypes the film depicts?

The Need for More Leaders, Especially Women Leaders

The work of the contemporary school principal continues to intensify, and the role's demands and complexity continue to increase. Many OECD countries, though, face principal shortages due to the imminent retirement of a large proportion of principals and other school leaders from the baby boomer generation, and statistics revealing a reluctance to apply for principal positions. These are important challenges to address. As a result, education systems and schools must prioritize developing high-quality, aspiring leaders and attracting the best possible candidates for school leadership positions. In a female-dominated workforce, identifying and developing the next generation of school leaders also requires encouraging talented women to take on these roles. Commentary and statistics reveal that some experienced teachers are reluctant to apply for principal positions (McKenzie et al., 2014).

> The whole goal of feminism is to become redundant. My dream is for a world where I won't have to call myself a feminist because there will be gender justice.
>
> —Chimamanda Ngozi Adichie, Nigerian author

According to University of Tasmania professor emeritus Bill Mulford (2008), education has entered the *golden age* of school leadership—a period in which interest and research in the practice of school leadership is higher than ever before. We know that principals can have a profound impact on a school, and that leadership "is second only to teaching among school-related factors in its impact on student learning" (Leithwood et al., 2004, p. 3). More than ever before, schools need to improve how they address the readiness gap, support current school leaders, and make the leadership role an attractive option for educators. Therefore, ensuring that more and more women seek leadership is crucial.

Next Steps in the Journey

Are you ready to aspire to leadership? You have a myriad of exciting opportunities to create meaningful change—to embrace *power to*! To ensure you stay inspired in spite of inevitable difficulties along the way, in the next chapter, we'll explore the still-existent gender barriers and what to do about them.

Step in for Further Reflection

The following activities provide you with valuable opportunities to reflect on the ideas, strategies, and concepts covered in this chapter. If you are approaching *Step In, Step Up* as a twelve-week journey, you can spread these out over several days.

You may complete them individually or with a group so you can share your thoughts and ideas. Keep a journal so you can revisit your thoughts as you travel this journey.

1. From your own experience in schools, do teachers (who are mainly female), as well as community members, have different expectations for female and male principals? Our discussions with female principals suggest this is the case. Do teachers and community members more tolerate and forgive behaviors from male leaders that they would less accept from a female leader because they are used to men in leadership roles? Do they have different and possibly higher expectations of female principals, particularly if, stereotypically, they perceive men as default leaders (Watterston, 2010)?

2. Complete these sentence stems by brainstorming at least six answers for each. Don't judge what comes to mind; feel free to spend just a few minutes, or an extended period of time depending on the ideas the prompt sparks for you. Try working with two sentence stems per day, journaling about the answers that intrigue you the most.

    ○ "If I could change one thing for teachers, it would be . . ."

    ○ "Teachers never have enough . . ."

- o "Considering my experiences as a teacher, I wonder about . . ."
- o "Considering my experiences as a teacher, I beat myself up over . . ."
- o "As an educator, I dream of . . ."
- o "I do a great job with . . ."
- o "As a leader, I could influence or accomplish . . ."
- o "I take a keen interest in . . ."
- o "I believe I'm getting better at . . ."
- o "For self-care, I'm at my best when . . ."
- o "The most impressive thing I've seen a school leader do is . . ."
- o "My leader role model is _____ because . . ."
- o "I can talk to _____ about my dreams because . . ."
- o "The difference I would like to make as a leader is . . ."
- o "I could become an inspiring leader because . . ."
- o "As a leader, I would like to be known for . . ."

NAVIGATING GENDER BARRIERS

GUIDING QUESTIONS

- What key roles and responsibilities do you see yourself having as an educational leader?

- How will you shine as a leader?

- Do you have any doubts about your leadership potential that resemble the barriers revealed by research on women in leadership? What are they?

We included the word *journey* in the title of this book for a reason: just as no teacher arrives in a classroom with all the skills, knowledge, and habits of mind that highly effective instruction requires, no one enters into school leadership with all the skills, experience, and confidence one needs to lead in a highly effective way. But becoming a leader isn't exactly smooth sailing, especially for women. Understanding what you might encounter—the winds and waves of gender barriers as well as the complexity of the work—will help you build the resilience and the skills you need to ensure the wind stays at your back and the waves don't swamp you.

> I am not afraid of storms, for I am learning how to sail my ship.
> —Louisa May Alcott (1832–1888),
> American author

We offer these brief descriptions of our own first steps on the school leadership journey.

A Word From Barbara

In the mid-1990s, a school district in midwestern Australia approached me to apply for an interim principalship of a small, rural school. My children were then three and five years old, and my husband's work at that time involved extensive travel. Relocating would have been a big decision even without the demands of the role and the expectations of a conservative farming community where most of my colleagues were males who had wives to support them in raising their young families. Yes, I was a capable teacher, and I had some leadership experience, but I was short on confidence to lead a school, even a small one. When the school hired me, I felt it dragged me to the role kicking and screaming, "I'm not ready. I need experience. They're going to find out I'm an impostor."

In hindsight, I know I fell into the trap, like so many other women, of assuming I had to have at least 80 percent of the skills and experience required before even trying for a position—counterintuitive given that you can't get the experience unless you seek the opportunities, step up, and lead!

A Word From Jane

I found myself in an educational leadership doctoral program, spurred on by my husband, who said, "You're already doing the research. Get the degree so that it is recognized." This wasn't an obvious career path; I have an MBA in finance and still do quite a bit of corporate consulting. But a school principal (with whom I eventually coauthored two books) had invited me to apply my executive-coaching skills to working with her staff years before instructional coaching grew into a hot topic. I paid my dues working side by side with the teachers in her school, helping them differentiate instruction as student demographics and curriculum demands went through rapid changes.

Soon, through word of mouth, school leaders called me in for coaching, conflict resolution, and other professional development; I took a partnership approach with school leaders across the United States and in other countries. When I look back, it amazes me how I developed as an educational leader in an organic, not planned way, as many, many women do.

Both of us could add to our stories, listing barriers we encountered or sometimes created ourselves. Hopefully, you've reflected on the guiding questions at the beginning of this chapter so you can compare the thoughts you have about becoming a leader with the difficulties other women have navigated.

Leadership barriers take many forms, from unconscious biases about looks or attire to blatant sexism around maintaining traditional patriarchal leadership expectations. Conversations with female educators have shown us that many cannot adeptly recognize these barriers, including those they create on their own. Instead, they often believe they themselves are the problem in need of a solution. We've observed that women underestimate their capacity for school leadership. Often, women have inaccurately high notions of the skills and experience that leadership requires, or they lack confidence and thus struggle to articulate their accomplishments or career aspirations.

Barbara's experiences guided her into research focused not only on women and leadership but also on championing school leadership development and professional learning more broadly. Recognition, recruitment, development, induction, transition, and ongoing renewal are essential, not just nice to have, to ensure that every school has high-quality and well-supported education leaders. To highlight the changes needed in each of these areas if women are to step in and step up, and to help you prepare to navigate the gender barriers in school leadership, consider the following.

- What women want
- What gets in the way
- What women can do

What Women Want

Just the United States and Australia alone have more than one hundred thousand primary and secondary schools, all of which need talented, high-performing leaders—several for each site (Australian Bureau of Statistics, 2018; NCES, n.d.b). Every student in every school deserves leaders who commit to ensuring incredible student outcomes by enabling teacher professional growth and engaging their school communities.

This vision can become reality only if schools tap as broad a talent pool as possible and ensure that their identified future leaders have equitable access to the leadership pathways at every stage of the leadership journey.

> A good leader inspires people to have confidence in the leader; a great leader inspires people to have confidence in themselves.
>
> —Eleanor Roosevelt (1884–1962), former First Lady of the United States

Leadership development is an ongoing process, with numerous transitional phases: preparation, onboarding, mentoring, and continuous learning. At each phase, systems need to recognize and accommodate the needs of future leaders of all genders through pathways and strategies that support and develop their unique leadership identities.

First and foremost, *women want the gender of those embarking on the school leadership journey to no longer influence their willingness or success.*

However, as discussed in chapter 1 (page 9), we know that in a wide variety of cultural contexts, people continue to identify leadership with maleness. Marianne Coleman, one of the world's most significant scholars in gender and educational leadership, continuously questions the underrepresentation of women in educational leadership roles and contends that leadership is a gendered concept. In the foreword of *Shaping Social Justice Leadership: Insights of Women Educators Worldwide* (Lyman, Strachan, & Lazaridou, 2012), Coleman explains the currency of this thinking:

> There is a widespread assumption that leaders "should be" male (Schein, 2007), and this expectation appears to hold good across continents and age groups and to a large extent is shared by both men and women. Assumptions that men are natural leaders create inbuilt barriers to women who aspire to leadership positions. Although the barriers are surmountable and are becoming more permeable, particularly in Western societies, there are still very firm expectations about the place of males and females . . . Gender stereotypes are particularly resilient, casting the male as generally assertive, strong, decisive, and able to see the "big picture" and the female as supportive, nurturing, and good at detail. (p. xiv)

As an educator who engages young students' hearts and minds, consider for a moment how gender stereotyping develops and affects expectations and aspirations. Research with primary students sheds light on the young age at which students internalize these stereotypes. In 2016, Education and Employers, a nonprofit organization in England, released a two-minute video in which a class of eight-year-olds are asked to draw a surgeon, a firefighter, and a pilot. Sixty-one of the students draw men, and five draw women. The video, *Redraw the Balance*, which brings to life the reality of gender stereotyping in primary schools, has had more than 35 million views (Chambers, 2018). You may view the video at the Education and Employers website (www.inspiringthefuture .org/redraw-the-balance).

In order to better understand gender stereotyping, the World Economic Forum, in partnership with OECD Education and Skills, the University College London Institute of Education, and the National Association of Head Teachers, undertook the biggest survey of its kind (Chambers, 2018). It asked primary students ages seven to eleven to draw a picture of the job they want to do when they grow up. According to the survey:

> More than 20,000 entries have been received and international participants include Australia, Belarus, Bangladesh, China, Colombia, Indonesia, Pakistan, Romania, Russia, Switzerland, Uganda and Zambia. . . . Analysis of the entries suggests the following:
>
> - Gender stereotyping starts at a young age and is a global issue—it was evident in every country.
> - Career aspirations are set at the age of seven and change relatively little between then and 18;
> - There is a significant mismatch between the career aspirations of children and labor market demands;
> - Less than 1% get to meet role models from the world of work visiting their school. (Chambers, 2018)

While these results may not surprise you, consider these gender biases' impact on future leadership candidates. The leaders young students know and what they see, either from their parents or their friends' parents' jobs or the roles they see on TV or in the media, hugely influence them.

What gendered notions of roles have you observed in your students, and how do these affect their aspirations? What can you do to challenge limiting notions of gender, raise students' aspirations, and broaden their horizons? How do you do this for yourself?

Second, *women want a world where gender has no influence on whether students aspire to become educators and education leaders, or leaders in any other field.*

However, more barriers loom when women assume leadership positions. As discussed in chapter 1 (page 9), they face a double bind. The world of work, and often society as a whole, critiques women with a more feminine leadership style as soft. Those with a more masculine leadership style are judged harshly for the same behaviors for which men are praised.

In the infamous Heidi versus Howard experiment at Columbia Business School, Professor Frank Flynn gave the same case study to two different groups of university business majors, changing only the name and gender of the manager (as cited in Sandberg, 2013). The students:

> Rated Heidi and Howard as equally competent, which made sense since "their" accomplishments were completely identical. Yet while students respected both Heidi and Howard, Howard came

across as a more appealing colleague. Heidi, on the other hand, was seen as selfish and not "the type of person you would want to hire or work for." (Sandberg, 2013, pp. 39–40)

Third, *women want a broader definition of leadership, which recognizes the values of both the archetypal male and female leaders and considers them essential and not a basis for criticizing either gender.*

It seems so self-evident that schools need to promote equal leadership access, leadership aspirations for girls and boys as well as women and men, and equitable interpretations of leadership qualities and styles. Yet they have a long way to go. Let's look more specifically at what gets in the way of equal access.

What Gets in the Way

Women may face many barriers in finding equal leadership access. Specifically, barriers that women leaders may encounter and struggle to navigate include the following.

- Gender expectations
- Barriers women themselves create
- Lack of self-care and sustainability

 WORDS FROM A LEADER

One of the barriers I had to navigate as a woman leader was the culture, beliefs, and practices that failed to recognize the leadership potential of women. I did this by doing my best work every day, building communities with other women, and demonstrating through results that women not only are capable of leadership, but when they are in leadership roles, the cultures of the communities in which they work are more humane, loving, and personal. (Joellen Killion, senior advisor, Learning Forward, personal communication, April 19, 2018)

Gender Expectations

Gender stereotyping, which arises from the expectations societies place on people based on their apparent gender, is a form of unconscious bias. Unconscious bias happens subconsciously based on people's personal, environmental, and cultural experiences. People make judgments and assumptions in a nanosecond, grounded in their beliefs rather than in facts.

As discussed in chapter 1 (page 9), *gender construction* is the meaning that people in a given group, culture, or society attach to being biologically male or female, actively built from possible traits and behaviors. Here are a few of the gendered expectations that women must navigate.

Unconscious Bias Creeps Into Hiring Practices

Gender stereotyping lies at the heart of the conversation on women in leadership at any level. In the work world, we observe unconscious bias in recruitment and promotion processes, work allocation, treatment of staff, and performance appraisals.

In an extensive literature review of women in educational leadership, Anthony Thorpe (2016) explores not only the representation of women in leadership structures but also where these structures represent women and how leadership is exercised. Not only do schools need to increase the number of women in leadership positions but also address deeper problems. Women appear to have positions of limited power or prestige. Further, "those positions defined as powerful, responsible, and prestigious are more likely to exclude care and less likely to be held by women" (Thorpe, 2016, p. 17).

And think about the impact of the wage gap: women need at least one more degree than men in order to earn the same salary as men do (Carnevale, Smith, & Gulish, 2018).

Teachers Have Unconscious Expectations of Male and Female Principals

Some teachers, particularly men, expect female principals to exhibit *taking care* behaviors rather than *taking charge* behaviors—behaviors they were unlikely to expect from male principals. Jo, an Australian principal, has called these cases "'I'm not your mum' moments."

Similarly, Jim Watterston (2018) observed that a large Australian school district anticipated that female leaders would have higher scores than their male counterparts in the areas of supportive leadership and school morale because of their more caring, relationship-oriented leadership style. The district found just the opposite; feedback for female leaders demonstrated lower ratings for supportive leadership and staff morale. With women composing more than 75 percent of the district's teachers, a number of theories might explain this. Perhaps female teachers have different and more critical expectations of female principals. Or, female principals may adopt a more dominant or masculine leadership style, believing that teachers expect this of school leaders.

Whatever the explanation, it highlights an additional complexity and challenge that has implications for leadership development programs.

In chapter 6 (page 99), we'll explore moving away from stereotypes and toward leadership archetypes. This involves articulating a group's values while still acknowledging individual differences and then naming the genders' positive archetypal values.

THINK ABOUT IT

Consider for a moment whether you have different expectations for male and female leaders. Make one list of leaders you admire and one list of leaders you disliked working for or with. Jot down a few notes as to why people made each list. What do you notice?

Women Are Less Likely Than Men to Plan Careers

Since the late 1990s, in our conversations with teachers, we have observed that while young male teachers eagerly seek career advancement, even actively planning their journey to the top, their female counterparts approach it less proactively. Further, many female principals only think about a leadership role when someone else suggests it or they are required to fill in for a short period and they find that they enjoy the role.

Traditionally, women face more difficulties in planning careers, because in one way or another, they need to deal with the expectations that they will take the lead in rearing children and managing family affairs (including caring for elderly parents and running a household). Women tend to put others before themselves in making career-progression decisions. Further, planning for career moves has stayed more part of male culture than female culture.

Women encounter more disruptions throughout their careers, including, as termed by the Global City Leaders Project, "the nexus of big jobs, small kids" (Spiller, 2017, p. 7). Even when women have opportunities open to them, given these complexities and connectedness to roles they play outside of their work life, those that require relocation often involve tougher decisions than men face because of family dynamics and societal expectations. Both men and women make difficult decisions when relocating, but women experience these challenges differently, as they take a weblike view of the impact and disruption on family life, including responsibility for a greater share of domestic circumstances.

THINK ABOUT IT

Explicit and subconscious messages about gender bombard people daily. Search YouTube (www.youtube.com) for the following videos.

- *48 Things Women Hear in a Lifetime (That Men Just Don't)* (HuffPost, 2015b)
- *48 Things Men Hear in a Lifetime (That Are Bad for Everyone)* (HuffPost, 2015a)

What gender biases can you identify? Before you watch the first video, consider three messages women receive that men don't. Were your points reflected in the video? After watching both videos, write down how you feel—what surprised you, challenged you, or resonated with you? What is one thing that you can do as an educator to address the issues raised?

Women May Judge Each Other Harshly

Former U.S. Secretary of State Madeleine Albright (2016) coined a well-known phrase when she was the U.S. ambassador to the United Nations and worked closely with the six other female UN ambassadors: "There's a special place in hell for women who don't help each other." Situations that demonstrate women's inhumanity to women include, for example, when those who have succeeded in climbing the ladder of success pull up the ladder because they feel that they toughed it out and thus others should too.

Australian writer, presenter, and commentator Jamila Rizvi (2017) says it's because women's expectations of how they should treat one another are much higher than how they expect to be treated by men:

> When you've worked hard, and done well, and walked through the doorway of opportunity, you do not slam it shut behind you. You reach back, and you give other folks the same chances that helped you succeed.
>
> —Michelle Obama,
> former First Lady of the United States

> *One 2008 study found that women who were working under female supervisors reported more systems of physical and physiological stress than did those working under male supervisors. I can't help but wonder if that was because the men supervisors were more supportive, or whether it was because when women supervisors were less than supportive, it came as more of a shock. We expect better treatment from other women at work. (p. 255)*

Albright (2016) firmly believes that "women have an obligation to help one another. In a society where women often feel pressured to tear one another down, our saving grace lies in our willingness to lift one another up."

Barriers Women Create Themselves

Another set of barriers involves women's own thoughts and actions. In chapter 7 (page 115), you'll have a chance to get specific about your own possible high-flying and limiting beliefs, and how you can address them, but some common ones follow.

Women Don't Know If They Are Ready to Lead

This phenomenon intrigued Jim Watterston, an educator and system leader, as he observed his career trajectory and those of teachers around him (as cited in Tarica, 2010). He took a particular interest in the stories of women who did and didn't become education leaders. It struck him that women in particular often talked of the same fraught path—they lacked confidence and had a nagging uncertainty about whether they were ready to lead. Those who did become principals shared the obstacles they had to overcome, including their own perceived lack of readiness. Watterston makes the point that overcoming obstacles is not about changing women but about changing the culture, including creating very explicit and diverse ways to engage women in leadership development opportunities (as cited in Tarica, 2010).

Women Assume They Need to Possess All Leadership Skills Before Applying

Part of women's reluctance to step up stems from a belief that leaders come fully prepared to lead, which may stem from misplaced ideas of perfection. Consider key research on happiness (Ben-Shahar, 2009). Are you a *perfectionist* who assumes that anything short of perfection represents failure? Or are you more of an *optimalist* who assumes that you will continue to learn and you need to understand and use the concept of *good enough*? Which describes how you think about the school leadership journey? See table 2.1 for a comparison.

Table 2.1: Comparing Perfectionists and Optimalists

Perfectionist	Optimalist
Journey as a straight line	Journey as an irregular spiral
Fear of failure	Failure as feedback
Focus on destination	Focus on journey and destination
All-or-nothing thinking	Nuanced, complex thinking

Defensive	Open to suggestions
Faultfinder	Benefit finder
Harsh	Forgiving
Rigid, static	Adaptable, dynamic

Source: Ben-Shahar, 2009, p. 18.

Women Equate Leadership With an Undesirable Definition of Power

During your reflective journey with this book, we want to ensure that you see school leadership as *power to* and not *power over*, as we described in the introduction (page 1). We demonstrate how we engage and influence outcomes in the multidimensional and collaborative nature of our work in education—working with and through others to influence and inspire them. You'll have a chance to deepen your understanding of the beauty of leading with the right kind of power throughout these pages.

Women See the "Real" Work of Education as Direct Contact With Students

The motto, "We're in it for the children," serves women in education well but can also keep them from stepping forward or speaking up. Most teachers crave working with school principals and other leaders who truly understand what they face in the classroom, which means schools must have teachers as a core source for the leadership pipeline. Yes, many will have a calling to stay in the classroom, but is this your calling?

> What I know now is that gender equality or diversity work is action orientated. It is lived and practiced through our daily actions and interactions. In what is spoken and what is said without words. Culture, or normalized common-sense ways of behaving and believing is perhaps the most obvious obstacle and source of existential tension for women seeking and maintaining powerful positions.
>
> —Rachel Dickinson,
> assistant dean, Warwick Business School, Coventry, England

Women Fear Receiving More Intense Scrutiny and Criticism Than Men

You might call this the "Do I have thick enough skin to become a leader?" barrier. And the caution may be warranted. Perhaps through this journey, you'll find women with whom you can band together to tackle some suggestions in the What Women Can Do section (page 44).

Lack of Self-Care and Sustainability

In conversations with numerous female teachers, we learned that some women consider leadership only after their own children have grown more independent, because for them, career advancement and ambition don't sit comfortably with support of family well-being. Work-life balance presents a challenge for everyone, and the demands and stress of the role of principal can significantly impact well-being. A contributing factor that deters women from seeking principalships is that they see it as a less attractive option if the role impacts their personal well-being and life balance.

Numerous longitudinal principal health and well-being surveys indicate that principals have experienced increasing stress levels; these surveys recommend individual-, association-, and system-level implementation strategies to address and alleviate this stress (Pollack, 2017; Riley, 2017). However, these surveys also note that principals have high levels of satisfaction with the role. Inarguably, a principal's role has become more complex, now demanding skills as diverse as those needed to run a business. However, unlike CEOs who might be physically disconnected from their clients, principals have a constant and visible connection to clients, the students, and this familiarity brings joys and difficulties. Despite all the challenges, the statistics speak for themselves—in Australia, for example, 96 percent of principals would choose the role again if given the chance (Australian Institute for Teaching and School Leadership [AITSL], 2016).

Fundamentally, well-being and sustainability in leadership requires work-life balance, and for women in particular, this creates a weblike phenomenon. Women cannot isolate their work experience from their broader experiences of self and their everyday lives. They need to sustain and take care of themselves first; giving themselves permission to do so affects their productivity, impact, and influence. We will explore this focus further in chapter 3 (page 51). Women leaders' self-care is also crucial because it affects whether the leaders act as positive models and advocates for the role, influencing whether other women view leadership as feasible for them.

What Women Can Do

In chapter 1 (page 9), we discussed the need to address the readiness gap, support current school leaders, and make leadership roles an attractive option for future leaders. In a female-dominated workforce, identifying and developing the next generation of school leaders also requires encouraging talented women to consider and take on these roles.

Educator Jill Blackmore (2006) suggests that when choosing school leaders, systems need to promote multiple representations of and diverse approaches to leadership. This also promotes wider cultural and ethnic diversity and challenges the generally masculine representations of leadership. Such suggestions can address multiple barriers. For example, potential leaders may exit and re-enter the education workforce for a variety of reasons; multiple leadership models point out the diversity such candidates can bring to schools. Multiple models and leadership approaches include co-principalship, distributed pedagogical leadership, shared principalship, multi-campus principalship, and community-based principalship (Blackmore, 2006).

Schools and districts can support aspiring leaders to gain experience by offering work shadowing and internship opportunities or having them take leadership of specific projects or programs to flex their leadership skills and gain the experience they require. Given the feedback women have shared with us about not feeling good enough, having enough experience, or being 100 percent perfect, these are particularly attractive and flexible opportunities to build a repertoire of skills and leadership practices.

Fortunately, internationally, we've seen a push to get principal preparation right by firmly grounding it in the broader context of leadership development. Preparation program designers have accounted for the multitude of challenges inherent in attracting, preparing, appointing, and retaining high-performing school leaders.

In Australia, a national environmental scan of principal preparation programs highlights a desire for a more cohesive, systemic approach to school leadership development, including systematic approaches to succession planning and career development pathways (Watterston, 2015). But programs still need clarity on the necessary professional learning opportunities and the rationale for each; the support needed at each level and how to provide it; and internships or other ways to gain leadership experience. This alignment also requires a common understanding of the capacities that principals need. From a school leadership development perspective, Barbara calls pathways for leadership support the *three Ps*: (1) pipeline, (2) personalization, and (3) partnerships.

1. **Pipeline:** Identification, preparation, and ongoing development (creating a networked pipeline that enables aspiring leaders to step forward through varied, flexible, and diverse pathways underpinned by expected practices)

2. **Personalization:** Diagnosis and precision learning (recognizing and developing strengths, creating aspiring leaders' leadership identities, and matching professional learning opportunities to identified needs)

3. **Partnerships:** The power of the profession (mentoring, role modeling, and work shadowing)

So what can you do to prepare more women for—and add the feminine archetypal values to—school leadership?

WORDS FROM A LEADER

We've created avenues for professional development and career growth through a coaching module and a network of support. We have academic directors and school coaches—many of whom are women—who are the support network for our teachers. Through my leadership, we have created a council of academic directors who provide support to a group of seven to fifteen schools. Stellar teachers become mentors, mentors become school academic coaches, and school academic coaches become regional or group academic directors. This career ladder provides a structure and process for women to become leaders at their school and in their region. Our coaching module contains comprehensive content to improve our coaches' knowledge in curriculum, instruction, assessment, and team dynamics. We are proud of the quality of leaders we are generating to mentor, coach, and encourage others in our efforts to build capacity within our organization. (Karen Gayle, national director of curriculum and instruction, Imagine Schools, United States, personal communication, April 17, 2018)

Leadership development is a collective responsibility. Review the following leadership development reflections and strategies from the perspective of the individual leadership aspirant, the profession and the role it plays in supporting and informing leadership development, and the system (your sector, district, or central office) in providing the enabling conditions to articulate career pathways and ongoing capacity building. What else would you add to the list?

- **Address the readiness gap:** Systems need to get women into leadership positions—not by using quotas or favorable selection processes, but by getting everybody to the starting line. Like athletes in the hundred-meter sprint, each potential leader requires a different training regime to get to the starting line. That way, it's open to the best person to win the race, but individualized training provides each person with a chance to win.

- **Counter the belief that the principal role prevents women from directly impacting learning:** Women who take temporary positions as acting leaders frequently change this belief; they realize they can have a significant impact on more students if they lead. These interim opportunities address preconceived ideas and demystify the role.

- **Promote flexible work options for all:** Career breaks are a good thing; they promote a diverse view of school leadership and provide return-to-work and family-friendly work patterns. There are numerous pathways to senior leadership positions. Systemic practices regarding family leave, education sabbaticals, part-time positions, and other options can have a significant impact on the way people perceive opportunities for progression. The point is to do whatever it takes to effectively engage your most talented, creative, and committed educators.

- **Research the impact of merit and equity practices and selection processes, and increase career management support for women:** Ensure appropriate training for those involved in the selection processes. Women may lack the confidence to articulate their achievements or may see this as blowing their own trumpet. Some also assume others will see their achievements without their having to explicitly articulate them for selection processes.

- **Provide access to high-quality leadership programs:** Many systems have tinkered at the edges but not had a holistic career view or sense of responsibility to develop their school leaders. Think about formative student assessment that, in partnership with teacher and students, identifies learning needs, strategies to address those needs, and regular checkpoints to reflect on growth and understanding; likewise, you should diagnose before prescribing professional learning so it targets and meets diverse and identified needs. One size does not fit all. Doing this requires determining what school leaders need to know, understand, and do to succeed in their work (for an example, see the Australian Professional Standard for Principals [AITSL, 2016]; the Ontario Leadership Framework [Leithwood, 2012]; and the 4DTM Instructional Leadership Growth Continuum [University of Washington Center for Educational Leadership, n.d.]) so aspiring leaders can identify their strengths and challenges and inform their performance and professional learning conversations. Review the examples from Australia, Canada, and the United States. What do they tell you about the role of the school leader? What would you focus on to develop your leadership capacity?

- **Remember that women are less inclined to consider leadership roles unless someone suggests it to them or they become the *accidental principal*:** Current principals have a significant role to play in not only providing positive role modeling but also seeking, recognizing, and supporting the development of aspiring leaders (including those who don't know their own leadership potential). Principals can do the following to show women that they should consider leadership roles.

- Principals should be their own best advocates by articulating and displaying an obvious sense of job satisfaction; this goes a long way toward demystifying the role.
- Talent spotting may require education leaders to look beyond their leadership comfort zones to encourage people not like them and explore and develop others' leadership potential (Spiller, 2017).
- Mentoring, coaching, and support networks are critical to engage, invigorate, support, and sustain women in their leadership journey. Current leaders of all genders need to take on the crucial role of sponsoring potential leaders to open up opportunities, guiding aspirant leaders in how to be strategic in leveraging their allies to advocate on their behalf with a more explicit focus on career progression.

These strategies contribute to developing women's confidence and resilience so they feel able to drive their careers forward. Everyone has a role to play in leadership development.

Next Steps in the Journey

Think about your reactions and reflections to the gender barriers outlined in the previous section. Did you consider where you own challenges may lie in developing your leadership identity and what you could do about them? Remember, you bring many strengths to leadership that you will leverage to address your identified challenges. In the next chapter, we will explore how you can navigate your next steps in your leadership journey. Now, are you ready to hoist your sails?

Step in for Further Reflection

The following activities provide you with valuable opportunities to reflect on the ideas, strategies, and concepts covered in this chapter. If you are approaching *Step In, Step Up* as a twelve-week journey, you can spread these out over several days.

You may complete them individually or with a group so you can share your thoughts and ideas. Keep a journal so you can revisit your thoughts as you travel this journey.

1. Reflect on yourself in relation to this chapter's topics.

    o   Do you recognize when your unconscious biases show up in your expectations, behaviors, and responses?

    o   Do you take an active role in your own career planning, positioning, and preparation, including professional learning choices, qualifications, collegial support groups, and mentoring?

    o   How do you support and nurture women and girls in your circle of influence?

2. Use your journal to identify some specific motivations for your leadership journey.

    o   List five victories you've had as a leader.

    o   List three actions you could take to lead from where you are right now.

    o   Make three promises to yourself about your leadership journey.

    o   Plan one nice thing you could do for yourself each day for a week—and follow through—to ensure you stay energized for the hard work of becoming the leader you are meant to be.

FINDING TIME FOR THE LEADERSHIP JOURNEY

- How will you carve out time for the reflective practices that leadership development requires?
- What workplace expectations or personal habits get in the way of reflection, and what might you do to alter them?

As you delve into the third week of your leadership journey, hopefully you feel convinced that educational leadership needs more women and you've identi-fied a few key barriers that you're preparing to navigate. What's the next step? Finding dedicated time for the leadership journey for the following reasons.

- Developing management, scheduling, performance-review, and data-analysis skills requires practice.
- Developing as a leader requires reflection.

What is the difference between practice and reflection? A leader's role is not to simply get things done but to influence others in working toward an engaging, common pur-pose. It isn't what you say but what people see you doing that counts. James M. Kouzes and Barry Z. Posner (2010) summarize decades of research with this point: "It is not a question of 'Will I make a difference?' Rather, it's 'What difference will I make?'" (p. 1). They note that employees are most influenced each day by their immediate managers.

This means that whether you are a superintendent, a principal, or a teacher leader, what you do counts. To understand your impact requires reflection on both your experiences and what you observe in others. Think about it. You don't learn from experience; you learn from reflecting on those experiences and taking time to examine what happened and why. You learn from examining whether your actions and interactions had satisfactory results, how they affected others, what needs to change, and what it will take to make those changes.

Do you make time for reflection? Weekly, if not daily, do you find space in your day to revisit events, decisions, interactions, and outcomes, perhaps by journaling or by pondering questions you designed to consider the difference you are making? Becoming the best leader you can be requires regular reflective pauses.

So Much to Do, So Little Time

Perhaps carving out time for reflection seems nearly impossible. If you feel that life just keeps getting busier, you aren't alone. A destructive myth says that time and productivity have a linear relationship. This has too many people spending more time at their jobs and also working at home via 24/7 connectivity. But the relationship isn't linear; you aren't a machine. Eventually, your productivity drops. Performance expert Tony Schwartz (2010) writes:

> The way we're working isn't working in our own lives, for the people we lead and manage, and for the organizations in which we work. We're guided by a fatal assumption that the best way to get more done is to work longer and more continuously. But the more hours we work and the longer we go without real renewal, the more we begin to default, reflexively, into behaviors that reduce our own effectiveness—impatience, frustration, distraction, and disengagement. They also take a pernicious toll on others. (p. 4)

Further, women who work full time are busier than men; it's not your imagination. In just about every country and stage of life, women have less free time because they shoulder more household chores and caregiving tasks. In the United States, women spend at least ninety minutes a day more than men on meal preparation, chores, care for others, and general household management (U.S. Bureau of Labor Statistics, 2015). Similar figures in Australia reveal women

> My theory on housework is, if the item doesn't multiply, smell, catch fire, or block the refrigerator door, let it be. No one else cares. Why should you?
>
> —Erma Bombeck (1927–1996), American humorist

spend twice as much time on childcare and chores as men (Australian Bureau of Statistics, 2018). Women often have more responsibility for aging parents or fall into workplace patterns of picking up slack or caring for others that leave them with less free time as well.

Consider these two big truths about leadership and this crazy busy world.

1. **You cannot care for others unless you care for yourself:** At times, life may cause you to focus on others more than on yourself, or vice versa, but leadership research reinforces the interdependency of care of self and care of others. Follow the infinity loop in figure 3.1 to understand the importance of getting the balance right—and the systems nature of the relationship. Too much of one side brings its downside and a desire for the other.

When leaders support staff well-being, it has positive effects on staff retention, job satisfaction, and productivity as well as on student outcomes (MindMatters, 2016).

Leaders who model work-life balance can better lead collaboratively for collective teacher efficacy, the "level of confidence a group exudes in its capacity to organize and execute the tasks required to reach desired goals" (Sun & Leithwood, 2015, p. 569).

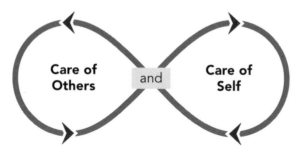

But leaders who fall short on work-life balance struggle to lead collaboratively (Edge, 2014).

But leaders who focus on their needs without paying attention to the staff's motivational, situational, and emotional needs will be judged as uncaring, resulting in decreased teacher job satisfaction, engagement, and effectiveness (Edge, Descours, & Frayman, 2016).

Figure 3.1: Infinity loop diagram representing care of others and care of self.

2. **Your staff need to see you model a good work-life balance:** As a role model, let your staff see that it is both possible and acceptable to honor their own needs, even in the face of daunting workloads. Further, teachers report increased job satisfaction, loyalty, and effectiveness when leaders care not only for their staff but for themselves as well. The result? Collective efficacy, one of the very top strategies for improving student achievement, which has an effect size of 1.57 on student learning. When a strategy has an effect size of 0.4, it equates to students achieving a year's growth in a year (DeWitt, 2017). Thus, teacher collective efficacy has tremendous power; in part, creating it depends on your ability to balance your life.

A Word From Barbara

I've engaged with designing and delivering professional learning and leadership programs since the late 1990s. And I prioritize sustainability and well-being practices as critical pieces for insight, reflection, and action. Over the years, I've seen how challenging leaders find it to take time for themselves, even small moments during the day—and, ultimately, how it energizes leaders when they commit to and model taking time to rest, reflect, and reset. Prioritizing and privileging these practices—being allowed to or permitting themselves to take time for themselves and reflecting on the significant benefits in doing so—causes both surprise and relief.

As one experienced principal described, "This has also been great for my personal development, the focus on the whole me, the interplay between deep purpose, self-care, and leadership ability . . . The well-being focus allowed me to give myself permission to take time." (Personal communication in the form of written feedback from a program participant, November 22, 2017)

Thus, besides to maintain your sanity, you have two big reasons to carve out time for priorities outside of work: (1) the importance of modeling and prioritizing self-care and, coming back to the focus of this chapter, (2) to engage in reflective practice. Let's consider how to find that time through the lens of neuroscience and what we know about fostering brain energy and bandwidth.

THINK ABOUT IT

Do you care for yourself? What would those closest to you say? How might others view your efforts to manage your work priorities and personal priorities?

Brain Energy and Bandwidth

Bandwidth, defined simply, is your mental capacity, the fluid intelligence that affects how you process information and make decisions. While you can increase your overall bandwidth with good habits, it remains a finite resource. We'll work through how to gauge your current bandwidth and how you might increase it to find that reflection time.

Are you familiar with the *frog in the kettle* effect? It says that if you toss a frog into boiling water, it will try to jump out. However, if you put the frog in warm water and slowly turn up the temperature, the frog will settle in—until it's too late to escape.

This resembles how people have fallen into the traps of busyness and the consequences of 24/7 connectivity. People didn't really climb into the kettle of the internet until the 1990s, with smartphones following a decade later. The warm water of easy information access and worldwide connectivity allowed most to quickly get comfortable. The heat rose without people noticing it. Changes in workplace norms and technology caught many off guard; they accepted the changes as the new normal without considering whether they had compatibility with true engagement, effectiveness, and efficiency.

Your brain is rewiring to deal with the constant stimulation, interruption, and task switching that technology continues to drive. But your brain hasn't *evolved*. It takes generations upon generations for human systems to adapt to major changes. People are experiencing suboptimal use of their neuropathways driven by activities their brains aren't wired to handle. This explains much of the stress and lack of time so many people experience these days.

Here's how brain bandwidth works. By weight, your brain uses up a tremendous amount of fuel—just the prefrontal cortex, the home of executive function, uses up 20 percent of the body's available glucose. More important, you have only a finite amount of brain fuel available to do the following.

- Use your collaborative leadership skills.
- Engage in strategic thinking and other complex tasks.

- Exercise willpower to persevere.

- Stay calm and employ emotional intelligence skills.

- Avoid poor dietary habits.

- Get some exercise.

- Slow down and avoid impulsive decisions and actions.

Use up that limited fuel doing any of these actions, and you simply don't have it available for others. Do you notice that you have less patience after a long day at work, or that a cookie seems like a solution after a hard conversation?

Further, when you know you don't have enough of a key resource—time, money, relationship quality, health, safety, and so on—bandwidth goes down. You lose executive function and have less control over where you direct your attention. Sociologists Sendhil Mullainathan and Eldar Shafir (2013) describe how these scarcities cause tunnel vision—you focus on the scarcity at hand rather than your true priorities. This is why if you find yourself in a reasonably important meeting but you need to meet a crucial report deadline in a few hours, your mind defaults to that report rather than the meeting discussion.

Scarcity is real; bandwidth helps you exercise more control and more quickly recognize when scarcity is taking you in the wrong direction.

Let's look at three key factors that contribute to good bandwidth: (1) fueling your brain, (2) balancing your priorities, and (3) focusing your attention. Which one will help you carve out time for reflection?

Fueling Your Brain

Recommendations for sleep, diet, and exercise can fade into background noise, but you can't fool your body.

Sleep is crucial to your well-being, yet people too often dismiss it as a luxury. If on awakening you still feel tired, you simply aren't getting enough sleep. Most people need around seven hours a night—without it, willpower goes down, memory suffers, and you'll find it harder to consolidate learning. And, if you've spent a lot of time trying to learn something new or understand complex material, lack of sleep means starting over (Medina, 2014). Further, lack of sleep makes it tough to have patience with those around you. The cortisol spikes that lack of sleep causes actually kill brain cells. Lack of sleep decreases energy, efficiency, and effectiveness; it makes you take longer to accomplish things. Get that sleep, and you'll have more high-quality time for reflection.

A Word From Jane

I've worked as an executive coach for a large organization's highly selective leadership development program for several years and through several rounds of candidates. For the 2015 cohort, the program asked me to give a keynote speech at the kickoff banquet for candidates and their sponsors, mentors, and divisional leaders. As the banquet date approached, though, I couldn't help noticing that something seemed to have changed.

In the past, we hadn't had any problems getting the candidates to complete assessments or receiving 360-degree feedback from them and their sponsors, managers, and peers. But this time, getting the same information felt like pulling teeth! Further, the candidates kept postponing coaching sessions.

As my coachees complained of meetings, changing agendas, the call to do more with less, and so on, I realized that these people were overwhelmed—their brains couldn't handle the responsibilities or the pace of the demands.

So, I gave them, including the division leaders, a quiz during the keynote. Fifteen questions covered how well they fueled their brains, focused attention, and filtered information to keep the tasks at hand manageable. Out of sixty possible points, two-thirds scored lower than the cutoff for serious bandwidth deficit alert. One coachee scored ten points and emailed me that night, "I need to change *now!*" Discussions of bandwidth dominated the rest of the weekend in a good way as the attendees wrestled with what they needed to do to stay energized, efficient, effective, and engaged.

The quiz now includes thirty-two questions and is validated and part of my and my colleague Ann Holm's consulting services. Organization after organization learns that their workers are burning out when simple changes in office norms could prevent it. Brains need TLC to be effective!

Note, too, that too many people underestimate the importance of power naps. Closing your eyes for ten to twenty minutes improves mood, alertness, and performance (National Sleep Foundation, 2018). Jane's children quickly learned the benefits of listening when she asked, "Please, let Mommy close her eyes for just fifteen minutes and we'll have a much happier evening together!" A quick nap might be the best use of your lunch hour if last night's sleep left you feeling tired.

Diet comes next. Yes, your brain is what you eat. Executive function requires heavy glucose use, and boom-bust fueling with empty-calorie snacks or simple carbohydrates is not the answer. This creates a roller-coaster pattern that decreases your ability to pay attention, learn, and follow social cues. Bottom line—a healthy diet with treats in moderation leads to better overall bandwidth. Be honest with yourself. Does your diet help or hinder you?

Finally, your body was made to move. Exercise is not a luxury. In fact, it provides the fastest way to boost willpower, increase mental sharpness, bolster resistance to stress, and improve self-control in other aspects of life (Ratey, 2013). Know that even a five-minute walk around the block provides a significant boost in bandwidth.

If you wonder how you'll find the time to exercise, remember that the relationship between time and productivity is *not* linear. Schwartz (2010) reports that when professionals leave their desks midafternoon for an hour of exercise, they can leave the office earlier, not later, because they accomplish their work in less time. This shows how effectively exercise fuels the brain.

WORDS FROM A LEADER

We have to grow our physical, psychological, and emotional bandwidth to manage the complexity of "deep end" work. Being able to bounce back from rejection and disappointment isn't a luxury, but a basic necessity for us "deep end" leaders. As I described in *Swimming in the Deep End: Four Foundational Skills for Leading Successful School Initiatives* (Abrams, in press), I have an extreme self-care support team (massage, hair, coach, etc.). I do not consider self-care an indulgence, but an investment. If I want to keep doing good work, this "vessel" I am working with has to keep going and I have to care for it. We all need to take care of ourselves if we want to be able to swim in the deep end and not burn out. (Jennifer Abrams, American author and educational consultant, personal communication, November 28, 2018)

Remember, *fueling* means you increase that bucket of brain energy, increasing your efficiency and effectiveness. Fueling buys time; here's how. Jim Loehr and Tony Schwartz (2003) describe the two components of effective energy management.

1. **Rhythmic movement, between energy expenditure (stress) and energy renewal (recovery), called oscillation:** The real enemy of high performance is not stress but the absence of disciplined, intermittent recovery.

2. **Rituals that promote oscillation (rhythmic stress and recovery):**
   When repeated regularly, highly precise, consciously developed routines become automatic over time.

Do you have habits you could change that would help you find more time?

 THINK ABOUT IT

One of the best resources we've found for changing habits is *The Willpower Instinct* by Kelly McGonigal (2012). Its practical exercises help you set manageable targets and understand how to balance the *I will*, *I won't*, and *I want* aspects of developing new behaviors. And it features encouraging and entertaining anecdotes. Try it if you need to prioritize fueling.

Balancing Your Priorities

Balancing work and the rest of your life requires constant attention as demands and circumstances change. Consciously paying attention to key clues as to how well you are doing ensures that the effects of stress, lapses in concentration, and drops in effectiveness don't get out of hand. For example, answer the following questions to determine if you have balanced priorities. (These statistically validated items appear on Jane's bandwidth survey, which we describe on page 57.)

- When you're with people you care about, is your mind in the moment or back at work?

- Do you feel satisfied with the patience you have with the most important people in your life? With the amount of time you spend with them?

- Do you allow yourself to completely relax with some downtime—such as reading for pleasure, being mindful, or participating in a favorite hobby—or other such activities *not* linked to productivity? Downtime positively affects creative problem solving and accurate self-appraisal (Smart, 2013).

- Do you make time for self-care when you're ill? Or do you go against the recommendations from doctors and medical associations around the world to stay home and avoid infecting coworkers in a misguided drive to get things done?

We've already discussed the importance of leaders modeling and prioritizing, but remember that scarcity of the previous items leads to more tunnel vision—and lost bandwidth. Where might you lose time, energy, and effectiveness because of *I shoulds* or *I have tos* that don't account for the truth about how your brain works?

THINK ABOUT IT

How many items are on your priority list? The word *priority* appeared in the English language in the 15th century. There was no plural form of the word. There was just one very first or prior thing. Sometime during the Industrial Revolution, the plural form appeared (McKeown, 2014). Ponder this big truth: How can you have more than one *most important thing*?

In his book *Rest: Why You Get More Done When You Work Less*, Alex Soojung-Kim Pang (2016) critiques how people manage their time rather than their energy. In order to thrive, your brain needs rest every ninety minutes. People are born with good energy intelligence—that's why a toddler will play one minute and fall fast asleep the next. Pang (2016) challenges the no-rest *badge of honor* and lays out the case for deliberate rest through restorative activity. Rest your brain by going for a walk, taking an old-fashioned coffee break with others and talking about anything but work, or reading something entertaining and unrelated to your task. In other words, find an enjoyable, nonintellectual, playful activity that works well in fifteen- to thirty-minute bursts of time.

Focusing Your Attention

Neuroplasticity means that your brain is changing with the demands of the digital age. Again, though, these adjustments aren't making you more efficient; rather, they threaten your effectiveness.

Manoush Zomorodi (2017), a journalist for New York Public Radio, noticed how much trouble she was having with deep concentration. Friends told her similar tales about struggling with deep reading when they tried to reread favorite works of literature. Zomorodi was exhausted because her phone, if nothing else, filled every waking moment, and she lacked reflective solitude that formerly had driven her most creative efforts.

> Striving for excellence motivates you; striving for perfection is demoralizing.
>
> —Harriet Braiker (1948–2004), American psychologist and writer

So she started the Bored and Brilliant project in February of 2015 (Zomorodi, 2017). This podcast series gave people a set of challenges that they could complete to help them set aside their devices and work on creativity. She invited listeners of her *Note to Self* podcast to join in. Over twenty thousand people signed up initially. A listener survey revealed that people were well aware that their devices messed with their productivity. In some ways, they felt addicted and wondered if constant connectivity affected their health. Studies show that if you want to be creative, you need to get away from constant stimulation and find reflective time (Vartanian, Bristol, & Kaufman, 2013). Leadership requires creativity.

Having the ability to focus attention is vital for so many things. You've probably heard that engaging in handheld or hands-free phone conversations while driving makes your mind wander from the road as much as driving while intoxicated (Federal Communications Commission, n.d.). But have you noticed a change in reading habits? Can you engage with complex text as well as you used to? Researchers worry that internet habits, with the constant drive to interrupt and check links, email, and social media, are the root cause of changes in reading brain circuits (Wolf, 2018). You need the ability to both skim and read deeply.

 THINK ABOUT IT

If you have a hard time disconnecting from your device, check out *Bored and Brilliant: How Spacing Out Can Unlock Your Most Productive and Creative Self* (Zomorodi, 2017). The seven challenges start with simply tracking your device use and end with a goal-setting challenge that might come in handy on your leadership journey.

Perhaps the easiest way to work on focus—and increase your bandwidth—is to use the following three strategies.

1. **Stop multitasking:** Actually, there is no such thing. Multitasking, such as checking emails while in meetings or working on other tasks, really means task switching. Every time you switch tasks, your energy-guzzling prefrontal cortex has to signal one set of brain processes to stop and another set to start. This creates 50 percent more errors. Worse, it takes 50 percent more time to accomplish something (Medina, 2014). Further, younger people, so-called *digital natives*, do not multitask better; it is just their norm.

2. **Stop interruptions when you engage in executive function tasks or face-to-face interactions:** Turn off notifications, ignore your devices during conversations and meetings, and remove other distractions from your environment. Know that music may block distractions for you. However, interruptions such as ringing phones and loudspeaker announcements cause you to draw on that brain energy—and decrease bandwidth—to continue concentrating.

   Try checking emails only at set intervals during the day. If it makes you more comfortable, add an automated email response that says, "I check emails at set times during the day. Please call _____ if you need an immediate response." Even top executives who try this find that just about no one calls.

3. **Start blocking out sixty-minute chunks of time to work on important tasks:** Psychologist Mihaly Csikszentmihalyi (1997) pioneered the notion of *finding flow*, or getting into the zone. Professor Gloria Mark of the University of California, Irvine further supports his work with her discovery that it takes an average of twenty-three minutes and fifteen seconds to return to work after an interruption (Mark, Gudith, and Klocke, 2008). This start-restart phenomenon is similar to getting warmed up during physical exercise, stopping, and then having to start all over again. Close your door, ignore emails, or remove yourself to a quiet classroom, and you can do almost twice as much in the same amount of time. Right there, you gain thirty minutes for reflective practice.

One of the most useful concepts as you work on focus is *cognitive steps*: How many steps can you place between yourself and the temptations that prompt multitasking, interruptions, or loss of concentration? For example, if you're using your computer to compose a document, disconnecting from the internet places a step between you and the urge to check whether anyone has responded to a Twitter post or an email. Put your phone in a drawer if it tempts you. (One of Jane's coaching clients placed his in a box, taped it shut, and put it on a shelf in another room. He found his productivity skyrocketed due to the effectiveness of all these cognitive steps.)

 THINK ABOUT IT

The language of web development—*users* and *hits*—is the same as that of drug addiction.

Why has this *frog in the kettle* aspect of the digital age become so ubiquitous? Because technology is addictive. Checking email produces a dopamine hit—the same neurotransmitter that activates when the brain thinks it will receive other rewards such as fatty foods or recreational drugs. It isn't the email that you find rewarding but the anticipation of some reward, enticing you to check again and again. You may have heard of experiments in which rats could push one lever to receive dopamine or another lever to receive food, and they starved themselves because they had such a strong craving for dopamine (Wise, 1996).

Further, the internet and your devices are designed to keep you clicking. Zomorodi (2017) describes a conversation she had with Tristan Harris, who works in technology design. Harris points out:

> The most important thing to acknowledge is that it's an unfair fight. On one side is a human being who's just trying to get on with her prefrontal cortex, which is a million years old and in charge of regulating attention. That's up against a thousand engineers on the other side of the screen, whose daily job is to break that and keep you scrolling on the infinite feed. (as cited in Zomorodi, 2017, p. 92)

It takes bandwidth to focus. But focusing increases bandwidth. What habits will buy back time for you?

 WORDS FROM A LEADER

My most important source of support as a female leader has been a long-standing (over 20 years) community of highly successful female colleagues who care deeply about each other. (Joellen Killion, senior advisor, Learning Forward, personal communication, April 19, 2018)

Should your best first steps involve adjusting priorities? Fueling your brain through sleep, diet, or exercise? Or regaining productive habits for focusing?

Don't try to do it all. Choose something that sounds doable. Then consider choosing one of the following methods—Jane and Barbara's favorite methods for changing habits.

Jane suggests creating *why* and *how will I know* cards through just two steps.

1. Write down your goal and a reminder of why you are pursuing it—to find time to devote to your development as a leader. Including the *why* in goal setting greatly increases your chances of reaching that goal (McGonigal, 2012).

2. Decide how you will measure progress toward this goal in terms of gaining time. How will you know you have more time for reflection? Be specific. Motivation comes from seeing progress.

Jane often uses these *why* and *how will I know* cards to help clients set goals and monitor their progress. Figure 3.2 shows her own card for maintaining her deep-reading skills.

Why and *How Will I Know* Card for:
Engaging in and Enjoying Deep Reading

1	**Discovery:** What can I learn to further my effectiveness? • Am I selecting the deeper texts, in paper format, that contain the depth of knowledge I need?
2	**Challenge:** I need to get lost in deep texts and be in flow. • Am I reading for at least thirty minutes at a time without checking my phone?
3	**Personal Development:** Concentration for depth is a core habit of mind to cultivate as I grow older. • Am I excited and engaged in this effort?

Source: © 2019 by Jane A. G. Kise.

Figure 3.2: Why and *how will I know* card for maintaining deep-reading skills.

The term in each box—*discovery, challenge,* and *professional development*—gives a value or priority that Jane identified as key to this particular goal. The first sentence after each term states *why* she finds that value so important. The questions help Jane answer the question, "How will I know if I'm making progress?" to measure focus and progress.

Barbara also has a helpful personal practice. In one of her leadership programs, she invites wellness expert Shannon McNeill (http://thelivingwellstudio.com.au/shannon-mcneill) as a guest speaker to deliver a session on boosting life energy, stress resilience, and mental clarity. Barbara always develops a large mind map for participants to use as a targeted opportunity for reflection during the rest of the program. As a visual learner, she finds she can use it to encapsulate key messages, reflect after the session, and stay on track with her own health and well-being goals (or realize she has gone way off track!) in the following weeks.

Next Steps in the Journey

Remember, you're working on brain energy and bandwidth to create more time for the reflection required to become the leader you were meant to be. Give yourself the gift of reflection to constantly prepare yourself for leadership even as you do the work of leading. It's another *both and* paradox for leaders.

Now, let's get practical. Think of this chapter as a set of options for finding the time you need for the reflective journey. The following chapters ask you to complete activities, respond to questions, and ponder scenarios, and hopefully meet up with someone else on this same leadership journey, whether in person or via the internet. Where might you find the time? What did you learn about your bandwidth?

Step in for Further Reflection

The following activities provide you with valuable opportunities to reflect on the ideas, strategies, and concepts covered in this chapter. If you are approaching *Step In, Step Up* as a twelve-week journey, you can spread these out over several days.

You may complete them individually or with a group so you can share your thoughts and ideas. Keep a journal so you can revisit your thoughts as you travel this journey.

1. Choose one way you can carve out time for reflection by increasing your bandwidth. Set your priority focus, much like Jane's card does (see figure 3.2), and use this focal point each week or each day to reflect on whether you are following through. The most effective ways to increase bandwidth include the following.

    o   Identify the habit that interrupts your concentration the most, such as checking your phone, getting a snack, or talking to a coworker. Now, use the cognitive steps concept (see page 62) to put as many barriers as possible between you and that temptation.

    o   Improve your sleep habits. Avoid caffeine after 2:00 p.m.; sleep in a cool, dark room (make sure you dim your alarm clock or face it away from you); refrain from heavy eating in the evening; and limit alcohol.

    o   Rest your brain daily through an hour or so of *beach reads* (light, breezy reading), socialization, or other recreational activities with no real payoff. Choose something that feels like an escape. Let go of any guilty feelings that this wastes time. You are actually giving your brain a needed rest.

○ Build time into your schedule for meeting overruns and driving delays. Remember that you really can't be two places at once, so plan for the inevitable delays. This will decrease stress and the effects of scarcity that lack of time causes.

2. If you need more information or convincing, check out some of our favorite books and videos that informed this chapter. Remember, the more you know, the more you'll model good work-life balance and ensure that the environment you create as a leader allows everyone to become as energized, effective, efficient, and engaged as possible.

○ Fraser, A. (2011). *The third space: Using life's little transitions to find balance and happiness.* North Sydney, New South Wales, Australia: Penguin Random House.

○ Fraser, A. (2012, July 9). *Dr. Adam Fraser explains the third space* [Video file]. Accessed at www.youtube.com/watch?v=dpk _dssZXqs on September 4, 2018.

○ McGonigal, K. (2012). *The willpower instinct: How self-control works, why it matters, and what you can do to get more of it.* New York: Penguin.

○ Pang, A. S.-K. (2016). *Rest: Why you get more done when you work less.* New York: Basic Books.

○ Schwartz, T. (2010). *The way we're working isn't working: The four forgotten needs that energize great performance.* New York: Free Press.

○ Smart, A. (2013). *Auto-pilot: The art and science of doing nothing.* New York: OR Books.

○ Walker, M. (2017). *Why we sleep: Unlocking the power of sleep and dreams.* New York: Scribner.

○ Zomorodi, M. (2017). *Bored and brilliant: How spacing out can unlock your most productive and creative self.* New York: St. Martin's Press.

○ Blogs and videos at Pang's website: www.deliberate.rest

○ Videos exploring John Medina's 12 Brain Rules website: http:// brainrules.net/brain-rules-video

READYING YOURSELF FOR STEPPING UP

GUIDING QUESTIONS

- How do you influence, encourage, and inspire others in your current role or profession?
- How could you do that more at the next level of leadership?

Leadership is about impact and influence. At all levels, we expect our leaders to influence, encourage, and inspire those they lead. Having a powerful influence, through and with others, can do nothing short of empower people. The negative view of leadership and power we have heard from so many women, which we described in the introduction (page 1), challenges us as we ponder how to ensure that women see the school leadership journey as within their capabilities, exciting, and fulfilling.

Too many women believe they aren't ready to lead. Or, they don't look for opportunities to influence the systems that dictate what goes on in the classroom. This chapter will help you reflect on your perceptions of leadership, focusing on developing confidence,

> After more than five decades of observing leadership . . . I have come to this conclusion: *Leadership is influence.* That's it—nothing more; nothing less. . . . The issue is not whether you influence someone. What needs to be settled is what kind of an influencer you will be.
>
> —John C. Maxwell, American leadership expert

sharing success, and handling expectations—yours and those of others. You will reflect on your current internal narrative and what you might need to shift so you view yourself as a leader. While we will continue to revisit your theory of self in other chapters, here, you'll build recognition and understanding of your leadership strengths and style—and learn to own them.

"Why Me? I'm Not Ready!"

If you don't know whether you're really ready to lead, now is the time to get specific about what holds you back. Recall from chapter 2 (page 33) how most men aim early in their careers for a leadership position and then do whatever it takes to get there as soon as possible. In contrast, women wait until they feel completely prepared and have acquired all the necessary knowledge and skills to do the job proficiently.

Tanya Cooke, an Australian school principal, would agree that the "We're here for the children" idea held her back. She reluctantly found herself in the leadership hot seat when her principal left for another position. "I said to my school council, 'I didn't want it, I can't and I just don't want to,' and everyone around me said, 'Yes, you can'" (as cited in Tarica, 2010). Although the role's administrative demands and the prospect of losing touch with the classroom concerned her, she agreed to act in the role until the school found someone else. In the meantime, she started to enjoy the role and realized she could do it. Looking back on her experience, Tanya says:

> I love the fact that I had the chance to do it in an acting role first because in doing that I realized that I could make a difference for every child, not just the ones in my classroom. That was a really strong feature for me. (as cited in Tarica, 2010)

This hands-on opportunity showed Tanya that as a leader, she could be brave, shape learning while maintaining strong connections with both students and staff, and have a greater impact.

You may not feel ready to lead, but you can only gain confidence in your leadership abilities if you, well, lead! Much like when you climb onto a bicycle for the first time, wobbling, and someone who cares about you supports you, you can step into leadership surrounded by a circle of support—perhaps even women with whom you take this book's twelve-week journey. Sure, you'll wobble a bit, but as American writer Rita Mae Brown put it, "Good judgment comes from experience, and often experience comes from bad judgment" (as cited in Weekes, 2007, p. 111).

If you have fallen into the trap of believing that your leadership skills must be polished and noteworthy, now is the time to work on self-compassion. Carrie Dennett (2018) has summarized research that compares perfectionists with those who exercise self-compassion and found that the latter group not only experiences far less stress but also makes more progress toward self-improvement goals. Beating yourself up for what you have yet to learn is not just nonsensical but self-destructive. The path to self-compassion fits well within the recommendations we gave in chapter 3 (page 51) for improving your bandwidth. Dennett (2018) summarizes:

> *Start with mindfulness. Unless you pay attention, you may be unaware of the thoughts that play and replay in your head. Practice observing your thoughts—are they compassionate or critical? Be curious and nonjudgmental—criticizing yourself for being self-critical adds insult to injury. Remind yourself often that to err is human, and to forgive, divine.*

 THINK ABOUT IT

Tanya Cooke's story highlights the energizing and empowering elements of leadership. What lit your fire to consider leadership and explore it more fully in this book? Or, do you still need to develop the confidence necessary to consider leadership, and the self-compassion to give yourself time and permission to do so—without having to be perfect? If you aren't yet sure, this chapter will guide you through the possibilities that are open to you as you engage in your leadership journey.

The Benefits of Becoming a Leader

In the introduction (page 1), we shared the notion of *power to*, where people use positional power not as *power over* others but instead, altruistically, to influence goals, determine how they might use time and resources, inspire others toward a common vision, build an atmosphere of collaborative trust, and more. Pause for a moment. What one concrete change would you like to see in your learning community? What would energize you if you could set the course toward making it happen?

It's certainly not uncommon, no matter how experienced we are, that we need to reconnect with the concepts of *power to* and *power with* to establish important foundations and protocols for new teams, or reinvigorate existing teams, especially when educators feel powerless because of policies or outside forces that seem to undermine their efficacy. To address these challenges, leaders, and especially women leaders, need to identify where they want to have an impact. This is the moral imperative of their *why*—to provide the conditions that empower teacher collaboration.

A Word From Jane

I want students to find mathematics just as enjoyable as painting or reading or even as their favorite physical education activity. One year, a school principal gave me *power to* via asking me to work with her mathematics team all year long. The teachers were skeptical about my vision, saying they'd be satisfied with better test scores, even if students disliked their classes. But, after noting that it wouldn't hurt to shoot for both student knowledge and engagement, they dug in, working together to create learning targets, formative assessments, classroom activities, and interventions. During this seven-month project, I spent one morning using the team's intervention lessons with a dozen students. About three hours into the session, one student exclaimed, "Guys, we've been doing math for *three hours* and didn't notice. Wow!" The students showed increased understanding, and the other teachers reported similar moments. *Power to*, added to *power with*, resulted in the teachers accomplishing more than they thought possible.

A Word From Barbara

Power with is an important aspect of teamwork—to build collective efficacy and tap into intrinsic motivation. It's about empowerment, right? This is all very well when the team is humming along, but what about when it is stuck or on cruise control? As a deputy principal, I experienced a leadership aha moment when I could see artificial harmony getting in the way of healthy debate on my team. I needed to flip my negative *taking over* concept of power and recognize my role in influencing and creating the conditions for open conversations to occur. That meant using *power to* lead the team, solidifying the belief and confidence I had in my own abilities to make decisions, reinvigorate norms and processes, and motivate and create a narrative to get back to our *why* and what's important to us. Privileging time to do so provided a tangible impact on a re-energized team open to rigorous conversations and valuing each other's contributions to our collective work. I was stuck on *power with*, but while teams are interdependent, they also need a leader with *power to*. As a leader, *power to* informs *power with*—embrace it!

Perhaps you already know the impact you wish to have as a leader—your *power to*—but if you still don't know, consider one example of the impact you can have if you use your power as a leader: a better balance between the masculine and feminine archetypes, as discussed in chapter 1 (page 9). With more balance, values would shift and education policies might reflect both sides. Consider the importance of both and the dynamic tension between them that shapes educational decision making.

Table 4.1 provides a few examples of masculine and feminine emphases in education. What changes would you like to influence?

Table 4.1: Examples of Archetypal Masculine and Feminine Emphases in School Reform

Masculine Emphases That School Reform Promotes	Feminine Emphases That School Reform Has Disregarded
Data-driven instruction	Instruction based on student motivation
Teacher accountability and evaluation	Support for teacher development and growth
Technology as solution	Teacher-student relationship as solution
Standards and assessment	Curiosity, play, and flow in learning
Making students career and college ready	Educating the whole child

Where would you like *power to*? What goals would make leadership as exciting and fulfilling for you as it has been for us?

The Pedagogical Gifts of a Good Leader

We are keenly aware of the lack of status of teaching, arguably one of the most important professions on the planet. *Lack of status* means that others often make decisions for us. Think of the impact of government policies that may or may not reflect sufficient educator input. Enhancing the status of the teaching profession falls to leaders. To do this, you need a keen awareness of your pedagogical gifts. There is nothing prideful about stating your strengths. Rather, recognize this key fact: *Your gifts that make you a highly qualified educator, and that you will bring to leadership, aren't for you. They are for those you teach and lead. Identifying them, and advocating for being able to use them, are steps in unwrapping those gifts and putting them to maximum use.* Would you ever leave birthday presents still in their wrapping paper long after you receive them? Of course not! Unwrap those gifts and use them!

Emeritus Professor Frank Crowther is widely regarded as one of the world's leading advocates of the teaching profession. Much of his work focuses on teacher leadership. Throughout his book *Energising Teaching: The Power of Your Unique Pedagogical Gift* (2016), he challenges educators to take time to reflect on their gifts. How would you answer the following five questions adapted from Crowther's (2016) work?

1. Are your core values, hopes, and aspirations for the future clear to you and your colleagues?

2. What is your special gift for teaching and leading?

3. What do you do to enhance the quality of your whole-school workplace?

4. How do you enrich your school's distinctive pedagogy through your professional sharing and learning?

5. What educational philosophy guides your professional work?

How do your responses inform your view as to what makes a good education leader?

Consider how your answers align with research. When asked about the characteristics of effective leaders, New Zealand teachers listed *trust, respect, role modeling, good communication,* and *leading by example* as their top five (Moir, Hattie, & Jansen, 2014). Our experience and research into educational leadership highlight the need for integrated models of leadership that place greater emphasis on relational qualities as well as managerial skills. Key adjectives that appear throughout the literature describe effective leaders as *fair, supportive, collaborative, decisive, flexible, tactful, innovative,* and *persistent*; these attributes foster trust, an essential condition for school effectiveness.

Researchers Anthony S. Bryk and Barbara Schneider (2002) see *relational trust* as a social resource for school improvement—where *trust* is a resource with the potential to accelerate performance when people feel supported, assured, and open to engaging in collaboration.

Educator and author Stephen M. R. Covey (2012) describes *high trust* as a performance multiplier, a catalyst through which people work and learn together uninhibited by feeling self-protective and defensive. To create high trust, leaders must be credible. People's confidence in leaders (and leaders' confidence in themselves) is built around trust and what educational leadership expert John West-Burnham (2011) calls the *four Cs*.

1. **Credibility:** The extent to which a leader has integrity

2. **Consistency:** Authentic behavior, openness, reliability, "Do as I do"

3. **Competence:** Professional ability and expertise

4. **Confidence:** The basis of trust in leadership

He places these variables into his four Cs formula: credibility + consistency + competence = confidence (West-Burnham, 2011). Confidence is at the core. The leader who demonstrates these three factors inspires confidence, which is the basis of trust in leadership. As we see in the data throughout this book, for women, developing confidence is key. Of the three elements in West-Burham's model, it is how women reflect on their competence and leadership skills, without being perfect, that can build their trust and that of others in their ability to lead. Enacting all of these elements of leadership builds trust—and confidence.

Mike Helal and Michael Coelli (2016), at the Melbourne Institute of Applied Economic and Social Research, sought to answer the question, What makes a perfect principal? They investigated whether an equation could provide the answer. While the mathematics may be complex, the research had relatively straightforward results: principals significantly boost students' grades if they set goals, promote professional development, and encourage interaction among staff. Importantly, these interactions involve the principal learning alongside teachers about what works and doesn't work. They also found that a school's morale improves with effective principals (Helal & Coelli, 2016)—no surprise there.

In an education context, successful instructional leaders capture direct, evidence-informed approaches and use them to improve teaching and learning in their schools. They do this by creating enabling conditions that clearly and intentionally support the development of teachers' capacity to improve student learning. The collaborative nature of this professional work cannot occur without a foundation of trust and respect. Trust develops through everyday leadership actions and interactions, not through sporadic efforts such as *Today is trust day*.

Collaboration and Shared Leadership

As important as *power to* is, great leaders also know how to draw on *power with*, fostering collaboration and shared leadership to increase effectiveness. Michael Fullan (2011) wrote a deliberately provocative paper, *Choosing the Wrong Drivers for Whole System Reform*. He found that whether people agreed or disagreed, they viewed thinking about effective and ineffective policy drivers as a productive way of considering whole-system reform. While the following four drivers have a place, Fullan (2011) considers them "wrong" in that they alone won't drive success:

1. ***accountability:*** *using test results, and teacher appraisal, to reward or punish teachers and schools vs capacity building [intrinsic motivation];*
2. ***individual teacher and leadership quality:*** *promoting individual vs group [team] solutions;*

3. **technology:** *investing in and assuming that the wonders of the digital world will carry the day vs instruction [instructional improvement];*

4. **fragmented strategies** *vs integrated [allness] or systemic strategies. ([text added]; p. 5)*

Fullan (2011) wants education systems to see that individual and collective intrinsic motivation and the moral imperative of our work as leaders drive learning and teaching—the power of our work's relational nature.

Schools and education systems are focusing on transferring greater agency from the external to the internal, moving from isolation (practice shrouded in privacy) to interdependency, with networks of schools and classrooms working interdependently. By creating powerful professional learning cultures and implementing effective learning plans with their teachers, great school leaders improve teaching and student learning. Where schools and systems properly implement professional learning communities and consistently "focus on improving learning outcomes, they help teachers develop and integrate new learning into their existing practice" (Stoll, Harris, & Handscomb, 2012, p. 7).

THINK ABOUT IT

Where do you see Fullan's (2011) *right drivers* (intrinsic motivation, teamwork, instructional improvement, and allness) in play in your learning community? How do these drivers inform the leader you want to become through fostering motivation, inspiring teamwork, and engaging teachers and students in continuous improvement?

Allness affects all teachers and students. It focuses on coherence, rather than fragmentation of strategies and practice. Fragmentation is when we see, for example, standards for student assessments and teacher performance and development as discrete, autonomous boxes rather than interdependent, reinforcing components for learning and growth. Allness creates a shared understanding with a small number of ambitious goals and the support to achieve these goals (such as policies and capacity building).

In your current role, do you see fragmentation and separation of policies and strategies, or do they interconnect and inform each other? One can view the concept of allness from a classroom, school, or system perspective.

Research supports the effectiveness of intrinsic motivation versus extrinsic motivations (such as monetary rewards). Daniel H. Pink (2010) summarizes three key factors that drive intrinsic human motivation.

1. **Autonomy:** Having some say in what you do

2. **Mastery:** Believing that you can accomplish what you have set out to do

3. **Purpose:** Connecting your efforts with a meaningful goal, cause, or aspiration

Pink (2010) also points out that when people feel intrinsically motivated, they have more creativity, and they use their discretionary time to do whatever it takes to reach their goals.

Think about the students in your school. When they engage in something they find interesting, challenging, or rewarding, they are more likely to persist, find creative solutions, or come up with novel ideas. And teachers who work in a professional learning community will go the extra mile and support and advocate for one another when they are energized in working on something they all find important.

THINK ABOUT IT

Answer the following questions. How do your answers show up in the way you teach, lead, and interact with your family? Language reflects values and beliefs. What do these answers tell you about your values and beliefs?

- What do you consider important?
- What do you enjoy doing?
- What do you do well?

Leadership and Views of Power

So far, we've looked at building confidence, identifying and using personal strengths, and having an intrinsic goal as necessities for the leadership journey. A fourth necessity is viewing leadership and power in a positive way.

Researchers Francesca Gino, Caroline Ashley Wilmuth, and Alison Wood Brooks (2015) have found that women perceive professional power as less desirable than men do. Further, while women have more life goals than men, they place less importance on power-related goals. In its leadership development work with leaders around the world, Korn Ferry has used psychologist David McClelland's psychometric tools to uncover participants' social motives of power, achievement, and affiliation (as cited in Burnison, 2018). In Barbara's work with the Hay Group (now Korn Ferry), they observed school leaders' perceptions of power caused them to distance themselves from power for fear they will become motivated by it. Initially, school leaders associate power with self-aggrandizement, as opposed to a meaningful influence for empowering others.

As a school principal and as past chair of the Association of Heads of Independent Schools of Australia, and through her Churchill Fellowship research, Karen Spiller (2017) advocates that women should have an appropriate place to explore their understanding of power. This way, they learn to wield it in leadership roles and discuss ways they can exert power and influence that have compatibility with their beliefs and personalities. Spiller (2017) says:

> *"Power" is likely to remain a taboo for women as they consider their career options unless there is a more rigorous self-interrogation of the unconscious beliefs and biases they hold and an examination of their responses to or acceptance of "masculinized cultures of power." (p. 10)*

School leader Chris Cotton's metaphor of *the spaces between the pebbles in a jar* suggests that "leadership is not enshrined in structure, position or power relationships. Instead, it is a variable and fluid capacity, and it flows within and beyond an organization—it fills the spaces between the pebbles" (as cited in Jackson, 2017).

THINK ABOUT IT

What are your reactions to the phrases *positional power, power to,* and *power with*? How do you view the relationship between having power and having the ability to intrinsically motivate others? What does this mean for your school leadership journey?

Women have an image problem with power partly because they associate it with the masculine images of power and leadership, as discussed in chapter 1 (page 9). Educational leadership development training has emphasized the hard skills of administration, but based on research, it has begun to rapidly balance those with the soft skills involved in mentoring others, building trust, collaborating, and intrinsically motivating others. We devote chapter 8 (page 131) to working with your soft skills.

Personal Leadership Resources

Kenneth Leithwood (2017) in describing the leadership practices in the Ontario leadership framework (Leithwood, 2012) also highlights a small number of personal resources (cognitive, social, and psychological) that explain the variation in leaders' effectiveness. This points to evidence of an association between leaders' personal qualities and leadership success. This research has underpinned and informed school leadership frameworks in numerous OECD countries. The report *10 Strong Claims About Successful School Leadership* (National College for Leadership of Schools and Children's Services, 2010) shares compelling research that emphasizes a small number of personal resources or traits (as shown in figure 4.1, page 78) inform recruitment and development:

> *Our claim is that the most successful school leaders are open-minded and ready to learn from others. They are flexible rather than dogmatic within a system of core values. They are persistent in their high expectations of others, and they are emotionally resilient and optimistic. Such traits help explain why successful leaders facing daunting conditions are often able to push forward against the odds. (p. 7)*

While numerous traits are associated with leadership, Leithwood (2017) argues that these small but critical personal resources (outlined in figure 4.1, page 78), "are only those for which there is compelling empirical evidence suggesting they are instrumental to leadership success" (p. 38). As you reflect on these resources, consider the personal resources you bring to leadership and what you currently use, or could use, to support your leadership role. These are the resources that shape the leadership experience and our ongoing development.

Women clearly feel challenged and inadequate when they think they need to have done it all, or they need skills and competencies you would expect of more experienced school leaders. Most leaders, though, still have to work on some skills shown in figure 4.1 (page 78), even at the end of their careers.

In this book, we will spend the least time focusing on the cognitive resources involving day-to-day instructional leadership, although chapters 9 and 10 (pages 153 and 169) touch on problem solving. Chapter 8 (page 131) tackles ongoing development of the social resources through the framework of emotional intelligence. And, this entire journey is about bolstering your psychological resources. Practice self-compassion right now by identifying the resources you already have. Claim them, and get ready to use those gifts!

Remember that you're not meant to know everything, nor do we ever master all of these cognitive, social, and psychological resources. As many experienced, successful leaders will tell you, leaders are learners, and learning is lifelong—that's the exciting part! Don't expect to tie up learning in a neat little bow and check *I've arrived*. New information, new challenges, and different environments and contexts will always arise. For leaders, the key is the way they look at and respond to these challenges, internally and externally. Self-efficacy and confidence in leadership doesn't mean knowing the answer or immediately solving the problem; it means knowing that you have what it takes to figure it out or find a way, using all of the resources in figure 4.1 (page 78).

Cognitive Resources	Problem Solving
	Knowledge About Learning Conditions With Direct Effects on Student Learning
Social Resources (Emotional Intelligence)	Perceiving Emotions
	Managing Emotions
	Acting in Emotionally Appropriate Ways
Psychological Resources	Optimism
	Self-Efficacy
	Resilience
	Proactivity

Source: Leithwood, 2017, p. 38.

Figure 4.1: Personal leadership resources.

If you ever fall into the trap of self-doubt or lack of confidence, consider these five strategies for getting unstuck and finding time to evaluate your personal leadership resources and the changes you want to make to achieve your goals.

1. **Find your *why*:** *Why* lead? Think about how your answer taps into your intrinsic motivation, the moral imperative of teaching and leading, and your vision for engaging in this work. The power of finding your *why* is grounded in emotion and deep reasoning that enable you to persevere in adversity. Consider this as you look at Simon Sinek's (2009) TED Talk *How Great Leaders Inspire Action* (www.ted.com/talks/simon_sinek _how_great_leaders_inspire_action). Sinek explores the *golden circle*, a simple but powerful model for inspirational leadership, which starts with the question, Why?

2. **Take a strengths-based approach in your reflections:** Reflect on your strengths, and build on them. What energizes those personal resources that make you unique? Do more of what works well. Try exploring your strengths through the Virtues in Action (VIA) tool, based on researcher and scholar Martin Seligman's work (www.viacharacter.org/www/character). Find out more about your character strengths and your core capacities for thinking, feeling, and behaving in ways that can benefit you and others.

3. **Be present, mindful, and focused on the now:** Set yourself up for success. Be present with what you are doing in this moment—in action

and reflection—and don't get distracted by what you are not doing, should be doing, or need to do next (a bit like not fully enjoying your delicious lunch because you're wondering what's for dinner). Take a moment to reflect on any habits that distract you—those default settings that take you away from engaging in and enjoying what's important now.

4. **Make the small changes that make a difference:** While you may have the big picture of where you want to go and why, one big leap probably won't get you there. Everyone knows how paralyzing it feels when it all just seems too much and, perhaps, unachievable. Elite tennis players want to win, but during a match, they focus on the smaller pieces that will get them there. They don't think about the last set or the last game but stay fully prepared for the next serve and the next return. You know what you want to achieve; now break it down into smaller, more manageable actions.

5. **Focus on the things you can influence:** If something isn't under your control, be it forces in the community or forceful personalities across the hall, let it go and concentrate on the things you might gain *power to* change. Let's go back to you knowing your strengths and what energizes you. Who are you on the inside, and what do people see on the outside? How do you activate your leadership strengths and values in a way that connects with others' intrinsic motivations, values, and moral dispositions that led them to work in education? Engage others in your vision, recognize their gifts, and celebrate their contributions. Good leaders are good storytellers; share your story. As Sinek (2009) says, "People don't buy what you do; they buy why you do it."

Australian school and system leader Coralee Pratt finds journaling to be one of her key leadership journey strategies—and one of the ways she identifies her gifts and *power to* motivations. Faithful to the process since 2003, she enjoys reading through past reflections, notable quotes, and personal aspirations. Years ago, she journaled, *The more I learn about leadership, the more I feel inadequate. The vast amount of information, opinion, advice, and theory about leadership styles and how to develop the skills is making me feel quite overwhelmed.* She said, "This prompted me to consider how to support the potential leaders within my sphere of influence" (as cited in Watterston & Watterston, 2010, p. 32).

You have potential within you to open up worlds of possibility that are uniquely yours. That should inspire, energize, and empower you. As a leader, how will this potential shape the way you want to lead and the way you influence others? Your attitude has a powerful effect on whether you succeed. Henry Ford (1947) said it best: "Whether you believe you can do a thing or not, you are right" (p. 64).

And remember—taking care of yourself is a key part of your leadership journey and your life journey. Reflect on the two big truths in chapter 3 (page 51): (1) you cannot care for others unless you care for yourself and (2) your staff need to see you model a good work-life balance. That's fundamental to building leadership sustainability. We cannot emphasize enough the importance of privileging time to create rituals that sustain your energy and inspiration and reinvigorate your work.

When you are *in flow*, you fully engage all sources of energy—physical, emotional, mental, and spiritual (or moral purpose). Loehr and Schwartz (2003) developed this concept of full engagement when they researched ways to increase capacity for sustained leadership and peak performance and build endurance, strength, flexibility, self-control, and focus. These four energy sources are highly relevant not only for leadership but also for life. These are not either-or aspects of life; seek alignment, and integrate self-care into every day. Consider what you might start doing, stop doing, and do more of.

Next Steps in the Journey

Take time to challenge your mental models of leadership; reflect on and consider your experience, your observations, the preceding chapters, pearls of wisdom from other women leaders, your values, and your beliefs. Bring these thoughts together to discover your inner long-term vision. Start to create your leadership philosophy.

With potential, you grow. Your leadership philosophy will develop over time. Present it in a way that is uniquely yours, whether through narrative, poetry, a graphic, a manifesto, or a storyboard (see the following reflection exercise for examples).

Step in for Further Reflection

The following activity provides you with an invaluable opportunity to reflect on the ideas, strategies, and concepts covered in this chapter. If you are approaching *Step In, Step Up* as a twelve-week journey, you can spread out over several days.

You may complete it individually or with a group so you can share your thoughts and ideas. Keep a journal so you can revisit your thoughts as you travel this journey.

In the programs they facilitate, D. Trinidad Hunt and Lynne Truair, two leaders in the field of women in educational leadership, emphatically encourage an approach that creates a living philosophy of leadership—"living" in the sense that it changes, deepens and evolves as you grow and develop as a leader. They share a very practical leadership process that fires up those neuropathways that we explored in chapter 3 (page 51) to optimally foster your brain energy so you develop a leadership philosophy.

As you develop your leadership philosophy, it begins to improve, refine, and polish your leadership competencies.

Making personal changes might be easier than it initially appears if you understand a little bit about the brain and neuroplasticity. The brain is an instrument you can use to implement change easily. As you reflect and put your thoughts on paper, you are creating new neural pathways in the brain. If you reread your goals daily or even weekly, you strengthen a new mental map. This process replaces old habits with new thoughts that lead to a desire for action and change. The inner work is the first step. Then you can move from an internal process to an external active process, taking steps that lead to the change you desire. D. Trinidad Hunt offers these thoughts about leadership:

> *Essentially, we are already leaders. . . . The only question we want to answer is, "What kind of leader do I intend to be?" Thus action is usually values based. . . . Values are our ethical and moral compass and help determine when to say yes or no to something. Our values naturally lead to action or how we behave with others in life.*
>
> *Consider these three steps:*
>
> 1. *Brainstorm ten to twelve of your top professional values. These would be the things you believe are vital to the well-being of yourself and others, as well as the educational system in which you work.*
> 2. *Pick your top five to seven values from the longer list.*
> 3. *Trinidad often refers to W. Edwards Deming, the father of total quality management, who said in a seminar she attended that it is impossible to lead without a philosophy of leadership.*
>
> *In this final step, develop your philosophy of leadership in either a mind map or a written statement. Don't be concerned if you can't finish it immediately. Just jump in and get started. This philosophy will be a living document, changing and growing as you grow personally and professionally.*
>
> *Finally, remember that you are laying a new neural map in your brain. This will be the first step in a natural, positive growth process that will eventually take you where you wish to go in life. (personal communication, April 15, 2018)*

Figure 4.2 (page 82) shows different ways of developing a philosophy of leadership. From our experience in numerous workshops, some women started with these types of examples as a sketch for further writing. Others have said that it was enough to just have the key ideas and values as a constant reminder.

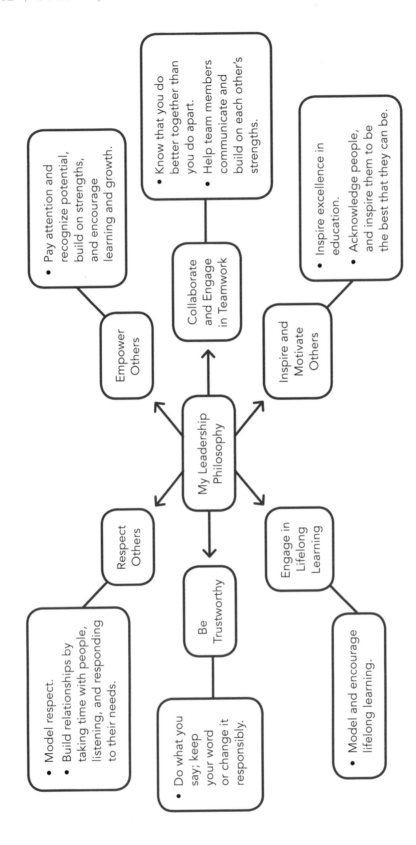

Source: © *2018 by Trinidad Hunt. Used with permission.*

Figure 4.2: Example leadership philosophy mind map.

TAKING THE PATH TO MATURITY

GUIDING QUESTIONS

- At what development stage do you find yourself?
- How have you felt stuck in neutral in your development?
- What adjustments might you make to meet those you lead where they are during change?

Too often, people think that adults have arrived when they've actually barely made it to the first stage of adulthood—that crucial time where you leave self-centered childishness behind and wrestle with fitting into a community, learning to collaborate, and embracing community values. Successful leadership, though, requires moving to a higher level of maturity, where, rather than seeking simple answers, you can see the merits of other viewpoints and grapple with ongoing paradigms. Making this move even more difficult is the nonlinear, spiraling nature of development. When you take on new roles or responsibilities, you often move *backward* to an earlier development stage.

Let's look at how the development stages become visible through the actions, reactions, and beliefs of a school leader who has

> If any human being is to reach full maturity, both the masculine and feminine sides of the personality must be brought up into consciousness.
>
> —M. Esther Harding (1888–1971), British-American psychoanalyst

assumed a new position. We will call her Shauna. Her story blends together the stories of several school leaders Jane has coached.

> Shauna dreamed of starting a school from scratch, so accepting the principalship of an existing school that was recreating itself as a fine arts magnet school seemed like a great fit. "It's your show," the school district assured her.
>
> In her previous role, Shauna's work implementing a visiting artists program had cemented her reputation as a visionary yet collaborative leader. At this fine arts magnet school, she envisioned teachers tapping into the artistic pursuits most interesting to them—music, drama, creative writing, dance, photography, design, and more—to develop an arts-infused curriculum. And Shauna, in describing her vision for the school, emphasized that each teacher could choose. "Integrating the arts can make learning come alive. We have a blank slate that allows us to creatively meet the needs of our students, who are so diverse in cultural backgrounds, diverse in interests, and diverse in how their hunger for learning is best kindled."
>
> But from just about day one at the new school, she met with resistance. Most of the staff had stayed out of convenience, not out of excitement for the new program. Shauna soon learned that many of her teachers had never set foot in the theater and art museum a few blocks from the school. She quickly arranged field trips to those sites as part of professional development the week before school started.
>
> But as the school year got underway, instead of bringing ideas to the table, teachers brought questions, concerns, and complaints. They didn't have time to plan all of this. Students would fall behind in reading. Shauna's strategic plan didn't provide enough details. They wanted examples. Shauna found herself pleading with her increasingly disengaged staff, "You have a wonderful blank slate."
>
> "They're lazy," Shauna found herself thinking. "And they don't have a creative bone in their bodies. I need a whole new staff."

You may wonder, "Didn't Shauna see that her vision overwhelmed the staff and they needed more direction? Why didn't she work more collaboratively?" But to understand Shauna's developmental needs, a better question to ask is, "Shauna, how might you make sense of your actions?"

Shauna would probably indicate that she wanted to set free everyone's creativity. That's what the fine arts are all about. Getting her to better understand the teachers' viewpoint would require different kinds of support, depending on her development stage, or she simply wouldn't have the capability to make the shift.

We use lots of tools in leadership coaching, but one of our foundational premises is that adults are at various stages of development. The framework that this chapter presents describes the increasing stages of complexity and perspective taking that adults master as they mature. People of any age may be at any stage, depending on whether their experiences and decisions fostered growth or stagnation, but older people are more likely to have reached the higher stages.

In her book *Changing on the Job*, leadership development advisor Jennifer Garvey Berger (2012) gives three reasons to pay attention to someone's current development stage.

1. Instead of judging others when they fail, you can parse out what they weren't ready to handle. Thus we'd reframe, "Shauna ignored teacher needs," as "Shauna inappropriately applied the golden rule because she assumed everyone would crave the blank slate approach that motivated her."

2. You can tailor support to match developmental needs. Shauna, especially when under stress, struggled to step into others' shoes. It stunned her when the focus groups she'd agreed to let Jane facilitate revealed that the teachers thought *she* was the lazy one because her plan lacked detail.

3. Most organizations run as if people operate at higher levels of development than they actually do. Couple this with the fact that most people backslide a bit when they take on roles with increased responsibility, and you have a perfect storm for leadership failure.

Once you learn about this framework, you may find it tempting to guess others' levels of development. However, doing so takes a great deal of study and practice. As a leader, notwithstanding the importance of clarifying your theory of change, know that context matters. Success in one context, as Shauna found, won't automatically mean success in another context, even when the contexts include similar priorities. A multitude of complex factors come into play. Like teaching a similar subject with a different class, you need to know not only your subject but, more important, your students—differentiation is key. In this chapter, we aim to help you discern your level of development, suggest ways to deal with complex issues (where, for example, both sides hold part of the truth), and show you how to improve the perspective taking that your leadership role requires.

This chapter will help you consider your ability to think independently and paradoxically, both of which require higher levels of adult development to do well, while simultaneously working within your community.

Stages of Adult Development

Besides Jennifer Garvey Berger (2012), others such as psychologist Angelina Bennet (2010) and management guru Robert Kegan have contributed to adult development theory (Kegan & Lahey, 2009). The following descriptions of adult development draw from all their perspectives.

THINK ABOUT IT

Invest the time to complete this reflection exercise before reading further so you can discern your own development stage when you read on. Journaling concretely about a real dilemma you have faced will provide needed material for identifying your current development stage.

Think of a difficult situation or decision you recently faced. Take several minutes to write about it—how you reacted to or processed things, what actions you took, and what you thought and felt about it (Berger, 2012).

In other words, tell a story about it. Take your time, perhaps as long as thirty minutes. You'll use it to think about your development. Set this aside while you read an overview of the stages.

Pre-Adult Development

By definition, children aren't mature. That's why adults don't let them drive cars, vote, or drink alcoholic beverages. Although most people progress to the first stage of adult development before entering the work world, a small percentage—perhaps 10–15 percent—never quite make it (Kegan, 1994).

People at this stage only see things from their perspective, often called the *self-sovereign mind.* And they avoid delving into complexities, preferring simple cause-and-effect answers or clear positions on even the messiest of issues. While few adults and even fewer leaders get stuck at this stage, note that most people temporarily backslide as they take on new roles. Thus you need to keep this stage on your radar.

Every stage has strengths and shows development from the previous stage. Those with a self-sovereign mind have usually identified their consistent likes, talents, and attributes. And they generally have a keen awareness of their own perspective. However, they have the following weaknesses.

- They struggle to empathize because they can only fathom their own perspective. They see other people as either helpers or barriers.
- They know the rules, but will devote effort to getting around any that inconvenience them.
- Their motivation to follow rules often flows from fear of retaliation or of getting caught.

Think about Shauna for a moment. While this was not her true level of development, she did lose track of other perspectives and categorized her staff as barriers to the magnet school program. Remember, she'd gained a reputation as a collaborative leader, but the pressure of feeling unsuccessful—and disliked—kept her from accessing the ways she usually worked with other perspectives.

It is dangerous to assume that other people have caused all problems that occur, as Shauna did. Leaders need an objective way of teasing out their role and others' roles in things that go wrong. Otherwise, like Shauna, they select the wrong solutions. It is equally dangerous, though, to assume that everything is your fault. Take a moment and contemplate: Do you overemphasize blaming others? Blaming yourself?

THINK ABOUT IT

Revisit the situation or decision you journaled about for the "Think About It" activity on page 86. Consider problems you have faced. Whose perspectives did you consider? For what did you take responsibility? Who else was responsible and for what? Did you feel tempted to put yourself at the center of your mindset? In other words, did you backslide to the self-sovereign mind? Occasionally, situations warrant this, but usually, it leads to poor leadership perspectives.

Adult Development Stage One: The Socialized Mind

Most adults find themselves at the socialized mind stage of development. The essence of this stage involves fitting into a community. This means valuing what the community values, whether that community is a family, a business, a school, a religious organization, a social or political group, or a combination of two or more of these.

WORDS FROM A LEADER

Know yourself first. Understand the values and principles that guide you and your decisions. Traditionally, we do not give attention to this space before starting a leadership journey, and it has to be a deliberate act. For me, it was a mentor who insisted I do this, and it has been invaluable. (Annette Rome, Australian principal, P–12 co-ed/single-sex school, personal communication, April 12, 2018)

You can celebrate people at this stage for their devotion to something bigger than themselves. After all, school leaders need to be in sync with their boards' values, and they want teachers to uphold the school's values. And you can only move toward a common vision if you agree on core values and align decisions and actions accordingly.

Reaching this stage also allows for successful collaboration through a shared purpose. You accept group norms and rules. You appreciate feedback or recognition that your efforts have made a difference.

At this stage, your notions of who you should become often come from the community. For example, recall your mental image of *school principal* from chapter 1 (page 9). People with a socialized mind might find that an image search on Google reinforces their view.

However, consider the following features of people at this stage.

- At this stage, people's core motivation comes from a desire for the community to accept and like them. This can work well in a stable organization. However, it can also make leaders avoid conflict or shrink from taking an unpopular stand.

- Their source of authority comes from the community or the people whose approval they seek. If such authorities give conflicting advice, a leader may truly not have strategies for making a choice and moving forward.

- They struggle to see perspectives other than the community's and may not fathom how people could hold a different, obviously "wrong" perspective.

- They are highly sensitive to feedback because of their desire to belong.

- They may bury thoughts and feelings rather than acknowledge that a community decision has made them uneasy or upset them.

Shauna operated from a socialized mind as she became principal of the magnet school. She accepted the vision that the school handed to her. The staff's waves of disapproval stymied her rather than prompting better perspective taking. She had become accustomed to using her genuinely excellent collaborative skills in a community of like-minded souls. The cumulative effect of these factors caused some backsliding toward the self-sovereign mind stage.

Shauna also assumed that all the teachers had the same needs. This may not have mattered in a less complex environment, but she was asking for big changes. She needed coaching to move from the golden rule to a more appropriate platinum rule, which we state as: *Do unto others according to their needs, not your needs.*

Coaching helped Shauna see that she needed to resolve the conflict between her self-images as team player and leader. This primed her to do the hard work of moving on to the next development stage.

 THINK ABOUT IT

Revisit the situation or decision you journaled about for the "Think About It" activity on page 86. Did you get caught between the roles you had, such as good mother, good teacher, and good leader? What choices did you have? Can you think of more alternatives you might have considered before making your decision? Did someone questioning community direction catch you off guard? Or did you struggle with hints of rejection from others? You may have felt the pull of the complexities that those at the next development stage have learned to handle.

Adult Development Stage Two: The Self-Authored Mind

At this stage, adults begin to actively explore other perspectives and consider the added value those might bring to a decision or a team. They can think independently from their community, using their own internal values, and they have clarity on how they chose those values. This internal compass helps them consider how they can operate in different environments. Note that you may use this compass well in one arena of your life and not as well in another.

Adults at this stage of development take complexity for granted. People with a self-authored mind are comfortable with ongoing tensions, such as gleaning data from standardized tests while also using teacher-created tasks to inform instruction; or setting a project's vision while also seeking input on that project. They know that one-size-fits-all disciplinary rules won't always work and feel comfortable making exceptions when the circumstances don't gel with a rule's intentions.

This stage marks the beginning of effective adult functioning, and perhaps 40 percent of adults reach this level (Kegan, 1994). Others see these adults as grounded and self-motivated. These adults have a congruence between who they are and the work they strive to accomplish.

This stage's strengths come with some warnings; just because you're aware of complexities and various perspectives doesn't mean you use the information well.

- Generally, people at this stage can see themselves quite objectively. They know their strengths and the blind spots they must continuously manage.

- Their inner values are so clear that they often know what is right with little deliberation. For this reason, though, they may find it tough to open up to new information and insights.

- They want others to recognize and thus benefit from their expertise and authority. However, they often use their strengths of intellectualism and rationalization as defense mechanisms, making it difficult for them to hear feedback.

For women, reaching this stage means comfortably managing the tension between traditional female roles in education and pushing for the needed feminine perspectives. They have the ability to step into the status quo, consider gender and generational differences, and find common ground where all genders can benefit from change.

 THINK ABOUT IT

Revisit the situation or decision you journaled about for the "Think About It" activity on page 86. If you encountered any gender stereotypes, how did you deal with them? How did you use different perspectives? How comfortable do you feel when a situation has no clear choice? In such situations, how would you determine the best possible outcome, the worst possible outcome, and the biggest risk? Keep asking until you understand the root of your motivations.

Think about how well you can work with the double bind women face: "In the workplace, women are expected to get ahead by some mysterious combination of femininity and intelligence while simultaneously getting things done and disguising drive" (Holland, 2017, p. 219).

Have you backed off when someone has accused you of not being ladylike or some other permutation of this double bind? Or have you built a support network, studied tactics for influencing perceptions of what is or isn't "ladylike," and forged ahead?

Adult Development Stage Three: The Self-Transforming Mind

Perhaps 1 percent of the world population reaches this stage, although more people may temporarily operate at this level of complexity (Kegan, 1994). Those with a self-transforming mind deeply know that they will *never* adequately reach their life purpose on their own with just their internal systems. And they usually have huge purposes.

 WORDS FROM A LEADER

The best advice I ever received in relation to leadership is to become curious about what other people think, value, and care about. Listen well to what they say and then look for common ground and mutual purpose. The more we can understand the people we lead, the more likely we will find ways to collaborate and work toward common goals. (Lucy West, American mathematics educational consultant and author, personal communication, May 30, 2018)

Instead of divides, the people at this stage look out and see one big community of humankind. Where others see differences, they see common threads. They constantly bring up wider contexts and help others see what is truly at stake and how they might go about working together.

You tap into a self-transforming mind when you help a team realize, "This is not about assigning consequences for behavior but about helping students embrace responsibility."

You tap into a self-transforming mind when you guide others in realizing and acting on the fact that students find mathematics taught well as enjoyable as the delight of a good book, the swish of a basketball hitting nothing but net, or the flourish of a great art project.

You tap into a self-transforming mind when the teachers you lead feel safe in opening their classrooms, their lessons, and their practices to their colleagues, knowing that collectively they can improve everyone's practice.

You tap into a self-transforming mind when you influence other leaders by saying, "This is too complex an issue to solve so quickly. Let's step back, ground ourselves in possible perspectives, and figure out what we can and can't fix long term."

THINK ABOUT IT

Revisit the situation or decision you journaled about for the "Think About It" activity on page 86. Before moving on, consider how your reflections on your story might inform a similar situation in the future. What development stage best describes you? What level of complexity and perspective taking are you ready for? Where do you need support and growth?

Reflection on People's Capacity

We realize that we've presented a quick run-through of this valuable framework. Our explanation is short because you develop not by reading but by reflecting. Invest the time to reflect for two big reasons. First, understanding your location on the spiraling path of development can help you target your best steps forward. Second, reflecting on this framework can help you create an environment where everyone can continue to develop. Instead of judging people for what they aren't yet ready to do, you can ensure that how you present change fits within their capacity.

Over the next week, work through the Step in for Further Reflection questions one at a time (see page 93). What next steps might you take? As you reflect, keep the following big points in mind.

- Pointing out to someone else, "Actually, you are at a lower stage of development than you think you are" does not help. Instead, use this framework to step back from judgment, redefine what he or she is ready to do, and support him or her in doing that.

- Underestimating your development stage is probably safer than assuming you are more evolved than those around you.

- When asking for big change, consider what people at each stage might need.
    - **The self-sovereign mind:** Personal benefits
    - **The socialized mind:** Clear group norms and values

- **The self-authored mind:** Acknowledgment of sticky issues and paradoxes
- **The self-transforming mind:** A chance to contemplate and make use of the view from thirty thousand feet

Next Steps in the Journey

As you consider your strengths, keep in mind that how well and how willing you are to use them in part depends on your stage of development. At which stage are you? Might a new position cause you to fall back a stage, as happened for Shauna? Reflecting on what your own behavior, reactions, and responses might look like at your current level of development, as well as at a lower one, can help you recognize which responses are helpful and where you might reach out to a coach or mentor to better navigate your new responsibilities.

The next chapter further explores knowing yourself, this time helping you discover and acknowledge your hardwired strengths and how they can contribute to your success as a leader.

Step in for Further Reflection

The following activities provide you with valuable opportunities to reflect on the ideas, strategies, and concepts covered in this chapter. If you are approaching *Step In, Step Up* as a twelve-week journey, you can spread these out over several days.

You may complete them individually or with a group so you can share your thoughts and ideas. Keep a journal so you can revisit your thoughts as you travel this journey.

1. Revisit the situation or decision you journaled about for the "Think About It" activity on page 86. If this situation or decision didn't provide insights into your current development stage, choose another dilemma, perhaps one in which you know you could have made better choices. Work through the questions in the "Think About It" boxes for each development stage.

2. Think through the following questions to further probe your current development stage. Consider, too, how your stage might shift depending on your comfort with a role.

   - When you receive negative feedback:
     - **The self-sovereign mind**—Do you argue with feedback because it just doesn't incorporate your perspective?

- **The socialized mind**—Are you sensitive to feedback because you need others to accept you?
- **The self-authored mind**—Do you single out feedback from those you respect? Does feedback need to match your carefully crafted ideals?
- **The self-transforming mind**—Do you request and welcome feedback, often reflecting on your thoughts and actions in the moment?

○ When things go wrong:

- **The self-sovereign mind**—Do you find fault with others?
- **The socialized mind**—Do you mainly experience the emotion of shame?
- **The self-authored mind**—Can you identify the role you and others may have played, both fairly and objectively?
- **The self-transforming mind**—Do you become introspective, wondering if you're living up to your beliefs?

○ When you face complex issues (the ones that create political divides):

- **The self-sovereign mind**—Do you assume there's a right and a wrong view?
- **The socialized mind**—Do you find it difficult to speak with people who hold a different view?
- **The self-authored mind**—Can you see the rationale behind other perspectives while at the same time remaining quite certain of your own?
- **The self-transforming mind**—Do you have awareness of the wider context and what disparate views might have in common?

3. To practice perspective taking, consider *Crucial Confrontations: Tools for Resolving Broken Promises, Violated Expectations, and Bad Behavior*. In it, authors Kerry Patterson, Joseph Grenny, Ron McMillan, and Al Switzler (2005) lay out a model for understanding how another person with sound reasoning ability can hold a position different from your own—a crucial skill for adult development. To build this skill, find someone

you trust who is willing to dialogue about a difficult decision, and follow these six steps.

    a. Let the other person know the issue you'd like to discuss and that you'll share how you came to form your position. Tell the person you would like to hear the same from him or her to increase your understanding of the issue.

    b. Before meeting, clarify your position. What do you believe? What evidence have you relied on? How can you clearly and succinctly explain both your belief and how you came to hold it? Think about how to state the facts without trying to persuade. This isn't easy, but it's the point of the exercise.

    c. When you meet, let the other person know, "We respect each other, so I'd like to take this opportunity to practice understanding the root sources of someone else's position. I will do my best to explain my belief, the evidence and experiences that formed it, and how it has influenced a decision I'm making. Then I hope you will do the same so I can understand how we came to hold different positions."

    d. Share your story. Then ask the other person if he or she has questions.

    e. Ask the other person to share. Give your full attention to understanding the foundation of his or her belief. Listen with curiosity. What new ideas or evidence do you hear? What might have kept you from knowing about them? Does anything in your development stage make it harder to understand this differing viewpoint?

    f. After the conversation, take time to reflect through journaling. How can you improve your ability to consider multiple sides of an issue?

4. We have based the infinity loops throughout these pages on *polarity thinking*, a specific philosophy and set of tools that Polarity Partnerships (www.polaritypartnerships.com), founded by Barry Johnson, developed. *Polarities* are interdependent sets of values that, over time, need each other. Both sides are incomplete and need the other side to capture the whole truth. Common polarities include individual and team, short term and long term, and justice and mercy. Having the ability to hold these kinds of paradigms in tension is a marker of adult development.

5. The reproducible "Individual Contribution and Collaboration Polarity" features a simple diagram you can use to start working with these values pairs. It provides sample prompts for the common education dilemma of individual contribution and collaboration.

    Often, people find one quadrant harder to complete than the others, indicating where their own experiences or biases may lie. Did this happen for you? What might cause that difficulty? Consider whether you or your team effectively balances this individual or team polarity. What steps might you take to get the best individual contribution and the best team collaboration? (To learn more about polarity thinking, check out Jane's [2014] book *Unleashing the Positive Power of Differences: Polarity Thinking in Our Schools.*)

Individual Contribution and Collaboration Polarity

Answer the following questions regarding the common education dilemma of individual contribution and collaboration.

What opportunities do you see when teachers use their strengths individually? • • •	What opportunities do you see when teachers collaborate? • • •
What problems do you see if you focus too much on teachers' individual contributions? • • •	What problems do you see if you focus too much on teacher collaboration? • • •

CHAPTER 6

KNOWING YOUR HARDWIRED STRENGTHS

GUIDING QUESTIONS

- Have you found the right balance between objectivity and subjectivity? Between logic and values?

- Identify some decisions you were part of that benefited when you employed these seemingly opposite sets of criteria. How can you improve your use of them to make better decisions?

- What praise and critique have you received for your leadership style?

An ongoing theme in this book is the need to add archetypal feminine perspectives and values to the masculine emphases that have shaped many current education policies and practices. Let's look at the ongoing efforts in reforming how reading is taught to gain an understanding of how these archetypes come into play and how your own hardwired strengths may influence your beliefs about literacy instruction.

Review these literacy skills. What elements might be missing from a literacy program that includes the following?

- Phonemic awareness
- Phonics
- Fluency

- Vocabulary
- Text comprehension

These components shaped the $1 billion-a-year Reading First grant program in the United States, introduced in 2002. Six years and billions of dollars later, researchers found that students at Reading First schools did no better than students at other schools (National Center for Education Evaluation and Regional Assistance, 2008).

What was missing? The Common Core State Standards architects tried to remedy the shortfalls in Reading First by paying attention to trends in the work world and the skills employers hoped to see in high school graduates. They added new emphases that have become buzzwords: *college and career ready, close reading,* and *informational texts.* They pushed back on the idea that students first learn to read and then read to learn, realizing the artificiality of that dichotomy (Sparks, 2012). Peggie McCardle of the National Institute on Child Health and Human Development points out, "The ramp up to learning from reading starts earlier and is just that, a ramp-up" (as cited in Sparks, 2012, p. 7).

Yet when one examines the National Assessment of Educational Progress scores (NCES, n.d.c), the first years of implementation of the Common Core State Standards, which were published in 2010, still haven't resulted in higher literacy rates. What's still missing? See the current and missing emphases in reading instruction featured in table 6.1.

Table 6.1: Current and Missing Emphases in Reading Instruction

Current Emphases in Reading Instruction	Missing Emphases in Reading Instruction
Proficiency	Engagement
Critical thinking	Creativity
Utility	Interest
Complexity	Cultural diversity
Knowledge building	Emotional intelligence building

Too many reading initiatives have emphasized everything in the left column and neglected the right column, leaving out many elements of reading instruction that motivate students and go beyond teaching skills to teaching with a whole-child approach. Eleven-year-old students told Jane the following things about reading in her November 2003 doctoral focus groups, which illustrate the need to motivate students:

It's kinda boring just sitting there and doing work. Like in a reading class, we'll have to read a book and then write a paper on it, read a book, write a paper, like that. . . . If I get into it and it's a good book, I won't stop reading. I'll walk with the book, sittin' there reading it. When it's a book I'm into, I almost, like, talk to the person in the book; you know what I'm saying?

I don't like my reading class. We do this easy work. Cat, mat, sat, fat. What is that? (Laughter from other focus-group students.) And spelling. And then we got these big old books and you gotta do these little listening journal things and you need to put this cat, rat up on the sticky notes . . . Oh yeah, if I see a real good book, I'd be like, "I wish I was in that book, I wish I could meet those characters, I wish I was flying with them," and all that.

Former teacher and staff development leader Donalyn Miller (2009) emphasizes the research-based effectiveness of giving students classroom time to read books of their choosing as a literacy strategy. She summarizes:

We have turned reading into a list of "have to's," losing sight of the reality that students and adults are more motivated by "want to's." . . . And that kind of instruction is a guarantee that most of them will never read, not in the summer, not at home, and never again when their formal schooling ends. (Miller, 2009, Location No. 2388)

Now, take a look at the lists of traditional masculine and feminine values in table 6.2 as identified by Gerzema and D'Antonio (2013). Can you see the relationship between the left-hand columns in this table and table 6.1 and the relationship between the right-hand columns?

Table 6.2: Traditional Masculine and Feminine Values

Traditional Masculine Values	Traditional Feminine Values
Analytical	Passionate
Linear	In flow
Logical	Intuitive
Objective	Empathetic
Goal directed	Creative

Would it overstate it to say that archetypal masculine ways of thinking drive the current state of reading instruction, and that reading instruction lacks the balance that feminine ways of thinking would bring?

Also consider these other popular educational policies and strategies. Do they stem from the left-hand lists or the right-hand lists?

- Principal and teacher evaluation systems
- Content standards and pacing guides
- Formal response to intervention (RTI) programs
- Technology as solution
- Data-driven instruction

None of these are problems in and of themselves, but have you seen them implemented in lopsided ways that lead to new problems and dilemmas? In this chapter, we'll look at the power of bringing both the masculine *and* the feminine to the table when making decisions, forming policies, and setting strategic directions. We'll also examine how each leader, whether male or female, leans toward a more masculine or feminine style in his or her hardwiring and how that affects his or her perspective on leadership.

 THINK ABOUT IT

Before moving on, consider at least one initiative in the previous bulleted list. What about it do you like or dislike? How do these elements you like or dislike compare to the masculine and feminine values we've discussed?

How Thinking and Feeling Preferences Impact Leadership

Let's bring these ideas of masculine and feminine archetypes into the realm of daily decisions so you can explore which of your personal leadership strengths connect more with those archetypes. Chances are, you've had a few lively discussions in your education career regarding how you discipline students or how you discipline your own children.

Jane has used the following exercise countless times with both students and educators— and often has to coach the adults to rethink where their thoughts go *first*, not how their training might inform their thinking. That first reaction often reflects our hardwired preferences for which areas of the brain we use most in decision making—the criteria that first come to mind. If you can, discuss the following scenarios with someone with whom you don't always see eye to eye on discipline issues to compare notes as to how your responses might reflect your strengths.

- You have a firm classroom rule: no sweet snacks. A student dashes in the door a minute late and tells you, "Our power was out this morning, we only had cold water, and I didn't get breakfast. Can I please eat this bag of Lucky Charms and a donut? It's all we had." Is your *first* thought to stick to the rule or make an exception?

- Your team is discussing setting consistent policies when students are late to class. Are your *first* thoughts focused on consequences or on ideas to motivate students to get to class on time?

- You're observing a peer using a new teaching strategy that is a true stretch for him or her. Do you tend to *first* wish to communicate how he or she might improve or on what went well?

- Your professional learning team meets regularly. Does time spent on relationships within the team during those meetings *first* strike you as a waste of time or as a valuable use of time?

In each of these scenarios, the first potential response uses a more logical approach to decisions, perhaps using if-then or pro-and-con reasoning and considering the precedents you might be setting. The second potential response uses a more subjective but still rational approach of considering the impact on the people involved, personal values, and the role of relationships in motivation. Both responses are valuable. In fact, most decisions require using both sets of criteria to find the best alternative. However, you've probably noted in discussions about incidents such as these scenarios that some people consistently rely on logic while others more often consider the impact on people.

Looking at your first responses can help you determine the criteria you naturally employ when making decisions. Swiss psychiatrist Carl Jung (1971) notes the following two different decision-making approaches that people use.

1. Those with what Jung named the *Thinking* preference look first at logic: cause-and-effect, if-then, pro-and-con, and measurable criteria. Note that people with this preference resist making exceptions with the logic, "If I make one exception, I'll have to make more and soon I'll have

chaos." This preference sees fairness as giving everyone an equal chance and emphasizes justice.

2. Those with what Jung named the *Feeling* preference look first at personal and community values, as well as how a decision might affect people. Thus when asked to make an exception, they will consider the impact on an individual and deal separately with any unintended consequences of making exceptions. This preference sees fairness as giving everyone the chance they deserve, or need at that moment, and emphasizes mercy.

In decision making, the subjective approach of the Feeling preference is equally as important—and as rational—as logic and objectivity. How many logical decisions fall flat because leaders ignore the values and feelings of those charged with implementing them? Of course, if a leader who prefers Feeling makes decisions so illogically or inconsistently that predictability vanishes, problems arise as well.

Neuroscience backs up the assertion that these are hardwired differences in how we make decisions. Neuroscience and personality type expert Dario Nardi (2011) finds significant correlation between personality types and the areas of the brain's cortex that are most active in individuals. For example, two of the sixteen personality types, ones that use Thinking in their inner world, show active use of their brains' logic centers but very little use of the main auditory processing centers. They seem to rely on internal, logical models instead of input from others.

In contrast, two types that use Feeling in their introverted worlds show the *most* activity of all the types in the main auditory processing centers, but very little use of the logic centers. They show a keen interest in others' input and are innately good at listening. That's only about 7–10 percent of the population. What do the rest of people do? They judge what a person says, or they think about how they will respond. They do not give their full attention when others speak.

Apart from type research, using brain imaging, researchers have found that when the brain's logical neural network lights up, it suppresses the network for empathy, and vice versa. Either you go into if-then, pro-and-con mode or you consider human costs (Jack et al., 2013). The brain requires us to consider the two sets of equally valuable criteria sequentially, not simultaneously.

What does this mean for education policy? One example is that much support for zero-tolerance policies comes from focusing too much on the Thinking preference's view of fairness as consistent implementation of a rule, as well as its focus on cause-and-effect reasoning. Leaders who lean toward Thinking criteria assume that if leaders have zero tolerance, then students will less likely engage in those behaviors, or that expulsion is a natural consequence. Leaders who focus on Feeling criteria are often aware of reasons to make exceptions or ways in which such rules might unfairly impact certain students. Does your learning community include voices for each side?

To understand your hardwired strengths, review the descriptors in table 6.3. First, consider which list you find more natural for you. Then, consider how those descriptors tie to the masculine and feminine archetypes that are the focus of this chapter.

Table 6.3: Descriptors of Thinking and Feeling Preferences

Descriptors of the Thinking Preference	Descriptors of the Feeling Preference
Logic	Values
Consistent rules	Rules that account for individual circumstances
Results	Harmony
Objective, impersonal criteria	Criteria formed from motives and values of those involved
Employment of skepticism	Employment of trust
Causes and effects and pros and cons	Common ground

How Decision-Making Preferences Impact Leadership

Research indicates that more than 80 percent of business leaders around the world prefer Thinking, and traditional leadership literature emphasizes Thinking traits. We know, too, that about 60 percent of men prefer Thinking and 60 percent of women prefer Feeling (Myers, McCaulley, Quenk, & Hammer, 1998; Schaubhut & Thompson, 2008).

However, when women who naturally prefer the logical stance move into leadership, what labels do people often sling at them? Similarly, how do people label men who operate from the Feeling function? You probably can think of a few labels for the genders that people simply don't use in polite conversation. Yes, feminism is for everyone!

No leaders can operate at their best unless they ground their leadership in their preferred way of making decisions and then gain methods for accessing the other. Individuals and the world of education lose when these gender stereotypes prevent leaders from acting from their natural strengths. They can never quite become the leaders they are meant to become, nor can they bring much-needed balance to the realm of education policy.

As noted in *Collected Works of C.G. Jung* (Jung, 1971), Jung first developed the type framework in 1921, and the mother-daughter team of Katharine Briggs and Isabel Myers (Myers et al., 1998) made his theory accessible and useful through the well-known Myers–Briggs Type Indicator (MBTI®). Besides the Thinking-Feeling dichotomy for decision making, they identified three other dichotomies, as follows.

1. **The Extraversion-Introversion dichotomy:** Action and interaction energize those who prefer *Extraversion*. Solitude and reflection energize those who prefer *Introversion*. Think about how this colors your natural perceptions of classroom participation, collaboration, group work, silent reading, and more.

2. **The Sensing-Intuition dichotomy:** You might describe those who prefer *Sensing* as detail oriented; they accurately draw on past experiences and what their five senses tell them. They first "see the trees." You might describe *Intuitive* types as big-picture people; they trust the connections, themes, and analogies their minds devise. They first "see the forest." In education, this preference pair affects the way you learn to read and do mathematics, the test questions you write, your choice of content areas and university majors, and more.

3. **The Judging-Perceiving dichotomy:** Those who like to plan their work and work their plan are known as *Judging* types; they like gaining closure and coming to judgments (they are not more judgmental). Those who prefer to keep options open longer in order to seek more information, or perceptions, are called *Perceiving* types (they are not more perceptive).

Type isn't destiny. It points to patterns in human behavior and development, not what any individual will do at a given moment. However, as the discussion of Thinking and Feeling in this chapter reveals, these preferences have an impact on your leadership approach.

Your Decision-Making Style and Leadership

Let's look at three ways in which your decision-making style might influence your leadership priorities: (1) the brain's inability to be simultaneously empathetic and logical, (2) the need for feminine values in leadership, and (3) how you define your path.

The Brain's Inability to Be Simultaneously Empathetic and Logical

You can learn to become a better listener and use tools and protocols that improve your logic, but remember that researchers have found logic and empathy to be mutually exclusive processes (Jack et al., 2012). Knowing which you favor allows you to build strategies and scaffolding tools to include both equally valuable sets of criteria into important decision processes. Recall your responses to the scenarios given earlier in the chapter. Did you initially react more logically and objectively, perhaps indicating a Thinking preference? Or more empathetically and subjectively, perhaps indicating a Feeling preference?

WORDS FROM A LEADER

A skill I've learned that has been crucial to effective leadership is deep, committed listening; it is often the only tool needed to solve nearly every problem, communicate personal regard and respect, and honor each person's story as a part of the tapestry of humankind. (Joellen Killion, senior advisor, Learning Forward, personal communication, April 19, 2018)

Yes, you can do both. Note, though, that women who prefer Thinking may have a difficult time unearthing which comes more naturally to them because so many cultures condition women to seek harmony and care for individuals. These questions may give you a few clues: As a child, did you feel more or at least equally comfortable with male playmates? Did you struggle to understand girl "drama"? Are you more likely than women you know to get over things simply with a good night's sleep? Women who prefer Thinking report all these things.

Jane and her type colleagues find over and over in their consulting work that people more frequently criticize Thinking women than Feeling women. Why? For "hard" or "bossy" behavior (for example, stepping outside the boundaries of traditional female roles), even when they behave no differently than the men around them. Jane can summarize what so many Thinking women have told her after learning about type:

> *The type vocabulary gives me words to describe what I've experienced. For forty years, my mother has tried to change me from being a Thinker into being a Feeler. And it hurts. Now, though, I have words that say I'm normal, not horrible, and just different from my mother who has her own type-related strengths and struggles.*

The best type of leader to be, of course, is who you are. We've seen cultural shifts when the masculine-feminine debate changes to a Thinking-Feeling debate and people understand how individuals with both decision-making styles populate different genders. People stop stereotyping and start accepting logical and values-driven behavior from colleagues of all genders.

THINK ABOUT IT

Search Google images for the statement, "My daughter isn't bossy. She has leadership skills." Study the memes that result and answer the following questions.

- In your school, have you seen examples of people judging girls and boys differently for the same behaviors? Does this apply to cultural differences as well?

- How might you use the images you found to have a productive discussion about ensuring your learning community values students for who they are and doesn't judge them differently based on gender? What other facts from this book might help your learning community rethink the truths and stereotypes around gender differences that have helped or hurt all students?

Do you recognize your strength as more Thinking or Feeling? How can you help spread the word that your emphasis on either objectivity (Thinking) or subjectivity (Feeling) depends on this innate personality preference and not on gender? Do it for the sake of the girls and young women you lead so that others will no longer accuse them of bossiness but instead recognize their leadership potential.

If you look at women's employment reviews, certain words show up repeatedly, like *bossy*, *abrasive*, *strident*, and *aggressive*. This is when women lead; words like *emotional* and *irrational* are used when they *object*. In reviews, men are exhorted to be more aggressive in the workplace, but not so with women.

—Julie Holland,
American psychiatrist

The Need for Feminine Values in Leadership

The importance of recognizing and using your strengths goes far beyond your personal development and influence as a leader. Reframe much of the advice that female aspiring leaders commonly receive, that strange mix of being told to be more assertive while simultaneously being warned not to be too tough, through the lens of Thinking and Feeling. Thinking women hear that they should tone down their natural strengths, while Feeling women feel pressure to act out the strengths of the Thinking function without losing their soft touch.

Even more significantly, though, if women can't speak up in their natural styles, the impact of their messages may be lost. Reconsider the following list of popular education policies and strategies and add others that come to mind.

- Principal and teacher evaluation systems
- Content standards and pacing guides
- Formal response to intervention (RTI) programs
- Technology as solution
- Data-driven instruction

Now that you know more about how the masculine and feminine archetypes play into how these are implemented, what would you like to have *power to* change? How might your preference for Thinking or Feeling influence this? Can you see how, because more women prefer Feeling, getting more women at the leadership table can drive more balanced decision making if they use their natural strengths?

How You Define Your Path

Whichever way of making decisions you find more natural, you need to know how to use both Thinking and Feeling to make good decisions and to lead well.

In just about every conflict situation in which someone asks Jane to facilitate a resolution, misunderstanding around this basic difference in the criteria people use to make decisions lies at the heart of the conflict. Without a vocabulary to celebrate the strengths of objectivity *and* subjectivity, people become entrenched in their own positions, and the results can get messy.

If Thinking types don't carefully consider more subjective criteria when setting policies or making major decisions, Feeling types might criticize them for the following.

- **Not acknowledging their or others' emotions and feelings:** Remember that you can use emotions as data for decisions, and emotions may have as much—or more—to do with leading change as any objective set of facts.

- **Giving too few compliments compared to criticisms:** Remember that people who prefer Feeling may assume that they are to blame when things go wrong. They may also doubt that there is such a thing as constructive criticism.

- **Accepting compliance rather than striving for collaboration:**
  Thinking types may struggle to read the climate they've created.
  Who might you consult for objective input regarding how to create
  buy-in for change?

- **Displaying conditional respect (appreciating people for
  accomplishments) at the expense of unconditional respect
  (appreciating people for who they are):** People need both kinds of
  respect. Remember to express what you value about people without
  discussing accomplishments or performance.

- **Being too strictly business:** In chapter 8 (page 131), we'll look more
  closely at the human need for social connection—it's actually the default
  brain mode. Move outside your normal range of conversational topics
  to share personal facts, details, or insights about yourself and underlying
  emotional tones.

If Feeling types don't carefully consider more objective criteria when setting policies
or making major decisions, Thinking types might criticize them for the following.

- **Giving meaningless, *fluff* feedback:** This leads Thinking types to
  ponder, "What are you buttering me up for?" Practice giving specific,
  direct feedback to others.

- **Not understanding the precedents and unintended consequences
  that flow from decisions:** Ask yourself if-then and cause-and-effect
  questions such as, "If we do this, then what scenarios could possibly
  result?" and "If I make this exception, then what other exceptions might
  we need to make in the future? Will that be good or bad?"

- **Making decisions that they can't support logically:** Yes, sometimes
  values trump logic. However, you can explain values-based decisions in
  a straightforward way, such as, "Our top collaborative value is trust.
  The other possible solutions could rattle trust because _____ and
  therefore, I concluded . . ."

- **Not holding firm or being wishy-washy:** Feeling types often say
  things like, "We can revisit this choice later to see how it is working
  out." Sometimes, this is appropriate, but it also leads to uncertainty and
  perceived lack of commitment. After logical consideration (using pros
  and cons, for example) and a review of your values, consciously decide
  whether to take a tough-minded stance, and hold firm.

- **Getting too personal in terms of relationships:** Remember that to some people, business means business. They prefer not to turn their work relationships into friendships.

Use these critiques and suggestions as clues to your natural strengths. For what have people criticized you? How can you use these strengths without falling into their traps? What next steps might you take to ensure that you make optimal decisions?

Next Steps in the Journey

The personality type framework doesn't box you in. Instead, it points to your starting place on the lifelong journey of personal development and allows you to learn from millions of others who are ahead of you on that path. When teams use the language of personality type, they replace labels such as *bossy* and *wishy-washy* with neutral terms such as *Thinking* and *Feeling*. If you are interested in learning more about this power-ful tool for coaching and personal development, contact Jane via https://janekise.com /contact-me to receive a decision-maker code that will give you one-time access to the TypeCoach Verifier (www.type-coach.com). Through this interactive online experience (*not* an assessment or questionnaire) you will identify your four-letter personality type code and receive a six-page report about your type in education.

Step in for Further Reflection

The following activities provide you with valuable opportunities to reflect on the ideas, strategies, and concepts covered in this chapter. If you are approaching *Step In, Step Up* as a twelve-week journey, you can spread these out over several days.

You may complete them individually or with a group so you can share your thoughts and ideas. Keep a journal so you can revisit your thoughts as you travel this journey.

1. Read these quotes from students in their early teens who received in-depth training about their hardwired strengths. After reading them, consider the questions that follow.

   "I *know* I'm a Thinker because sometimes I blurt out things that might hurt somebody, but not on purpose, because that is what I'm thinking. I don't like to put myself in someone else's shoes."

   "I think I am a Thinker because people have responsibilities, and if they don't do them, I don't care about their excuses. I would rather think about things than help people."

"I'm a Thinker. When someone is sad, I don't really feel sad with them or try to help them feel better. I try to give them good and logical answers, which would probably make them feel better."

"I prefer Feeling. I feel bad or happy when people tell me what they feel. My friends are the most important to me. I listen to everyone's problems if they tell them to me. If I let someone down, I feel so bad that I can't think straight."

"I am a definite Feeler. I care for people. When I grow up, I want to help people by being a physical therapist. I also have a lifelong dream to go to another country and help homeless, war-torn, or other less fortunate people. I also believe family and friends come way above business and school."

"I am sure I am a Feeler. I always sympathize with other people and relate to their feelings and thoughts and problems. Sometimes, I can be a little judgmental, but not too bad. I really try to look for the good in people."

- o Consider the strategies students use when interacting with others. Which quotes remind you of your teenage self as well as the students you have worked with? (Note that the quotes may seem rather one-sided; this reflects the fact that adolescents are not fully developed and often only use their strengths.)

- o Do the quotes remind you of different reactions to policies, rules, events, and circumstances you've seen that surprised or annoyed you? How do the Thinking and Feeling decision-making preferences provide some insights into your reactions?

- o How might your education environment put Thinking and Feeling girls and Thinking and Feeling boys at risk in different ways?

2. Consider the following suggestions for developing your decision-making skill set.

- o If you prefer logic (Thinking), try the following.

    - • Think through a past decision that had a suboptimal outcome, and consider why it occurred. Did you consider all the different stakeholder groups? Did they have issues or concerns that you didn't factor into the decision-making process? How did that affect the decision's quality, acceptance, and implementation?

- Choose a meeting, relationship, or project in which you had unsatisfactory results. List what role you played and what you might have done more effectively. Ignore all external factors and, instead, concentrate on the impact of your ideas and actions. Where were you to blame?

○ If you prefer empathy (Feeling), try the following.

- Think through a past decision that had a suboptimal outcome, and consider why it occurred. Did it have unintended consequences? Did you accidentally set precedents? Did some facts you relied on turn out to be opinions? Where might logic have improved your decision?

- Write down the pros and the cons of choices you face. Fill in, "If I do ____, then ____ might happen" to practice if-then thinking. Or, use a matrix. List your options in the first column. Add columns for objective criteria: time needed, cost, level of support, and so on. Then, rank your alternatives on each criterion, assign one point to the top item, two points to the second item, and so on, and add up the points. Which gets the best rating? Figure 6.1 (page 114) shows a sample matrix for changing meeting times.

Options	Cost	Rank	Precedents to Consider	Rank	Potential Unintended Consequences	Rank	Total
Before school	Overtime for hourly employees	3	This slot's time constraints may keep teams from taking extra time when needed	1	Meetings cut short before decisions are made	3	7
Rotating schedule		1	People may expect convenience and reset all school meeting times	2	Uneven attendance	1	4
Late start	Employees and parents may incur daycare costs	2	This could plant seeds that teacher needs always come before parent needs	3	People are tired	2	7

Other generic logical criteria that might be used include:

- Time involved
- Consistency with employee contracts
- Space limitations
- Past performance information
- Data from employee performance, progress toward goals, and so on
- Survey data

Figure 6.1: Decision—Changing meeting time matrix example.

CHAPTER 7

CHALLENGING YOUR HIGH-FLYING AND LIMITING BELIEFS

GUIDING QUESTIONS

- What career move do you want to make next?
- What would you consider an audacious role for you right now—the one that you ultimately want but feel you're not ready for? Why don't you feel ready for it?
- What gets in the way of pursuing that audacious role?

You've made it halfway through this journey to new levels of leadership. You have found the leader within, and you're ready to forge ahead—you've discovered your high-flying beliefs about leadership. You are aiming high, stepping out of your comfort zone, and stepping into preparing for audacious opportunities. Positions you once thought were unattainable, limiting your options and beyond your capabilities, are now achievable. You've started to recognize and define your unique leadership style and identity, and what you'd like *power to* accomplish, which your reflections in previous chapters have stimulated. You're clarifying your strengths and how to use them to address the opportunities and challenges ahead. So you're nearly there!

Do you consider yourself ready for a leadership role? In what ways do you feel confident about becoming a leader? In what ways do you feel you might lack readiness or have impediments? Figure 7.1 (page 116) shows two continuums for leadership readiness. Where would you place yourself on these continuums?

If you're taking this journey with other women, ask them where they would place themselves. Then, ask some men at your level to do the same. Where do they place themselves on these continuums? Finally, ponder how you compare and whether you're flying high in your beliefs about your leadership potential or stuck in beliefs that might limit your potential.

Strength	0	1	2	3	4	5	Struggle
Learning on the job will provide the rest of what I need to lead.							I need significant training, preparation, and practice before I'll be ready to lead.

Strength	0	1	2	3	4	5	Struggle
I'm fully prepared to step into the next level of leadership.							I need much more preparation before I'll be ready to consider the next level of leadership.

Figure 7.1: Continuums for leadership readiness.

Women are often tentative in describing their skills and experience and are more likely to express doubt in their abilities. As we discussed in chapter 2 (page 33), men often express more confidence and boldness, even if they are less qualified (Helgesen & Goldsmith, 2018; Kay & Shipman, 2014). While you need self-confidence to succeed as a leader (Who wants to work for someone who doesn't think she has any business taking charge?), appearing self-confident has shaped up to create another double-bind issue for women.

Laura Guillen (2018) studied how others perceive women's self-confidence at a large, male-dominated company. She discovered that even among high-performing workers, self-confidence did not necessarily equally translate into influence for women and men. For women, influence was associated with warmth (for example, caring), and women's self-reported confidence did not correlate with how confident they appeared to others:

> While self-confidence is gender-neutral, the consequences of appearing self-confident are not. The "performance plus confidence equals power and influence" formula is gendered. Successful women cannot "lean in" on a structure that cannot support their weight without their opportunities (and the myth) collapsing around them.

Popular messaging about how women must change to appear more self-confident as a key to their success isn't just false. It also reflects how the burden of managing a gender-diverse workplace is placed on the female employees themselves. (Guillen, 2018)

In other words, women face real barriers, as chapter 2 (page 33) outlined. However, your own beliefs shouldn't form a barrier. In this chapter, we will continue to identify your beliefs about leadership and how you see yourself as a leader in order to more deeply explore what might help and hinder your ambition and growth. Now, let's explore your leadership mindset.

Deselect Your Default

Now that you have identified your strengths and how you can use them to address the opportunities and challenges ahead, you feel ready to begin your leadership journey. You're ready to go . . . but then, you select your default. Instead of considering what you would bring to a leadership opportunity, how you would shape and contribute to the role, how you will grow into the role, you select your default position, which is to immediately question whether you are good enough, ready enough, or capable enough. This one screams to you, "Not me! Why me? I'm not good enough! Other people are much better than me, know more than me, or are more confident than me! I haven't led, so how can I do it?"

Where does this come from? Leadership expert John C. Maxwell (2014) says people never outperform their self-image, calling this the *law of the mirror*. He sees people with incredible potential destroy their chances of doing something great and not become who they want to be. The operative word here is *potential*. Women perceive that they need to arrive with experiences to show they are *fully qualified* and *job ready* to successfully apply for a job they have never done before. We need to redefine their notion of readiness to lead. While, yes, leadership positions require a certain level of experience and skills, we also need to come to a leadership role acknowledging and understanding our potential, and be prepared to grow *into* the role and become the leader that role requires.

> "Be yourself, everyone else is already taken" (attributed to Oscar Wilde). The point is to become yourself, to use yourself completely—all your skills, gifts, and energies—to make your vision manifest. You must withhold nothing. You must, in sum, be the person you started out to be, and enjoy the process of becoming.
>
> —Warren Bennis (1925–2014), American scholar and organizational consultant

Successful leaders are continually learning and developing their skills and attributes on the job.

Nancy Badore, former executive director of the Ford Motor Company's Executive Development Center, has found that it often takes women ten years longer than men to realize how good they really are. She reflects that you'll find it difficult to contribute until you've moved beyond wondering if you're good enough (as cited in Vukovic, 2016).

In relation to school leadership, we have observed and discussed with numerous male and female colleagues how women have a less strategic focus on developing and managing their careers and how men are more prepared than women to develop their skill base *on the run*. This means men use their experience in the new position to improve their performance. In contrast, women think they have to fully prepare themselves before they consider such moves. They limit their capacity to take on these roles and are reluctant to apply until they feel perfect.

Women also seem to believe they need experience in a particular role before applying for it, consciously or subconsciously activating what one could loosely describe as the *80/20 rule*—women will only consider applying for leadership positions when they have 80 percent of the experience and skills required. They commonly do not apply for principalships unless they feel certain they can fulfill all job requirements (Maunder & Warren, 2008) and have previously done all aspects of the role. The dilemma discussed in chapter 4 (page 67) rears its head; women deem themselves not qualified enough, or in need of more experience than their current leadership experience provides, and therefore avoid taking on something bigger. Marianne Coleman (2007) concurs, commenting:

> Women tend to be more lacking in confidence than their male counterparts. Men on the whole will apply for a job without having all the necessary examples of qualities that the job states. Women are much more hesitant to put themselves forward without having most, if not all of the qualities that the job has asked for. (p. 8)

Leaders are learners. Reflecting, learning, and developing while on the job *is* part of the job. Stepping into leadership inevitably involves facing unanticipated responsibilities and obstacles, as Robin, one of Barbara's colleagues, discovered when she took on a principalship role. She started teaching in the 1970s, a time when most principals were men. It wasn't until someone tapped her on the shoulder, when someone actually recognized those skills and qualities within her, that she was willing to take that extra step (Watterston & Watterston, 2010).

Much like Tanya's journey in chapter 4 (page 67), Robin had the opportunity to act in the role when her principal suddenly took another post. At the age of thirty-eight, overcoming self-doubt and her own perceived lack of readiness, Robin became one of the youngest female principals in the state at the time. Her perception was that everyone else had more expertise, knowledge, and confidence than she had. She is emphatic in her advice about not thinking that you can't do it or pressing the deselect button before giving leadership a go.

Replicated in the statistics beyond the education sector, women initially feel unequal to the task of leadership. Robin looks back on her career as a pathway of opportunities:

> We need to get the message to women to find ways to develop confidence in their leadership abilities, which will continue to engage their passion and purpose for teaching in strategically seeking their career pathway. . . . As an experienced principal, I now know that failure is not something to be feared, but a natural consequence of learning and dealing with problems. (as cited in Tarica, 2010)

Ponder this research, experience, and advice, and then consider where you lack confidence or inclination to articulate your achievements and desire for career advancement. Considering these thoughts, allow yourself to remain open to possibilities that will give you courage to tackle the next steps. As Robin did, see obstacles as gifts that can build your "confidence muscle" regarding your capacity to lead and add to your development while you gain others' recognition and support.

So you might be ready, but will you apply? Do you possibly underestimate your capacity for a top leadership position because you have unrealistically high expectations of the skills and experience that the position requires? Are you possibly afraid of failing?

> You can either waltz boldly onto the stage of life and live the way you know your spirit is nudging you to, or you can sit quietly by the wall, receding into the shadows of fear and self-doubt.
>
> —Oprah Winfrey,
> American media executive

If so, look back at chapter 4 (page 67), where you considered how you view and what you value about leaders and leadership. How can you leverage your strengths that you reflected on in chapter 6 (page 99)? Focus less on your limitations and more on what you do well. Take a strengths-based approach, and communicate your leadership identity with confidence.

Embrace Your Confidence

"Evidence shows that women are less self-assured than men—and that to succeed, confidence matters as much as competence" (Kay & Shipman, 2014). Women are more likely than men to choose leadership tasks based on their confidence level. We rarely have conversations with women leaders, with experience levels from emerging to executive, where we don't see glaringly apparent implications of the confidence gap. Journalists Katty Kay and Claire Shipman's (2014) felt prompted to write their essay "The Confidence Gap" when they made similar observations across many diverse fields of work:

> To our surprise, as we talked with women, dozens of them, all accomplished and credentialed, we kept bumping up against a dark spot that we couldn't quite identify, a force clearly holding them back. . . . In two decades of covering American politics as journalists, we realized, we have between us interviewed some of the most influential women in the nation. In our jobs and our lives, we walk among people you would assume brim with confidence. And yet our experience suggests that the power centers of this nation are zones of female self-doubt—that is, when they include women at all.

In other words, if you're still working up the courage to step out in leadership, know that you are in good—and massive—company!

 THINK ABOUT IT

Go to *The Atlantic*'s website (www.theatlantic.com), and search for the essay "The Confidence Gap" (Kay & Shipman, 2014). In it, you'll find a link to a video interview with the authors (The Atlantic, 2017). As you watch it, think about the following.

- How do you second-guess yourself, ruminating and dwelling on what you did or didn't do? Do you stay stuck or acknowledge what happened, let go, and move on?
- How do you judge your performance? Do you judge it through the lens of what you could have or should have done, or do you think about what went well or even better than you expected?
- In applying for a new position, do you think about what you don't have or do have and whether it's not enough or good enough?
- How do you stop yourself from projecting what other people think?
- What is under your control that can change how you feel and how others perceive you?

You might also consider taking the authors' confidence quiz (https://theconfidencecode.com/confidence-quiz) to gauge your current level of self-confidence.

Overwhelmingly, self-doubt feeds the confidence gap, which plays a pivotal role in women's perceived readiness and their negative evaluations of their abilities. Men also wrestle with self-doubt, though, as Kay and Shipman (2017) share in their interview, women doubt themselves more and back themselves less. Best-selling author, women's advocate, and sought-after international speaker Margie Warrell (2016) says that of all the barriers women still face, one of the biggest is lack of self-confidence:

> We get caught up second-guessing our value, beating ourselves up, talking ourselves down and apologizing for our opinion. We work hard to do a great job, whilst juggling all facets of our lives, keeping all the balls in the air, set high bars for ourselves and continuously fall short of the measures we have set for ourselves. That little voice in our heads just doesn't let up, continuously critiquing what we haven't yet done or didn't do.

Over and over, women mention the key role that mentors, friends, and colleagues play in providing the motivation and encouragement, along with the knowledge and advice, they need to overcome the confidence gap. We will explore how to encourage more women to lead in chapter 11 (page 185), but for now, note the impact of these supportive relationships, and become your best advocate. Self-advocacy may seem like an unrealistic concept if you underestimate your abilities. It may seem unrealistic where self-doubt feeds the need to be perfect; where a lack of recognition and confidence deepens those doubts; or where your ability to navigate affirmation and recognition meets with self-sabotage. Many invisible barriers coat women's progression at any level, double coated by their lack of confidence (Rizvi, 2017).

Shift Your View on Vulnerability

Leadership is an act of vulnerability. Shift the paradigm, and look at vulnerability from an empowering perspective. You need to have courage to show vulnerability, stepping out as a leader in spite of the trepidation and fear of failure you may feel. Instead of looking at failure as a dead end, reframe it as an opportunity to expand your definition of success. Sometimes, you need to get out of your own way and turn challenges into opportunities.

There's a great saying, "Growth and comfort can't ride the same horse" (Warrell, 2015). Take comfort in feeling uncomfortable as you step into leadership—that way, you'll find joy and excitement in stretching your growth. Remember, you grow into your potential as a leader. You don't need all the answers; with a growth mindset, you can find them when you need them most.

THINK ABOUT IT

If you feel unsure of the wisdom of vulnerability, search for Brené Brown's (2010) TED Talk *The Power of Vulnerability* (www.ted.com/talks/brene _brown_on_vulnerability).

After watching the video, ask yourself the following questions.

- "Am I willing to let go of who I think I should become and be who I really am?"
- "Do I have the courage to be imperfect?"
- "Where do I lose out and sabotage myself by trying to be perfect?"
- "How do I show compassion for myself?"

Don't Get Derailed by the Impostor Syndrome

We can all identify numerous moments throughout our lives and careers in which we have felt way out of our depth—completely fraudulent, even. Many of us face the *impostor syndrome* phenomenon when we find ourselves in unfamiliar roles or challenging situations in which we feel vulnerable, underqualified, or inexperienced.

Remember in chapter 5 (page 83), we discussed how people often spiral back in stages of maturity as they assume new responsibilities. As the two of us chatted about this phenomenon, Jane shared that she has found that impostor syndrome (Clance & Imes, 1978) often arises when someone asks her to facilitate conversations around specific conflicts, dilemmas, or needs for new strategic direction. She has written about these fields, taught tools for working with and through them, and done the work for years, yet she still sometimes questions her effectiveness.

Everyone is a work in progress. Like Jane and Cassandra Erkens (see page 124), you need to recognize the value of these impostor moments and learn from them, continuously "sharpening the saw," as Covey would advise (Franklin Covey, 2018). Don't let them dilute your ambition, permanently impact your confidence, or make you take a step back. The impostor syndrome derails many people. It's the way you reflect, reframe, and reset that counts. Remind yourself that you reached your position by being the person you are, and as Annette describes, focus on what you bring to the role:

One of the barriers I had to navigate as a woman leader was trying to forget I am a woman and instead focus on what I believe I know and can do. It is easy to feel inferior when others are often so very good at blowing their own trumpet. (Annette Rome, principal, St Margaret's and Berwick Grammar School, personal communication, April 12, 2018)

A Word From Jane

You'd think I could say to myself, "Yes, you are qualified." But the realization that improper facilitation could take a team, school, or organization backward into more ineffectiveness rather than forward in a positive direction always gives me pause.

For example, I had facilitated a visioning day with a diverse teacher team that needed to get on the same page regarding its program's goal. A quick survey at the end of the day indicated that the team members believed they'd established a productive level of agreement. They asked me to return for another half-day session to complete the process. And, as I prepared for it, I panicked. "I've used up my bag of tricks. Who am I to think I can help the teachers get from a general understanding to a practical set of values that can guide their programming decisions? I should tell them to find someone else," I told myself.

This impostor episode lasted a week. I began to productively plan for the session only after a chance conversation planted an idea that I could survey the team to provide evidence of common values. And yes, the session went well, as have all such sessions I've facilitated. Perhaps the panic keeps me humble enough to avoid any cookie-cutter approaches to such work. But it also wastes time that could go to creativity if I'd snap from "I can't" to "I've done this before" a bit faster.

We are all works in progress. As these reflections highlight, no matter what our experience, age or career stage, we will always have moments of doubt—small seeds or the larger challenges of the impostor syndrome. It's how we respond to these moments that matter. Let's explore what some of these responses could be.

WORDS FROM A LEADER

One of the fears I overcame is best defined as the *impostor syndrome* ("Do I have the right to be here? Why should anyone have to listen to what I have to say? Can I really do the job being asked of me?"). I did this by studying what was required in the task so I understood the depth and breadth of the challenges before me. Once I found my personal challenges within the bigger challenging task, I engaged in researching, learning, and creating alliances so I could fill in my own gaps. More important, however, I had to begin to trust myself and grant myself gentleness. Fortunately, over time, experience and previous successes have eliminated my need for positive self-talk; now the challenge is to continue my own learning and skill development as I strive to accept new and increasingly challenging tasks. (Cassandra Erkens, American author and educational consultant, personal communication, April 16, 2018)

Stand Tall in Your Self-Worth

Body language affects not only how other people see you but also how you see yourself. People instantly make inferences from nonverbal behaviors. Social psychologist Amy Cuddy is known for her research on stereotypes, discrimination, emotions, power, nonverbal behavior, and the effects that social stimuli have on hormone levels. In one of the most popular TED Talks, *Your Body Language May Shape Who You Are*, Cuddy (2012) reveals that *power posing*—or "standing in a posture of confidence, even when we don't feel confident—can boost feelings of confidence, and might have an impact on our chances for success." She found this message in the research from which the now frequently cited *Wonder Woman pose* (feet apart, hands on hips, a confident facial expression) has flourished.

Cuddy (2015) offers several key ways that people who are perceived to have power act. As an exercise, compare these examples of how they act to your own behaviors.

- **Initiate handshakes:** Do you wait for others to shake your hand?
- **Make longer eye contact:** Do you tend to look down or away?
- **Use broader hand and arm gestures:** Do you keep your hands by your sides?
- **Sit, stand, and walk with erect and open posture:** Do you slouch or sit and stand with arms folded or legs crossed?

- **Lean forward and orient their body and head toward others:** Do you lean away?
- **Have animated and self-assured physical expressions:** Do you hesitate?

Cuddy (2015) finds that those who expand their posture—think of standing with hands on hips or with arms in the air like a victorious athlete—begin to feel more powerful. This mindset shift promotes not empty vanity but increased confidence and power and decreased anxiety and self-absorption. Try this posture change to feel the difference it can make.

Note that checking messages on a mobile device places you in a slouching, power-draining position. Before important conversations or meetings, look up at your surroundings and other people, not down at your phone.

This perception of power reflection exercise guides you through applying Cuddy's research, but essentially, you can change other people's perceptions—and even your body chemistry—simply by changing body positions. Cuddy (2015) finds that power posing can stimulate chemical changes in the body, including a significant increase in testosterone (the dominance hormone associated with confidence and assertiveness), and a significant drop in cortisol (the stress hormone that produces an inability to adapt to highly stressful situations). These chemical changes affect behavior, leading to greater risk taking, an increased pain threshold, a higher ability to think abstractly, and a greater likelihood of performing well in stressful situations.

Cuddy's research has sparked heated debate in the research world, with attacks and counterattacks on her research's replicability and the assumptions of researchers who refute her. We argue it's glaringly obvious that if you sit hunched in a meeting or an interview, or look at the floor while giving a keynote address, others will not see you as powerful or confident. You may doubt whether two minutes in the Wonder Woman pose before such an event will change your life—although Cuddy claims that a staggering number of women have reported that their lives did change as a result. But boosting confidence by standing tall, giving a firm handshake, making longer eye contact, and other social norms does make a difference.

Your body language and nonverbal communication also reflect your internal thoughts. Going back to this chapter's title, and the focus of challenging your limiting beliefs, reflect on those little voices that tell you you're not ready, the job is too big or too important, and you don't have what it takes. Changing your self-talk and developing your self-image so that you can stand tall in your self-worth builds your concept of how you currently—and how you will in the future—value yourself. To do this, Maxwell (2014) offers the following advice.

- **Guard your self-talk:** Tell yourself you can and will do better.

- **Stop comparing yourself to others:** Focus only on what you can do today to improve where you are now.

- **Move beyond your limits:** Identify something you believe about yourself, determine how it holds you back, and then recreate that belief. Make sure you also create a statement to affirm that new belief. Tell it to yourself over and over again.

So, how can you develop your personal agency? By doing something you have the power to do: changing how you speak. Take time to practice positive self-talk that puts you firmly in command; think about your thoughts, feelings, actions—and their impact on yourself and others. When you review Margie Warrell's (2018b) phrases on page 129, identify where you may spiral into self-talk traps that magnify the negative. And don't forget those positive affirmations, such as "I am enough."

Reach Your Potential Through Growth

Addressing your limiting beliefs also requires you to consider your leadership potential and effectiveness, together with the skills and dispositions you bring to your work that make you successful. This doesn't occur in a vacuum. Women in particular tend to expect that others will recognize their work's value without their having to articulate it. Don't expect others to know about the significant contributions you have made and success you have had. Acknowledge your own expertise and success, and use this in your conversations around advancement, in, for example, applications and interviews, which we will explore more fully in chapter 11 (page 185).

An aspiring leader in one of Barb's women in leadership programs shared how mentoring, a key element of the program, enabled her to articulate pride in her achievements. Instead of shying away from affirmations, she became more explicit about her goals: to become more ambitious and to network more. These personal reflections and insights, in tandem with her mentor's support and coaching, revealed to her that the answers come from within and helped her uncover her own solutions.

> Believe that everything is a possibility and then ask what you need to do to make it a reality.
>
> **—Lauren McGoodwin,** founder of Career Contessa

Drawing on her personal experience and doctoral research, Jill Berry (2016), author of *Making the Leap: Moving From Deputy to Head*, articulates the qualities that make a good teacher and leader of learning and how they inform the transition to other leadership roles. She finds the challenge in moving from deputy to head (assistant principal to principal) of particular interest; in this move, preparation as deputy will get you partway but not all the way there.

As we've highlighted previously, you learn by doing the job. For many women, this requires a shift in thinking and a shift in what it means to come fully prepared. This also means reflecting on assumptions you make about a role when you have yet to be in that role. Berry (2017) writes about what she learned from her transition from deputy to head:

> When people say it can't be done or you don't have what it takes, it makes the task all the more interesting.
> —Lynn Hill,
> American rock climber

> *The foundation of a strong headship involves clear vision and values, integrity, a commitment to working hard and continuing to learn, and the capacity to build your resilience over time.*
>
> *I learned a lot about the nature of the move and how it feels to make that leap. If you're considering it, here's what you need to know. There is a paradox at the heart of this transition: in some respects, being a deputy appears the best possible preparation for headship, giving a senior leader a taste of what ultimate school leadership involves. However, in many ways, being a head is a quite different professional identity. As deputy you often act as a buffer between the staff and the head. As the head you are one step removed from this.*

Australian Stacie Hansel had young children when she transitioned from school principal to a director in the central office of a large state-based education system. She describes the transition as exciting; she loved the challenging work and stayed present for her family. In looking back at her career trajectory, Stacie, who was eventually promoted to executive director, shares this advice:

- *Take every opportunity that is meaningful to you—don't wait to master the skill set.*
- *You don't have to know all the answers; admit that you don't know yet and build the capability of others around you to collectively learn how to learn.*
- *You'll earn respect from your peers (male or female, younger or older) by the work that you do.*
- *Believe in yourself.*

- *Be resilient. Getting it wrong is not a career stopper. It's the opportunity to learn and grow through self-reflection and ask respected colleagues for advice.*

- *Everyone has strengths and weaknesses—know yours.*

- *Know that along the way there will be times when you get the balance of home, kids, and work life wrong . . . and that's OK.*

- *And it's also OK to say out loud that I like what I do, I enjoy going to work, I enjoy being at work, and I enjoy the challenges it brings. (Stacie Hansel, personal communication, April 20, 2018)*

Next Steps in the Journey

An important part of leadership development is making meaningful connections with others. You learn from and find support in others' stories. Build and use your professional network and engage in learning opportunities to strategically benefit your career development. Don't apologize for this. In the next three chapters, we'll look at managing emotions and communicating with others, verbally and nonverbally, to negotiate, empower, or persuade.

Step in for Further Reflection

The following activities provide you with valuable opportunities to reflect on the ideas, strategies, and concepts covered in this chapter. If you are approaching *Step In, Step Up* as a twelve-week journey, you can spread these out over several days.

You may complete them individually or with a group so you can share your thoughts and ideas. Keep a journal so you can revisit your thoughts as you travel this journey.

1. Now that you've considered how the confidence gap might limit your beliefs, revisit these questions.

   - What are your key strengths?

   - What gets in your way and has the potential to derail your ambition and belief in yourself (challenges, impostors, and defaults)?

   - How do you take time to build the habits that shape and display confidence to nourish the leader within? For example, creating space to come down from a busy mind or a stressful day and stepping back into the present can be enormously helpful. When we are present, we are more likely to gain perspective and see that we have the resources and power to regulate our response to pressure. Try this simple step—S-T-O-P, a ninety-second breath meditation (Goldstein, 2013).

- **Slow down:** Switch off automatic pilot. Slowly breathe, press your feet down, or slowly stretch.

- **Take note:** Notice with curiosity and openness what is happening, here and now. What is your mind telling you? What is happening in your body? What actions are you taking?

- **Open up:** Make room for difficult thoughts and feelings. Acknowledge them as natural and normal, and let them come, stay, and go in their own good time.

- **Pursue values:** Remember your values, and take action, no matter how small the actions; act mindfully on those actions.

2. Warrell (2018b) provides a powerful tool for improving your ability to show confidence—phrase variations that help you consider how to increase the power of your communication style. The following list of examples will help you practice speaking more powerfully so that, with time and practice, you gradually embody the presence of a powerful woman who commands attention and influences outcomes. The first phrase or sentence uses qualifying, passive, and imprecise language, and thereby limits your power, presence, and impact on others. The second phrase or sentence uses positive, specific, and declarative language and puts you firmly in command, making others want to listen to you.

   - "I think I can do that." ⇨ "I can do that."

   - "I should do that." ⇨ "I could do that if I wanted to."

   - "I'm hopeless at . . ." ⇨ "I'm learning how to . . ."

   - "I will try . . ." ⇨ "I will do . . ."

   - "I'm nervous." ⇨ "I'm excited."

   - "I hope I can . . ." ⇨ "I'm confident I will . . ." or "I know I will . . ."

   - "It's really hard." ⇨ "It's a great challenge."

   - "Might you be able to do this for me?" ⇨ "Would you do this for me?"

   - "I'm no good at . . ." ⇨ "I have yet to learn how to . . ."

CHAPTER

8

EXPLORING EMOTIONAL INTELLIGENCE

GUIDING QUESTION

- How is emotional intelligence different from being resilient, kind, and empathetic?

- What skills or capacities do you need as a leader in order to work with your and others' emotions?

Most organizations, including schools, can relatively easily assess whether a leader has mastered hard skills such as planning, budgeting, and giving feedback. They find it harder to assess the soft skills involved in using emotions properly in leadership and decision making that have proven to be the more important components of leadership effectiveness—and people have a harder time learning the soft skills (Weite, 2013).

Leadership is about impact and influence. How do you recognize and manage your and others' emotions to inform your interactions for positive impact and influence? Doing so is an important part of who you are and how you lead.

Leaders who have low emotional intelligence (EQ) will find it nearly impossible to create the conditions necessary for collective teacher efficacy. As we discussed in chapter 3 (page 51), collective teacher efficacy—teachers' confidence that their hard work will have the desired results (Sun & Leithwood, 2015)—may just have the biggest effect size on student learning of more than 150 strategies (DeWitt, 2017). The leadership skills you need to build *collective efficacy*—motivating others around a common purpose, establishing an emotionally safe environment, and providing individual coaching and support—all require EQ.

In this chapter, we'll look at four major areas of EQ that most EQ models incorporate: (1) emotional self-awareness, (2) self-management of emotions, (3) social awareness of emotions, and (4) relationship management. You'll have a chance to assess yourself on eight key skill sets and consider some development suggestions for your leadership journey. Let's begin with a definition of EQ.

A Definition of Emotional Intelligence

While researchers, psychologists, sociologists, and others have been investigating EQ since the 1940s, psychologist and science journalist Daniel Goleman popularized the concept in his 1998 book *Working With Emotional Intelligence*. In this book, he defines EQ as "managing feelings so that they are expressed appropriately and effectively, enabling people to work together smoothly toward their common goals" (Goleman, 1998, p. 7).

A misconception exists that women have more EQ than men, but EQ involves more than just the "touchy-feely" stuff of the feminine stereotype. Components of resilience and self-efficacy also factor in. Goleman (1998) cites research that shows individuals have strengths and weaknesses that may or may not track with gender patterns. While, in general, women do have the edge in emotional awareness, empathy, and interpersonal skills, men do better at self-fulfillment, optimism, flexibility, and stress management. Because you need EQ to develop and motivate others to move toward common goals— in other words, the heart of how we define leadership—understanding your EQ strengths and struggles is a vital part of your journey.

> One looks back with appreciation to the brilliant teachers, but with gratitude to those who touched our human feelings. The curriculum is so much necessary raw material, but warmth is the vital element for the growing plant and for the soul of the child.
> —Carl Jung (1875–1961),
> Swiss psychiatrist and psychoanalyst

Another common misconception is that leaders shouldn't show emotions. Women in particular come under fire for showing emotions, especially if tears emerge, whether they stem from frustration, anger, happiness, sadness, empathy, or tragedy. The result of this judgment that displaying emotion is bad? Because they flatten out women's normal ebbs and flows of estrogen, which heighten emotional sensitivity, some women turn to selective serotonin reuptake inhibitors (SSRIs), an antidepressant. The use of antidepressants has increased dramatically since the year 2000, and women are two times more likely to take them than men, especially SSRIs (Holland, 2017).

SSRIs decrease irritability and aid impulse control, helping patients behave in a more accommodating and cooperative way. They can be a godsend for women who suffer from depression. However, categorizing expression of negative emotions as pathological has a major downside, as psychiatrist Julie Holland (2017) explains:

> I had a patient who called me from her office in tears, saying she needed to increase her antidepressant dosage because she couldn't be seen crying at work. After dissecting why she was upset—her boss had betrayed and humiliated her in front of her staff—we decided that what was needed was calm confrontation, not more medication. . . .
>
> Unrestricted growth, the type seen in many corporations, has a different name in medicine. It's called cancer. Checking corporate malignance is perhaps the most important reason to rely on emotional authenticity. If I give into my patient's request to ratchet up her happy pill dosage, her boss's emotionally incorrect behavior remains unchecked, and the unrestricted growth of corporate greed and malfeasance continues unfettered. It's not easy. I, like my patient, have teared up in a meeting with my boss, or worse, my boss's boss, and crying is the last thing anyone wants in the office. But that part of ourselves that gets us misty-eyed when something is amiss is a vital feedback system that the corporate world needs. (pp. 222–223)

The world of education equally needs the vital feedback system of emotions.

The importance of managing emotions skillfully has become even more crucial because research shows how positional power—*power over* that lacks *power with* or *power to*—actually blunts empathy and other aspects of EQ (Useem, 2017). Think about spectacular leader derailments that make the news headlines, which result from poor business decisions, sexual misconduct, embezzlement, and so on. Those in power lose perspective as well as some abilities that helped them climb the ladder. According to journalist Jerry Useem (2017):

> Power, the research says, primes our brain to screen out peripheral information. In most situations, this provides a helpful efficiency boost. In social ones, it has the unfortunate side effect of making us more obtuse. . . . Less able to make out people's individuating traits, they rely more heavily on stereotype. And the less they're able to see, other research suggests, the more they rely on a personal "vision" for navigation.

This may seem like a remote worry at your stage of the leadership journey, but now, not when leadership pressures increase, is the time to build your conscious use of EQ skills. Know that as a school leader, understanding and improving your EQ not only readies you to improve staff EQ but also has an amazing number of personal benefits. Review the following impacts of heightened levels of EQ (Gujral, Gupta, & Aneja, 2012).

- Higher individual well-being
- Higher resilience levels
- Lower stress levels
- Better physical health
- Higher-quality work performance
- Better psychological health
- Better self-efficacy
- Better relationships
- Higher overall life satisfaction
- Lower burnout levels

Does anyone *not* want to develop a healthy level of EQ or *not* think EQ is important for effective teaching and learning?

Figure 8.1 shows a general EQ model for school leadership and the skill sets that these major areas of EQ include.

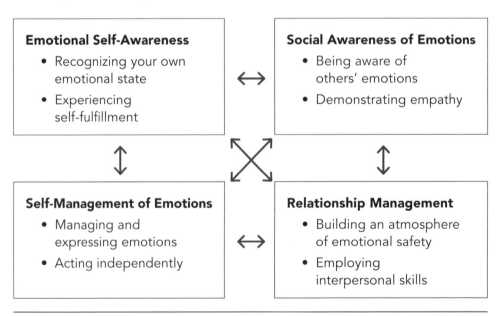

Figure 8.1: General EQ model for school leadership.

Leaders need to be aware of their emotions and use them appropriately. However, EQ also involves others' emotions, and leaders must know how to consciously recognize and influence those emotions in healthy ways.

As you read through the following sections that explore these four areas, think about the areas you do well, the ones that your position draws on the most, and where you might need to concentrate your development efforts.

Emotional Self-Awareness

How often do you slow down to consider how you feel and what prompted those feelings? Conscious, healthy use of emotions begins with recognizing the emotions that surface, their causes, and their influences. Following are two core skill sets of self-awareness: (1) recognizing your own emotional state and (2) experiencing self-fulfillment.

 WORDS FROM A LEADER

One of the fears I overcame was acknowledging my own vulnerability, a fear of failure. I did this by sharing a very important story from my teenage years at a whole-school assembly, a story I had never fully told. It was by showing my own vulnerability that I actually faced it truly for the first time in thirty years. I am still susceptible to the claws of fearing failure, but I have a greater sense of self-awareness and try to manage it. To be honest, I think it is a lifelong struggle for so many of us. (Linda Douglas, principal, Ruyton Girls' School, Australia, personal communication, April 18, 2018)

Recognizing Your Own Emotional State

Jane has coached several leaders who recognized their emotional state only after it got them into trouble. One high-level school leader didn't realize how frustrated she was by two colleagues' inability to support a mandate she'd given them until she lost her temper with them in a public meeting. This destroyed trust.

Another school principal thought she had full control of the emotions that a life-threatening illness caused until she lost control and began crying in a meeting where appearing so vulnerable was unwise.

Both scenarios illustrate how ignoring or lacking awareness of your emotions can have unintended consequences. Figure 8.2 (page 136) shows two continuums regarding your skills with recognizing your emotional state. Take a few moments to consider where you fall on these continuums. Perhaps even take the time to call some examples to mind and jot down a few notes.

Strength	0	1	2	3	4	5	Struggle
I'm aware of my emotional state and how it affects others.							Often, it surprises me when others tell me I seem angry, frustrated, or otherwise upset.

Strength	0	1	2	3	4	5	Struggle
I can tell when my emotions might be affecting my judgment or reactions.							I often lack awareness of my emotions.

Figure 8.2: Continuums for recognizing your own emotional state.

To improve your skills with recognizing your emotional state, ponder exactly what you are feeling. Some people have a limited vocabulary of emotions. For example, they think they are angry when, in fact, they may feel frustrated, hurt, shocked, or disgusted. Each of these emotions requires a different response. Search for an emotions chart online using the keywords *emotions chart for adults*. One of Jane's favorites, designed by Gloria Wilcox (n.d.), places six core emotions in the center, with each spoke naming related emotions that nuance how that core emotion might be experienced or expressed. (Go to https:med.emory.edu/excel/documents/Feeling%20Wheel. pdf to view this emotions chart.)

Use the chart after a meeting (or while watching a movie) to reflect on exactly which emotion you feel, and consider how your response to it might differ if you named your feelings in different ways.

Being aware of your emotions such as impatience and frustration is crucial to leadership, as they lead to low impulse control. "But I don't act impulsively," you might say. Note that interrupting others, finishing their sentences, and rushing decisions are all impulsive acts.

Of course, every EQ skill is as dangerous when overused as when underused. If you constantly tune in to your emotions such as anxiety, fear, embarrassment, or other barriers, they'll, of course, get in your way. Note that you won't necessarily best deal with these emotions by calming yourself, trying to ignore them. Instead, work on reframing them, perhaps through journaling. For example, reframe anxiety about an important meeting as, "I feel excited about the possibility of influencing how we craft this policy, and I want to come prepared," and acknowledge that it is normal to feel your stomach flip-flop. Such reframing allows adrenaline to work for you instead of against you.

Experiencing Self-Fulfillment

Do you have personal goals? And do you feel that your efforts bear fruit? Most leaders who answer *yes* to those questions demonstrate an optimism and enthusiasm that helps motivate their team. Having an accurate picture of your accomplishments makes you neither arrogant nor meek; rather, it gives you a healthy self-image that fosters more achievement—achievement of the right kind, that is, that fosters more optimism and well-placed self-confidence.

Think about the messages women receive as they ponder stepping up to leadership positions. Traditionally, you probably heard some variation of "Don't toot your own horn." We can think of at least three problems with this saying. First, as we discussed in chapter 7 (page 115), people simply don't note your contributions unless you draw attention to them. Second, being aware of your accomplishments energizes and encourages you to do more. And third, letting others know what you have accomplished often creates a pathway for receiving resources for doing more.

Citing the truth that a phenomenal number of successful people are deeply unhappy, author Elisa Albert (2017) describes a set of more affective goals for self-fulfillment, ones that have nothing to do with money, power, or influence. Consider the goals that her questions might spark for you:

> What kind of person are you? What kind of craft have you honed? What is my experience of looking into your eyes, of being around you? Are you at home in your body? Can you sit still? Do you make me laugh? Can you give and receive affection? Do you know yourself? How sophisticated is your sense of humor, how finely tuned your understanding of life's absurdities? How thoughtfully do you interact with others? How honest are you with yourself? How do you deal with your various addictive tendencies? How do you face your darkness? How broad and deep is your perspective? How willing are you to be quiet? How do you care for yourself? How do you treat people you deem unimportant? (Albert, 2017, pp. 201–202)

Adding these sorts of goals to work-related goals can help strike the right balance between humility and arrogance, a balance that leads to effectiveness and fulfillment. Figure 8.3 (page 138) shows two continuums for self-fulfillment. How would you rate yourself on these continuums on both achievement goals and affective goals?

Strength	0	1	2	3	4	5	Struggle
I set and accomplish my goals.							Setting goals reinforces my disappointment in what I've failed to accomplish before.

Strength	0	1	2	3	4	5	Struggle
I like a challenge.							I don't feel capable of having a positive impact in most areas of my life.

Figure 8.3: Continuums for experiencing self-fulfillment.

To improve your self-fulfillment skills, examine what activities you consider in and out of your comfort zone. Not all challenges have to fall completely out of your comfort zone. Draw a circle, and inside it, list activities that you find easy. Draw a circle around the existing circle, and place in that circle the activities that you find a little more difficult. Continue to add expanding circles, listing activities of increasing difficulty. Where could you take just one step out of your current circle? Use that step to boost your confidence for the next step.

If you worry that you concentrate too heavily on self-fulfillment, schedule time to focus on activities that someone else finds important, especially for those people closest to you who may also need your attention. You might also try bringing to mind a few hubris-dispelling episodes from your past to ensure that you don't become overconfident or truly arrogant.

Self-Management of Emotions

Recognizing emotions represents the first step toward effectively working with them. Ignoring them seldom solves anything, but rather can increase stress, decrease opportunities for needed support or celebration, and result in unintended consequences. A huge part of managing emotions requires that you preserve your capacity to do so, as we discussed in chapter 3 (page 51) with bandwidth. Note that teachers report increased job satisfaction, loyalty, and effectiveness when their leaders care not only for those around them but also for themselves. A leader without work-life balance discourages others from striving for it in their own lives (Skakon, Nielsen, Borg, & Guzman, 2010). And without that bucket of bandwidth, you'll find EQ just about impossible. Following are two core skill sets of self-management of emotions: (1) managing and expressing emotions and (2) acting independently.

Managing and Expressing Emotions

Emotional expression is an important contributor to motivating others in authentic ways, yet many leaders try to contain emotions. Figure 8.4 shows two continuums for managing and expressing emotions. Where do you fall on these continuums?

Strength	0	1	2	3	4	5	Struggle
I accurately share my emotions most of the time.							I tend to withhold my emotions, or I am vague about what I am feeling.

Strength	0	1	2	3	4	5	Struggle
I know when and how to share emotions appropriately.							Expressing emotions seems like a sign of weakness in most situations, so I don't express them.

Figure 8.4: Continuums for managing and expressing emotions.

To improve your skills with managing and expressing emotions, listen to a talk from a leader you consider genuine. (You might check the TED website [www.ted.com] for eighteen-minute presentations that communicate huge ideas.) How and why does this leader tap emotions? How might you do the same while feeling authentic? Make some notes on when you should and shouldn't share emotions at work, and evaluate them with someone who shares emotions more easily. When, why, and where might you be too sparing in sharing emotions?

If you tend to overuse emotional expression to the point where others tune you out, practice getting to the bottom line sooner. Before meetings or other situations in which you can anticipate what people will discuss, decide, "What is my main message? How can I express my feelings most succinctly?" Likewise, set negotiated time limits on expressing or discussing emotions. For example, you might say, "Let me vent for a minute. Then we can discuss the solutions."

Note that managing stress well enables you to manage other emotions. While people once viewed stress as categorically bad for them, newer research indicates that how you deal with stress determines how it affects you. Psychologist Kelly McGonigal (2015) points out that stress is not only normal but also inevitable if you pursue worthy goals, develop relationships, or are fortunate enough to live a long life. Take time to journal about how, in a past stressful situation, you made use of the four factors that define *hardiness*, or the courage to grow from stress.

1. Stress is normal and an opportunity to grow, not a time to catastrophize.

2. Engage with life and others, rather than isolating yourself.

3. No matter the circumstances, you can continue to make choices.

4. Caring for yourself—physically, emotionally, and spiritually—is key to growing from stress rather than experiencing its downside.

How can you use what you've learned from past stressful situations when, inevitably, stress again emerges?

Acting Independently

In general, women prefer a more collaborative leadership style, seek input from stakeholders, and work for consensus. However, leaders also need to take necessary stands, and this requires acting independently. How difficult do you find it to take a stand when others disagree? Figure 8.5 shows two continuums for acting independently. Consider which end you lean toward.

Strength	0	1	2	3	4	5	Struggle
I know which decisions I should make on my own, and I feel comfortable making them.					I struggle to make decisions without consulting others.		

Strength	0	1	2	3	4	5	Struggle
I am comfortable with my self-worth and with standing up for what I value.					I tend to need assurance from others and struggle to stick to views that go against those of the majority.		

Figure 8.5: Continuums for acting independently.

To improve your skill set for acting independently, think about whose approval you seek. After you share a decision, a presentation, or a new idea, do you look to a few individuals' reactions as the litmus test? While you may need your superior's approval in order to have success, you also need to know how to realistically assess your performance. Before an event, try defining what success would look like in your view, and then grade yourself before receiving others' feedback.

If you sense you might act *too* independently, revisit whether others might have legitimate concerns regarding one of your decisions. Check in with individuals directly affected by your decision. What can you learn from their pros and cons concerning your choices?

Social Awareness of Emotions

As we've mentioned before, your and others' emotions provide data as valuable as any hard data about test scores, classroom observations, or other common tools for data-informed decisions. People simply can't leave their emotions behind. In the modern workplace, researchers have found that when people pause from focusing on specific tasks, their attention defaults to social cognition. They think about themselves and their relationships (Lieberman, 2013). Following are two core components of social awareness of emotions: (1) being aware of others' emotions and (2) demonstrating empathy.

Being Aware of Others' Emotions

Some people can read a room and understand both the general mood and individuals' moods. Others only realize these things later, when someone else informs them or some action brings attention to the emotions in the room. Figure 8.6 shows two continuums for being aware of others' emotions. Consider where you fall on them.

Strength	0	1	2	3	4	5	Struggle
I can accurately assess others' emotional state, and I take time to do so.							I'm often surprised by the emotions others express.

Strength	0	1	2	3	4	5	Struggle
I pick up on group undertones and emotions, grasping others' levels of enthusiasm, trust, fear, stress, frustration, and other feelings.							I tend to focus more on tasks and goals than on group dynamics.

Figure 8.6: Continuums for being aware of others' emotions.

To improve your skills in being aware of others' emotions, do the following exercise. After a meeting, take time to reflect on the emotions others experienced during the meeting. Compare notes with someone who you believe exhibits high awareness of others' emotions. Where his or her impressions differ from yours, ask for an explanation of what he or she saw, heard, or experienced. Look for patterns in what you missed.

If you are overly sensitive to others' emotions, strive too hard to keep everyone happy, or worry to distraction if someone is upset, you might benefit from setting boundaries before interacting with others. When does this sensitivity get in your way at work? Do you spend too much time listening to others' problems? Do you experience stress from trying to meet competing needs? Do you worry over how to communicate tough messages? Make a list. Then, choose an area that would benefit from more objectivity, and make a plan to find a better balance between objectivity and sensitivity.

Demonstrating Empathy

Showing true *empathy* means not just recognizing someone else's emotions but also understanding what causes them and their potential ramifications. Thus a school leader might recognize annoyance, but without empathy skills, he or she could attribute that annoyance to the wrong thing—perhaps an early meeting time—rather than the true cause—such as a teacher's belief that the leader didn't hear his or her voice.

Empathy is undoubtedly a core leadership skill. Overuse and underuse of empathy cause equal harm, as with all these EQ components. However, people usually quickly and harshly judge women when they fail to get empathy just right. When women empathize but still insist on an unpopular yet wise course of action, they may receive labels such as *coldhearted*. And accommodating emotional needs may, of course, result in the label *too soft*. It is true that overuse of empathy may encourage someone to indulge in self-pity, for example, rather than employ skills that lead to resilience. Too much empathy can also get in the way of a leader's independence.

Goleman describes three kinds of empathy, which spark different parts of the brain (as cited in OWN, 2016).

1. **Cognitive empathy:** Understand others' viewpoints and perspectives. Leaders will find this useful for communication and performance feedback, but they can also twist it to manipulate people if they lack concern about their emotional impact on others.

2. **Emotional empathy:** Tap into the social brain's functioning for rapport or chemistry. Leaders critically need this to lead others, foster harmony, and have general leadership likability. They'll have difficulty employing this kind of empathy, though, if they constantly experience emotional stress.

3. **Empathic concern:** Leaders often underrate this ancient mammalian system for parenting. One could describe empathic concern's actions as, "I see your need and spontaneously help out." In other words, leaders show concern by investing time in helping people learn and do better.

It creates the team atmosphere of putting others first. Overuse, though, can bog down progress toward goals if leaders don't also communicate high expectations.

To become a truly successful leader, you need all three capacities going at full strength. Each has critical powers but, as pointed out previously, they may become liabilities.

How do you solve this? Assess your acumen with empathy in relation to your independence level *and* your interpersonal skills. Consider where you'd place yourself on the empathy continuums in figure 8.7. If you have confidence in your empathy skills, revisit them in light of the behaviors we describe in the figure.

Strength	0	1	2	3	4	5	Struggle
I easily recognize others' emotions and what triggered them.							I strive to keep emotions separate from work.

Strength	0	1	2	3	4	5	Struggle
I care about and take care with others' feelings.							I often discover I've inadvertently hurt someone's feelings.

Figure 8.7: Continuums for demonstrating empathy.

To improve your empathy skills, read a book with literary merit or watch a character-driven movie, and name the characters' motivations and why they do what they do. This research-based strategy effectively improves leaders' empathy (Chiaet, 2013). Check your understanding of the characters with other people—friends, book club members, or a discussion group at an online site such as Goodreads (www.goodreads .com). Empathy means understanding another's viewpoint even if you disagree with its merit.

If your empathy sometimes undermines your independence, reflect on a decision or situation in which you believe you were too accommodating, and learn from it. Did the situation have unintended consequences? What precedents might you have set? What other choices could you have made? What are the pros and cons of each choice? If you do ____, then what might happen? Might a new precedent be set? What can you learn? What questions can you ask yourself when you face future dilemmas and need to balance empathy, fairness, and your own needs?

Relationship Management

Of course, leaders need to do more than recognize others' emotions and empathize; leaders also need to understand how to work with emotions to motivate people, create effective workplaces, and more, without manipulating people.

WORDS FROM A LEADER

I wish I'd known earlier as a leader that relationships matter more than strategy, and that change in others begins first with change in me. (Joellen Killion, senior advisor, Learning Forward, personal communication, April 19, 2018)

You may know that the physical needs of food, shelter, and water form the foundation of Abraham H. Maslow's (1943) hierarchy of needs. Research indicates that good relationships represent a more foundational core need for human survival (Lieberman, 2013). Remember the stories of infants in institutions who were fed and clothed but kept in cribs with little adult contact? Without human interaction, they failed to thrive and many did not survive (Hughes, 2013). People need other humans as much as or more than they need food and water.

Too many leaders, especially women, feel isolated in their roles. If this describes you, take the opportunity to gather with other female leaders. Whether you call it a *support group* or an *accountability group*, you need a safe place and caring relationships. These are key resources for your leadership journey and overall health.

Further, school leaders need to manage external relationships with parents, the community, school district personnel, and so on. Following are two core components of relationship management that leaders need: (1) building an atmosphere of emotional safety and (2) employing interpersonal skills.

Building an Atmosphere of Emotional Safety

The biggest task that school leaders face requires them to ensure an environment where people effectively collaborate toward a meaningful vision or purpose that personally inspires them. Leaders take what they know about the organization and the goals and use both strategic thinking and EQ to guide and motivate people.

However, building this collective teacher efficacy requires leadership expertise in the following EQ skills.

- **Inspiring group purpose:** People who feel connected to an organization's purpose and values have more effectiveness than competent people who lack connection to that purpose (Coyle, 2018). Read that again—a school benefits more from inspired teachers than from the absolute best teachers who aren't inspired by the school's purpose.

- **Providing teachers with individual support:** Holding teachers accountable makes up only one side of the equation for developing effective teachers; the other side requires the leader to support them as they grow. Think, for example, of the different levels of support that teachers need in order to implement the same new strategy, depending on their experience levels, individual strengths, and content-area expertise. Collective teacher efficacy flows from all teachers experiencing the levels and forms of support they need to learn. It takes empathy, listening, and coaching skills for school leaders to provide that.

- **Creating an atmosphere of safety and trust:** The number-one predictor of effective teams is an atmosphere of safety and belonging (Coyle, 2018). Team members consistently describe such atmospheres as like a family.

In his book *The Culture Code: The Secrets of Highly Successful Groups*, Daniel Coyle (2018) summarizes decades of research on what it takes for people to feel included in a group and lists three key leadership behaviors that create such a safe space. First, the leader invests his or her *energy* in the immediate exchange. Group members feel safe sharing problems and mistakes because the leader listens intently and ensures that no one critiques or judges them. Second, this *individualized attention* makes each group member feel like a unique and valued person instead of a problem to solve or a nameless face in the crowd. Third, the leader makes it clear that the relationship and the safe space are *ongoing*. When we know we are safe, we can tell the "friend or foe?" filter in our brains that developed back in caveman days to take a break. Safe in an atmosphere of unconditional acceptance, we can freely seek help to meet high expectations.

If that sounds like a huge, nebulous responsibility, perhaps that lends weight to the premise that developing EQ is far more difficult than mastering the technical leadership skills. Use the two continuums in figure 8.8 (page 146) to reflect on your skills in building an atmosphere of emotional safety.

Strength	0	1	2	3	4	5	Struggle
My team members willingly share struggles and mistakes.							My team members seldom share struggles but rather share only what is going well.

Strength	0	1	2	3	4	5	Struggle
People seek me out as a good listener.							Instead of deeply listening to other people, I jump to trying to solve their problems.

Figure 8.8: Continuums for building an atmosphere of emotional safety.

To improve your skills in building an atmosphere of emotional safety, model how to share mistakes. Bring your lesson plans for critique, use examples from your practice, or admit when you've misinterpreted someone's actions. When team members see how much they can learn from sharing mistakes, they will gain confidence to share their own.

One potential downside of focusing on emotional safety is possibly neglecting progress toward student achievement goals and other aspects of your overall purpose. Keep in mind that you can do both simultaneously. Do the work of change while building the trust necessary for change by meeting people's needs, listening to them, and otherwise investing in them.

Employing Interpersonal Skills

In addition to listening skills, leadership requires collaborative skills, coaching techniques, and good feedback skills. Again, these skills lead the way in creating an atmosphere of safety and belonging, the number-one predictor of effective teams (Coyle, 2018). Team members consistently describe such atmospheres as being part of a family. Examine your interpersonal skills using the continuums in figure 8.9.

To improve your interpersonal skills, explore whether you have a good awareness of attitudes, workloads, relationships, and other key contributors to various staff members' productivity. Meet with colleagues from different areas, and note anything that surprises you. How can you build better awareness of your school or office's atmosphere? This is key to effective work relationships.

Strength	0	1	2	3	4	5	Struggle
I tend to work effectively with others.							I seldom find working with others advantageous for me.

Strength	0	1	2	3	4	5	Struggle
My staff seek coaching and feedback from me.							My staff seem a bit afraid of my feedback.

Figure 8.9: Continuums for employing interpersonal skills.

If you struggle with giving effective feedback, consider these four basic approaches to feedback, as those who prefer them might describe them.

- **Just the facts:** Start with clear expectations and let me ask questions. Then, use those expectations to let me know where I succeeded and what I might do better. I don't need fluff, but if you haven't clued me in to what I'm supposed to do, don't tell me I didn't do it!

- **Be my encourager:** I need a clear picture of what you expect, but if things don't go well, I already feel guilty enough. Don't yell at me or seem harsh. Instead, give me one or two solid suggestions, explain how they fit with what I do well, and point out what I'm doing well.

- **Be my partner:** Ask me what I felt went well and where I should improve. That's the starting place. We can set expectations together and brainstorm where I need to concentrate my efforts.

- **Be an expert and a sounding board:** Ground your critique in sound theories and practices and be ready to explain why I need to change. Chances are, I'm operating out of my own well-grounded ideas. I'm willing to change if your suggestions are more effective.

Which most resembles your approach? Which least resembles how you deliver feedback? Consider how you might do more of the latter.

Can you see how easily you may give feedback that someone else can't handle? Implement the platinum rule for feedback: *Do unto others according to their needs, not your needs.*

Next Steps in the Journey

Just like leadership development, improving your EQ skills is a lifelong journey. While wisdom doesn't always come with age, most people whom we view as truly wise have developed their EQ as well as their cognitive capacity.

If you're keeping a journal as you journey through these pages, note the EQ skills you're using well and ones you might target for improvement. Know, though, that it's often easiest to develop a particular skill when a specific responsibility, goal, or situation requires it. In chapter 12 (page 203), you'll have a chance to revisit how EQ fits with your next steps in the leadership journey.

Step in for Further Reflection

The following activities provide you with valuable opportunities to reflect on the ideas, strategies, and concepts covered in this chapter. If you are approaching *Step In, Step Up* as a twelve-week journey, you can spread these out over several days.

You may complete them individually or with a group so you can share your thoughts and ideas. Keep a journal so you can revisit your thoughts as you travel this journey.

1. Think about three leaders you admire. Without reading further, quickly list five things you admire about them.

    Now consider: Which of these characteristics involve EQ? IQ? Accomplishments? Most people find that what they admire most in leaders reflects their EQ. How might you use this information as motivation for continuing to improve your EQ capacity?

2. This chapter asked you to reflect on your EQ capacity and where you need to improve or tone down certain skills. However, don't try to change everything at once. Instead, use the following process to choose a few focuses for making the most of your EQ as a leader.

    ○ Select one current goal to use as a lens for thinking about EQ. The goal could focus on working on a project for which you have some leadership responsibility, enhancing a specific relationship, or improving a team atmosphere that is key to your leadership effectiveness or the next leadership position to which you aspire.

    ○ Use the reproducible chart "EQ Components for Development" on pages 150–151 to help you identify which EQ components you might need to develop to progress toward this goal. In the chart, highlight up to three components that you find most pertinent to your selected goal, and use the sentence starters as prompts to record both why you are focusing on this EQ skill and how you will measure progress in improving your skills.

○ Select just one EQ component for now. Look back at this chapter's section that describes that component to find suggestions for developing it. Set a *what* goal and a *why* goal, as described in chapter 12 on page 203, to help you follow through on this commitment. The answers you gave in the reproducible chart (pages 150–151) provide much of the input.

EQ Components for Development

My focus goal for evaluating my EQ development needs:

Emotional Self-Awareness	Social Awareness of Emotions
Recognizing your own emotional state • Using this EQ component effectively is important to this goal because . . . • I will know that I have become more effective if I see . . .	Being aware of others' emotions • Using this EQ component effectively is important to this goal because . . . • I will know that I have become more effective if I see . . .
Experiencing self-fulfillment • Using this EQ component effectively is important to this goal because . . . • I will know that I have become more effective if I see . . .	Demonstrating empathy • Using this EQ component effectively is important to this goal because . . . • I will know that I have become more effective if I see . . .

page 1 of 2

Step In, Step Up © 2019 Jane A. G. Kise and Barbara K. Watterston • SolutionTree.com
Visit **go.SolutionTree.com/leadership** to download this free reproducible.

Self-Management of Emotions	Relationship Management
Managing and expressing emotions • Using this EQ component effectively is important to this goal because . . . • I will know that I have become more effective if I see . . .	Building an atmosphere of emotional safety • Using this EQ component effectively is important to this goal because . . . • I will know that I have become more effective if I see . . .
Acting independently • Using this EQ component effectively is important to this goal because . . . • I will know that I have become more effective if I see . . .	Employing interpersonal skills (listening, collaborating, coaching, and giving feedback) • Using this EQ component effectively is important to this goal because . . . • I will know that I have become more effective if I see . . .

chapter 9

MAKING YOURSELF HEARD

GUIDING QUESTIONS

- How does your communication style make others value your message, ideas, presence, input, and leadership capacity?

- How do you demonstrate that you understand the value of, and need for, the perspectives and issues women bring to education conversations?

Jane's colleague Beth Russell often describes the following statement from her mentor as some of the best advice she received in her early months as a school administrator: "They don't care how you *feel*, Beth. Give them *facts* to convince them this isn't working." She received this advice just after a meeting in which she gave a report to the school district's leadership team regarding implementation of a new scheduling system. As she described her frustrations with system glitches, she received stony stares and instructions from the team to speed up the process.

Her mentor, who had attended the meeting, followed up his advice with concrete instructions. He instructed her to log the number of hours she'd spent on the project, how many trips she'd made to the vendor, the increased time teachers were spending helping students fill out forms because of glitches, and so on. When Beth presented those data at the next meeting, the leadership team said, "This is terrible. You need an assistant."

As with so many things, we would find this funny if it weren't so real. As this chapter will convey, research indicates that the workplace still favors the male communication style—not because it has more value but because it has become the norm. People expect it. Much of the literature that encourages women to step up to leadership says, "Be more assertive. Speak up. If you want to make yourself heard in a man's world, speak like a man!"

Will that work? Not exactly.

Understanding and adjusting your communication style is crucial before stepping up in leadership—the stakes are high for you personally and professionally. Transitioning into a new role is also a time of change, not only for you as the leader but also for the team or the organization you are leading. It's also time bound in terms of your window of opportunity to succeed. The classic honeymoon period for a new leader lasts about ninety days (Watkins, 2013). That may be all the time people grant you to demonstrate that you can build relationships (with the fans, the power brokers, and the suspicious); gain trust (as you share expectations and articulate and live your values); and establish credentials (your visibility and the behaviors you exhibit).

In this chapter, we'll consider both the biological and cultural origins of gendered communication styles. You'll have a chance to consider how your style enhances and detracts from your ability to make yourself heard, as well as identify some concrete steps you can take to ensure that when you speak, people value your ideas.

To Be or Not to Be Assertive

Researchers Tessa M. Pfafman and Bree McEwan (2014) have interviewed women about the communication styles they admired in their female mentors and contrasted those styles with what the same women have themselves learned about communicating effectively in the workplace. Whereas they admired assertiveness in their mentors, it backfired when the women tried to behave assertively in male-dominated environments. Many interviewees reflected back on influential teachers, saying they were often assertive with students. However, these women had learned that it does not work to behave assertively with other adults. This study found that lack of assertiveness is a strategic choice women make, not a deficiency. Pfafman and McEwan (2014) report that women said they first need to be seen as "appropriate" females before people will see them as professionals. Otherwise, they risk their assertive behavior being interpreted as aggression:

> *Participants consistently described their male colleagues as being able to speak out assertively while they themselves had to strategically modify their own styles to accommodate their colleagues' [egos] and protect the relationship. They all recognized that attending to gender is part of their professional communication strategy. (Pfafman & McEwan, 2014, p. 216)*

Holland's (2017) succinct version bears repeating: "In the workplace, women are expected to get ahead by some mysterious combination of femininity and intelligence while simultaneously getting things done and disguising drive" (p. 219).

This "mysterious combination" poses an amazing dilemma, given that it involves half the world's population! Further, one of our themes for this leadership journey is that educators need to add the feminine voice to what has operated as a world of masculine making. Jennifer Palmieri (2018), former campaign communications director for Hillary Clinton, captures this sentiment well:

> *Men spent centuries building the professional world, devising rules to make sure it was a comfortable place for them and that it was geared toward their particular qualities and skills. Like any good guest, women have looked for clues on how we are to behave in this foreign land. We have tried to understand and follow the local customs. We have intuited that in this world we are to be obliging, calm under pressure, and diligent, and to always keep our emotions in check. Our adaptive skills have served many of us well. But we aren't in a man's world anymore.*
>
> *Now it's our world. And shame on us women if we don't do something to change the way this game is played so that everybody is able to bring their best to the effort. Let's embrace a new way of working that is equally geared toward our own qualities and skills . . . We have no idea what beneficial qualities we might be stifling in ourselves as long as we continue to follow an outdated set of behavioral rules that were designed to permit women to play a niche role in a workplace built for men. (p. 79)*

Many women haven't thought in much detail about how they actually communicate. Let's look at what research says about gender-based communication styles so you might identify how to make the most of who you are.

Why Men and Women Communicate Differently in the Workplace

Looking at why men and women communicate the way they do involves a tangle of nature and nurture. Recognize that differences in communication styles flow from many factors, including culture, training, brain anatomy, and social pressures. Understanding the sources of your communication strengths and struggles provides information on which are the most malleable as you seek to be valued and heard. And, enough truth surrounds differences in how the genders communicate to popularize books such as *Men Are From Mars, Women Are From Venus* (Gray, 1993), and to make it useful to contrast the styles. As you read on, consider where your communication strengths and struggles may come from: brain biology or cultural influences.

Brain Biology and Communication

Let's look first at biology. Organizational behavior specialists Susan S. Case and Angela J. Oetama-Paul (2015) reviewed the literature on brain biology and gender, summarizing the differences with a call to norm both styles' value:

> Policies that help people speak in their own voice take advantage of those differences and enable them to do their best, rather than women wasting energy in pursuit of surrogate masculinity. Because of brain differences, decision-making is more complex for women as they take in more factual and emotional information across their hemispheres than men, perceiving the human dimension of a business decision through discourse and context, with heightened sensitivity to personal and moral aspects of decision-making. Men rely more on calculated, formulaic, deductive processes from one hemisphere [of the brain], divorced from many human and personal dimensions of choice. Their approach is more analytic, extracting essential information deemed relevant. (p. 368)

In decision making, women consider a larger picture, a radar rather than a laser process (as described in chapter 1, page 9), including context and emotional sensitivity. Rather than suppressing these uniquely female characteristics, we should value them.

Note how the descriptions of men as analytical and women as emotionally sensitive tie back to our discussion of people's natural preferences for making decisions through the Thinking and Feeling functions (chapter 6, page 99). You might recall the discussion of the masculine archetype as a Thinking type and the feminine archetype as a Feeling type, but, in fact, as much as 40 percent of men prefer Feeling and 25 percent of women prefer Thinking (Center for Applications of Psychological Type, 2003). The same pattern of within-gender differences occurs when you look at the brain biology of male and female communication patterns.

EEG, MRI, and other advanced methods for recording brain activity provide more complex data that paint a complex picture of how the genders communicate. Neuroscience thinking as of 2017 says that when you look at group data by gender, on average, males and females have differences in how they use their brains (Denworth, 2017). However, when you look at individuals' brains, about half of people show some male characteristics and some female characteristics. Human brains feature a mosaic of male and female behaviors; gender does not determine them. You know this instinctively. For example, while boys on average may behave more actively, competitively, and assertively, you know active, competitive, and assertive girls as well. And, you know quiet, nurturing men who excel at language arts as well as more extroverted women who are top mathematicians. A preponderance of people are blends, and how you were nurtured probably has as big—if not bigger—an impact on your communication style as your brain's hardwiring.

Cultural Influences

However, biology doesn't explain all of the variation between men and women and how we communicate. Education, cultural norms around male and female behavior, experience, and skill development also influence how people's brains are wired (Nardi, 2011). In looking at cultural influences, note that in the world of business, broad agreement exists on what constitutes these gendered styles, although sorting out whether stereotypes cause the styles or they reflect true differences may be difficult. Executive coach and international keynote speaker Carol Kinsey Goman (2016) surveyed both men and women to understand how they view their own and each other's communication styles. She points out, "In the workplace, people are continuously—and often unconsciously—assessing your communication style for two sets of qualities: warmth (empathy, likability, caring) and authority (power, credibility, status)" (Goman, 2016). She finds that men and women see the strengths and weaknesses of the genders in the same way, as summarized in figure 9.1 (page 158). The infinity loop indicates that these are both interdependent; over time, we all need to draw on elements of both styles.

We can make the following conclusions about male and female communication.

- There are real differences in male and female communication styles, although many individuals blend the two gender styles and may display more of the other gender's style.

- While people reward men for using the male style, people see women as lacking authority when they use the female style and as too aggressive or ambitious when they use the male style.

- Examining components of the two styles can help you pinpoint what to do more of and what to do less of. Like it or not, women still need to attend to how others of any gender will perceive assertiveness and other behaviors, even as people work toward normalizing these styles as gender neutral.

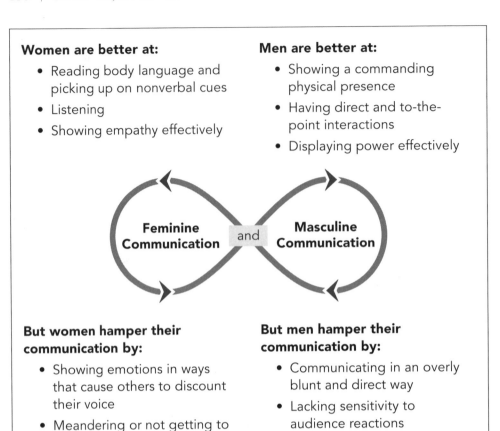

Women are better at:

- Reading body language and picking up on nonverbal cues
- Listening
- Showing empathy effectively

Men are better at:

- Showing a commanding physical presence
- Having direct and to-the-point interactions
- Displaying power effectively

Feminine Communication and Masculine Communication

But women hamper their communication by:

- Showing emotions in ways that cause others to discount their voice
- Meandering or not getting to the point
- Having a collegial, not powerful, presence

But men hamper their communication by:

- Communicating in an overly blunt and direct way
- Lacking sensitivity to audience reactions
- Being overconfident in their own opinions

Source: Adapted from Goman, 2016.

Figure 9.1: Infinity loop diagram representing feminine and masculine communication strengths and struggles.

Adding the Feminine Viewpoint to Education

Thus, a woman faces the personal dilemma of getting ahead via that "mysterious combination of femininity and intelligence while simultaneously getting things done and disguising drive" (Holland, 2017, p. 219). But society faces the dilemma that if women only communicate like men, it loses what the feminine viewpoint has to offer. And this viewpoint has a lot to offer, especially in education. As we discussed in chapter 6 (page 99), many major directions in education reflect an imbalance between the masculine and feminine archetypes. So what can we do? We can proactively and collectively champion the value of the feminine communication style in three ways.

First, women need to change the discourse surrounding leadership, success, and workplace priorities. Senior lecturer Maria Adamson (2017) has analyzed several celebrity CEO biographies, such as *Lean In: Women, Work, and the Will to Lead* by Sheryl Sandberg (2013) of Facebook. Consider Adamson's (2017) analysis of the common advice that women should balance different aspects of femininity through calculated, business-oriented, and efficient methods:

> *This balanced femininity, tamed in the interest of the market, poses little challenge to gendered power relations in contemporary organizations. In fact, through the promise of success and partial inclusion, it curtails the disruptive potential of the feminine and limits the possibility of imagining structural changes. (p. 315)*

In other words, defining *success* in terms of market goals decreases the impact women might otherwise have on social justice issues. This definition results in power relations between genders remaining unchanged. Gender inequality continues to be a women's problem rather than a structural problem that deprives society of half its workforce's many talents. In the short term, women no doubt need to alter how they speak in order to have an immediate impact, but danger arises when they change the content of what they say to only reflect traditionally masculine priorities (for example, How might things be different if, in the early 2000s, the feminine values that drive supporting teachers through mentoring and coaching had balanced the masculine drive supporting objective measures of teacher accountability?).

Second, when organizations discount feminine communication, that means they ask an amazing percentage of people to communicate without using their strengths. That's like asking a six-foot-tall swimmer to become a gymnast or a painter to communicate through poetry. In the long term, organizations must change so people value *both* styles for the significant contributions each makes to planning, decision making, and more.

Third, as long as people don't see women's views as valuable, fewer women will aspire to leadership—and fewer yet whose natural communication style fits with the feminine. In education, that means fewer leaders will challenge the status quo of what constitutes a good leader. Educational leadership specialists Margaret Grogan and Charol Shakeshaft (2011) find that women take a different school leadership approach than the traditional heroic, solitary, logical view of the role. They are far more likely than men to bring the following five leadership values (Grogan & Shakeshaft, 2011). As you read about each one, take time to consider how each influences your desire to step up as an education leader.

1. **Using a relational approach:** This represents *power with*, rather than *power over*, others. This approach facilitates the collective efficacy that, as you have seen, brings about real change.

2. **Emphasizing educational leadership as work toward social justice:**
   This encourages people to view education goals as broader than
   academic success and dependent on a wider range of societal influences,
   barriers, or problems.

3. **Embracing spirituality:** This provides women with a motivating
   force for leadership, meaning that they are purpose-driven to make a
   difference as leaders.

4. **Focusing on teaching and learning instead of power:** Women see their
   years in teaching as important and fulfilling work, not as a stepping-
   stone to more desirable positions. This leads them to include teacher
   wisdom and voices in leadership decisions.

5. **Recognizing and valuing that "women's work" on the home front
   builds leadership skills—they are not just the purview of the workplace:**
   This often results in women both modeling better work-life balance and
   creating an environment that honors people's lives outside school.

Look back through this list. Which values do you find compelling as you step up to
leadership? Which motivate you to improve your ability to communicate so people
will hear your ideas?

THINK ABOUT IT

In 2018, widely watched U.S. Senate hearings heightened awareness of how
men routinely interrupt women, but not other men. Where else have you seen
this behavior? Does it happen when women are in charge? Where women are
in the majority but men are in charge? How does this affect how others in the
organization view women?

Avoiding Gendered Communication Traps

Because we've been "strangers in a strange land" of communication norms created in
male-dominated societies, it can be hard to distinguish coping mechanisms from effective communication strategies. Women often find themselves falling into the following
four communication traps in earnest hope of making themselves heard. Think about
how these traps fail to allow the feminine communication style's gifts to influence
discourse around policy and direction.

1. **Apologizing:** A documented difference (Kay & Shipman, 2014) in the way women often communicate is the use of hedging phrases to lessen the appearance of aggressive behavior. Which of the following hedging phrases do you tend to use? What might you say instead to acknowledge the importance of your voice and ideas, rather than apologize for them?

   o "I could be wrong, but . . ."

   o "This is probably just my opinion, but . . ."

   o "I'm sure you've already thought of this, but . . ."

   o "I don't know if this is relevant, but . . ."

   o "I'm still thinking this through, but . . ."

   o "I'm sorry, but did you mean . . ."

2. **Avoiding conflict:** In the interest of wanting to be seen as nice, or out of fear of losing harmony, many women simply acquiesce instead of engaging when a clash of methods or opinions occurs. Chapter 10 (page 169) is devoted to strategies for having those hard conversations, but before you learn how to have those conversations, identify *why* you would refuse to back down. What values are worth fighting for? What behaviors are unacceptable and need to be called out? What, with regard to the classroom and students, do you consider non-negotiable? How did you come to those non-negotiables, and how can you support them in speaking with someone who thinks differently? For now, list some some quickwrite responses to these questions. Then use your list as examples while you work through some of chapter 10's communication strategies.

3. **Allowing male dominance to continue:** If you have a hunch that men are taken more seriously than women in your school or education system, track what happens during a meeting. Who speaks? Whose ideas do people acknowledge? Who gets interrupted? If the hunch holds true, bring your data to everyone's attention with the valuable point that the system needs everyone's wisdom to face the tough dilemmas in a rapidly changing world.

4. **Abandoning other women:** The Me Too movement has made it evident how banding together can make a difference. If you haven't thought in advance about when and why you will support other women, it can easily stun you into silence when put-downs, sexist remarks, belittling behaviors, and other inexcusable slights happen in front of you.

A Word From Barbara

During a leadership advisory meeting, I noted that one of the male leaders tended to talk over me. While I think he was driving for answers to some burning questions, I could feel my irritation growing. Rather than make it an issue, in a nanosecond, I thought, "What can I do through my voice and nonverbal body language so that I honor myself in this process?" My mantra is "Stand tall in your own self-worth."

In that particular meeting, I decided to speak more authoritatively, making direct eye contact with this particular person as I talked to him. When he spoke, I chose to look confidently at him and assume the classic open, calm, and confident seated pose suggested by Amy Cuddy (2015; see exercise 1 in the Step in for Further Reflection section on page 164). The result? He began deferring to me, used my name, and graciously acknowledged my time limitations for the meeting. Rather than trying to seize power, I simply redressed the imbalance—and it worked.

Talk with the women around you about these issues. How will you support each other? Here are a few ideas.

- **Take advantage of humor:** Saying with a smile, "You didn't really mean to say that, did you?" can keep tension from escalating and allow for apology.

- **Use data:** Yes, in a sense, this is a masculine strategy, but facts speak to everyone in different ways. For example, count the number of interruptions in a meeting; if gender imbalance has occurred, speak up with, "Excuse me, but is anyone else noticing this pattern? So far, someone has interrupted the person speaking a dozen times during this meeting, and ten of those times, the person interrupted was female. We need everyone's voice. What do we need to do so that we respect the person speaking?" If this seems scary, remember, band together.

- **Say, "Ouch":** Jennifer Abrams (2016), an expert on difficult conversations, states that if you can't say anything else, say, "Ouch." "'Ouch' truly says so much in so little space, allows for a pause in the conversation, doesn't let someone off the hook, and helps you to feel like you did speak up" (p. 68). She also recommends considering in advance how you might respond to situations like the following (Abrams, 2016).

- When you feel intimidated by someone shouting, name-calling, swearing, or threatening you
- When someone attacks your personality or identity instead of trying to solve the problem
- When someone brings up a valid but completely off-topic point
- When someone refuses to listen, acting as if an issue isn't worth talking about
- When someone has really triggered you
- When someone makes a racist, sexist, or homophobic comment

So, how do you ensure you communicate as effectively as possible? By analyzing how you communicate, thinking about your workplace's norms, and making the right adjustments. This takes planning. This chapter's reflection exercises are lengthy for that reason.

Next Steps in the Journey

You have a week to rethink how you present yourself, so take your time. Gather input from someone you trust if you aren't sure if you have good habits or self-sabotaging habits. Communication is one of the hardest—and most important—soft skills of leadership.

Remember, learning to make yourself heard affects more than just you. Doing so can help ensure the following.

- Half the population's ideas make it to the table.
- All people get to work from their strengths.
- People value important skills such as the ability to make sense of a decision's potential emotional impact, which is more feminine, as much as more masculine skills such as logical planning.
- You're working on your skills and voice so women around you and after you will also be heard.

Step in for Further Reflection

The following activities provide you with valuable opportunities to reflect on the ideas, strategies, and concepts covered in this chapter. If you are approaching *Step In, Step Up* as a twelve-week journey, you can spread these out over several days.

You may complete them individually or with a group so you can share your thoughts and ideas. Keep a journal so you can revisit your thoughts as you travel this journey.

1. The following exercise is designed to help you identify what to start doing, stop doing, and keep doing in your workplace communication.

   ○ **Step 1: Identify your strengths and struggles**—In a review of brain biology and gender literature, Case and Oetama-Paul (2015) have found the communication styles featured in figure 9.2 considered masculine and feminine. For each row in figure 9.2, determine which feature is more natural for you. Then consider the questions that follow.

Feminine	Masculine
Indirectness	Directness
Facilitation	Competition
Collaboration	Autonomy
Collegiality	Confrontation
Collective sharing	One-upmanship
Less talking	More talking
Supportive simultaneous talk	Change of topics
Supportive feedback	Disruptive interruptions
Person or process orientation	Task or outcome orientation
Relational practice	Referential practice
Status equalization	Status enhancement
Affiliation	Assertiveness

Source: Case & Oetama-Paul, 2015, p. 245.

Figure 9.2: Communication style differences by gender.

If you believe your use of a particular pair is balanced, think about the experiences, mentors, or training that may have influenced you. This might help you discover strategies for other pairs when you need the less-preferred side.

Consider which style in each pairing is more effective in your workplace.

- Of the twelve pairs, which three are viewed as most important?
- Given your answer to the previous bullet point, where might you need to develop communication skills?
- To complete this review of your communication style's effectiveness in your environment, refer back to figure 9.1 (page 158). Highlight which characteristics—on both the masculine and feminine sides—describe you. If you aren't sure, ask a colleague whom you trust to help you.

○ **Step 2: Consider body language**—Body language influences both how we see ourselves and how others see us. In what ways might you improve your body posture? Again, you may have to ask a trusted colleague.

Cuddy's (2012) TED Talk, *Your Body Language May Shape Who You Are*, is a fascinating introduction to her research findings.

Revisit the list of confidence-changing body language on page 124. As mentioned in chapter 7 (page 115), Cuddy (2012) found that those who expand their posture—think of standing hands on hips like Wonder Woman, or with arms in the air like a victorious athlete—begin to feel more powerful. This shift in mindset can increase confidence with a decrease in anxiety and self-absorption. Try it (in a private place, not during a meeting!) to feel the difference it can make.

○ **Step 3: Articulate a plan**—Use your responses from the first two steps of this activity to develop a plan for improving how you communicate. Use the reproducible "Polarity Thinking® Map for Communication Effectiveness" on page 168 to map out how you can improve your communication effectiveness.

In the chart, note the goal at the top: to be heard and valued. Note, at the bottom of the chart, the cost of not working on communication effectiveness: not being taken seriously. Failing to work on the weaknesses that are hurting you or failing to influence poor communication practices in your school can both lead to your own ineffectiveness.

In the chart's left column, fill in the three strengths and three struggles most key to improving your communication. In the right column, fill in the communication realities of your workplace.

Now comes the most important part. In the upper left (outside the chart), list one or two action steps you can take to improve your communication, such as body language. In the upper right, list one or two action steps you might take to match your style to your workplace or to influence communication norms in your workplace. The two sides may have identical steps. If so, you've found something to leverage for both improving your communication and fitting in!

Then, on the bottom left, brainstorm a few things that would warn you that you've started to fall into the traps your weaknesses might create. What would you notice *before* it becomes a problem? For example, you might note that you breathe a bit rapidly before a meeting—does that signify that you have an emotional stake in the upcoming discussion? Do you need to strike a power pose in your office or classroom before going to the meeting so you remain calm? Or, can you catch yourself talking rapidly, recognize it as a sign of nervousness, and slow down?

Finally, in the lower right section, brainstorm a few things that would warn you that people are being misjudged or undervalued because your workplace is overvaluing some communication styles over others. What would you notice before it becomes a problem? The previous example of counting interruptions might go here, or considering whether team time includes building relationships as well as task completion.

2. Partner with one or more women who are also working to make themselves heard and valued. Discuss how you might support each other. Here are some suggestions for what you might discuss in ongoing meetings, whether in person or virtually.

   - If you are in the same learning community or are often at the same meetings, you might give each other feedback on how you present yourselves.

   - You might use your meetings to discuss your action steps, what is working, and what might help.

   - Consider coaching each other via a quick web conference before important encounters where your communication style will matter.

   - How else you might support each other in making yourselves heard and valued as women in educational leadership.

Polarity Thinking® Map for Communication Effectiveness

Action Steps
How will we gain or maintain the positive results from focusing on this left pole? What? Who? By when? Measures?

To use my strengths more, I will:

Early Warnings
Measurable indicators (things you can count) that will let you know that you are getting into the downside of this left pole.

What I might notice that would prompt me to shift how I communicate:

I am heard and valued.
Greater Purpose Statement (GPS): Why leverage this polarity?

Values = Positive results of focus on the left pole

My top three communication strengths are:

1.

2.

3.

Values = Positive results of focus on the right pole

The top three communication strengths my workplace looks for are:

1.

2.

3.

My Workplace's Communication Needs

Communication in my workplace suffers when:

1.

2.

3.

Fears = Negative results of overfocus on the right pole to the neglect of the left pole

My Communication Strengths

My communication effectiveness suffers when:

1.

2.

3.

Fears = Negative results of overfocus on the left pole to the neglect of the right pole

I am not taken seriously.
Deeper fear from lack of optimization

Action Steps
How will we gain or maintain the positive results from focusing on this right pole? What? Who? By when? Measures?

To communicate more effectively at work, I will:

Early Warnings
Measurable indicators (things you can count) that will let you know that you are getting into the downside of this right pole.

What I might notice that would prompt me to influence workplace communication:

Source: © 2018 by Polarity Partnerships (www.polaritypartnerships.com). Used with permission.

CHAPTER

10

FINDING THE COURAGE FOR TOUGH CONVERSATIONS

GUIDING QUESTIONS

- Do you know when you need to speak up? Think of a time when you voiced a concern and a time when you failed to do so.

- Are you ready to speak up? Why or why not?

- Do you know how to speak up? What evidence supports your answer?

In the male-dominated world of banking, where she started her career, Jane gained way more firsthand experience than she wanted with engaging in difficult conversations. It all started when her manager, who had just taken over the team she'd been part of for about a year, contradicted her and said, "You're not as smart as you think you are."

Actually, the manager had given her misinformation so he could humiliate her in a meeting. While she had certainly overheard a good many remarks about why women shouldn't work in finance, this marked the first open hostility she'd experienced—and she knew she couldn't let it pass.

She hoped to address this first offense head-on, rather than turn to human resources. She discreetly sought advice from her former boss and a female mentor, and then asked the offending manager to schedule some time to talk, saying, "I believe you lied to me and set me up, and we need to have a conversation."

How did it go? Following the advice she'd received, Jane carefully laid out the facts from her perspective and asked the manager if his interpretation differed. She watched his demeanor deflate as she stayed calm and objective. No, this conversation didn't completely reform him, but after the conversation, he and Jane were able to work together.

Let's make this clear: Jane has never looked forward to these kinds of conversations. Neither of us wades into conflict lightly. But we've found that women who have avoided conflict in the past—and have had to live with significant consequences of that avoidance—feel motivated to learn how to speak up.

Jennifer Abrams (2009), author of *Having Hard Conversations*, points out that there are many reasons why most people don't like to have hard conversations with colleagues. Relationships mean everything in education, and so we mostly like to avoid bad feelings. She continues:

> *Teachers just aren't a confrontational group. In our field, unlike banking, which is transactional in nature, we are about more than that. We are about helping people grow up to be good human beings, not just doing a deposit or withdrawal of funds. We are in schools to transform students and help them develop, not just do transactions and call it a day. Relationships are everything in this field. We actively shy away from causing bad feelings. We purposefully did not become litigators, ready to depose others on the spot. We get anxious if a little dander is raised. We worry a lot.*
>
> *Yet telling truth to one another, as coaches, as administrators, and as colleagues, is one of the most important ways that we grow personally and professionally. (Abrams, 2009, p. 2)*

Abrams (2009) rightly says that the logical, fact-driven culture of banking immersed Jane in tasks that developed her skills in taking a logical, fact-driven approach to difficult conversations. Jane might disagree that people find these conversations any easier to have in the world of banking, especially when gender issues raise their ugly heads, but generally in the world of business, addressing such issues is the norm.

In contrast, the values-driven world of education fosters a different view of conflict. The "If you don't have anything nice to say, don't say anything at all" world of education (and most nonprofit organizations) values kindness and diplomacy over candidness or exploration of differences of opinion. And what happens? People bury their feelings and agree to act professionally, allowing the pressure to build until someone explodes. Or, they fail to take time to reflect on what has made them uncomfortable— or on how their behaviors affect others. Way too often, we've had school leaders ask for recommendations for antibullying materials or a well-being program only to discover that the leader is the most caustic person on the team—and the damage to collegiality and trust can be huge. Jane has facilitated interventions in several schools where conflict erupted to such an intensity that it interrupted teaching and learning. In one case, the teachers threatened to settle things in the woods after school!

Consider the upsides and downsides of candor and diplomacy, as shown in figure 10.1. The infinity loop emphasizes the systems nature of interconnectedness. An ongoing tension exists between each side, requiring conscious thought and management to stay on the upside of both. Where have you seen educators overuse or underuse candor and diplomacy?

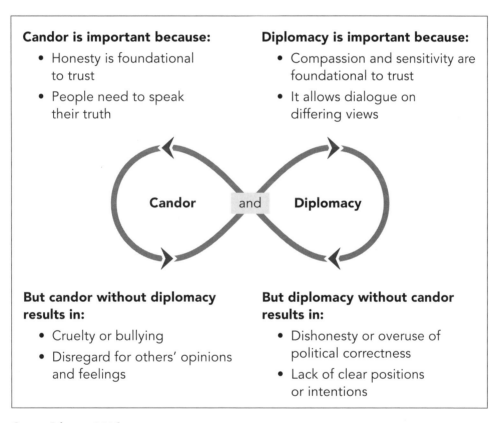

Candor is important because:
- Honesty is foundational to trust
- People need to speak their truth

Diplomacy is important because:
- Compassion and sensitivity are foundational to trust
- It allows dialogue on differing views

Candor and Diplomacy

But candor without diplomacy results in:
- Cruelty or bullying
- Disregard for others' opinions and feelings

But diplomacy without candor results in:
- Dishonesty or overuse of political correctness
- Lack of clear positions or intentions

Source: Johnson, 2016.

Figure 10.1: Infinity loop diagram representing candor and diplomacy.

Note that ignoring either candor or diplomacy can lead to mistrust, loss of relationships, and more. So how do you steel yourself to have honest conversations about things that matter while ensuring that relationships stay intact and everyone moves forward together? In this chapter, we'll look at how you can increase your capacity to handle conflict and recognize when and how to speak up, and we'll provide a few techniques for preparing for hard conversations.

Your Capacity for Difficult Conversations

Whether you find yourself in the "I simply hate and avoid conflict" camp or the "Bring it on!" camp, consider that either attitude, similar to the candor and diplomacy dilemma, can bring problems. While we wouldn't call it a happy medium, a balancing point exists between these extremes where you *know when* you need to lean in to conflict and you *know how* to do it.

How close have you gotten to that balancing point? Identifying your starting place is your first step toward understanding your capacity. Craig Weber (2013) uses the term *conversational capacity* to describe a team's ability to successfully engage in effective, balanced, nondefensive dialogue—to have those hard conversations. But you can consider your individual capacity as well.

Weber (2013) describes the following useful guidelines for understanding when you might try to minimize conflict and when you might try to "win." Which descriptions fit you? Are they helpful or harmful in the long run?

- You minimize conflict when you know you should address an issue but don't do it in order to avoid discomfort, maintain harmony, stay in your comfort zone, protect relationships, or, in general, play it safe. You might withdraw or discuss things behind others' backs, change the subject, or even pretend you agree and bury the resulting resentment.

- You go for the win when you know you're right and you bring up the issue to ensure that everyone agrees with you. You keep talking (probably more loudly), stop listening, construe your opinions as facts, and dismiss others' viewpoints.

Neither strategy—minimizing conflict or going for the win—helps with relational trust and collective efficacy. And everyone does both. Consider the following for yourself and then for your team to understand patterns in employing these strategies.

- What triggers you to minimize conflict, for example, specific topics, values, or individuals?

- What triggers you to set out to win, for example, specific topics, values, or individuals?

A second component of your capacity for difficult conversations is your EQ. What EQ goals did you set for yourself in chapter 8 (page 131)? How might these affect your capacity to work with conflict?

A third component is your ability to handle stress. Again, a misnomer suggests that all stress is bad for you. In truth, a good deal of the stress you experience comes from relationships and from difficult challenges that you surmount, including professional goals.

Do you want a life devoid of people and challenges? If not, stress is a given, especially for leaders. Instead of avoiding stress, you need to work with it. In chapter 8 (page 131), we asked you to reflect on the four key factors of *hardiness*, the ability to grow from stress. Are you growing from the inevitable stress that stems from relationships and professional challenges? If not, consider journaling, using the following Think About It questions to increase your hardiness.

THINK ABOUT IT

Think of a stressful situation you face or might face as a leader, and answer the following questions.

- Do you see stress as a normal part of leadership, or do you have to fight off the thought, "Why me?" How might you normalize the stress?
- How do you stay engaged, even during the stress? Do you continue to do your favorite activities? Do you invest in your relationships or withdraw from them?
- Have you identified the choices you have control over? Are you making them?
- Think back to chapter 3's information on bandwidth (page 55). How well do you meet your bandwidth needs? Your physical, emotional, social, and spiritual needs?

Your capacity to work with conflict, your EQ, and your ability to handle stress add up to your ability to speak up when you need to do so.

When to Speak Up

Let's consider four measures that can help you decide when it's appropriate to speak up: (1) your values, (2) the significance of the issue, (3) your understanding of the situation, and (4) your emotional readiness.

Your Values

Most people know many things that they value, but sometimes, they don't realize the importance of a value until something threatens it or it disappears. Or, as one of Jane's colleagues puts it, "You might not know it's a value until it gets stomped on!" (personal communication, September 15, 1996). For example, one of the finance teams Jane was part of in her first career didn't know how frequently humor played a part in their ability to work together until a new leader declared joking a complete waste of time.

Start by clarifying your values and the role they play when you speak up. Many values card sort activities are available online. Jane's (Kise, in press) book *Holistic Leadership, Thriving Schools* also has a companion set of cards. Why use cards rather than work from a list? Because your working memory can only hold about seven separate pieces of information at any given time (note how basic phone numbers are just seven digits and fairly easy to remember, whereas credit card numbers take far more effort to memorize (Miller, 1994). When you sort through a stack of cards, one per value, a desk or table becomes an extension of your working memory, freeing up your prefrontal cortex to concentrate on how each value might affect your leadership priorities.

Although you could also capture the information on a whiteboard or in a computer mind-mapping program, the mobility of the cards allows ideas to remain flexible longer. Cards give you an easier way to consider possibilities, changes, synergies, and other ways to sort your values, and thus explore them longer before cutting off options.

The second key step in looking at the role that values play in conflict is to consider how clear expectations are schoolwide. At one school, for example, the principal saw patterns of racial bias in how teachers treated students in the hallways, whereas the lack of these patterns in his classroom observations had pleased him. He realized that teachers' professional development work hadn't addressed how cultural diversity might affect how they perceive students outside of class and what equity looked like. He realized he needed to establish clarity before having hard conversations.

Leaders can't say, "My staff isn't meeting expectations," if the leaders haven't set the expectations.

Thus, clarifying your values and whether you have communicated your expectations that flow from them guide you in knowing whether you need to speak up.

WORDS FROM A LEADER

As a leader, I have to deal with the fear of not pleasing everyone. I realized I never would so I had to make the best decisions, given the information I had at the time, that supported the vision and mission of the organization, even when that made people upset and sometimes mean. I did this by being clear on the vision and mission of the organization and how I was to help support staff to meet that goal, and I did it by being consistent in my message and actions. (Karen Gayle, national director of curriculum and instruction, Imagine Schools, United States, personal communication, April 17, 2018)

The Significance of the Issue

The cliché "Choose your battles," has merit. Ask yourself the following questions to ponder whether you should tackle or ignore an issue.

- "How much will it matter ten minutes from now? Ten days from now? Ten years from now?"
- "Will not addressing it potentially lower my opinion of someone or my ability to work with that person?"
- "Does it have the potential to grow into a bigger problem?"
- "To what depth does it connect to my core values and trigger a wish to take action?"
- "Might it disempower me or dishonor who I am if I do not act?"

In a way, these are basic questions, but if you are a conflict avoider, they serve as motivators for the hard work of preparing for a hard conversation.

Your Understanding of the Situation

If a situation triggers your emotions, know that trying to ignore them or calm down before taking action is the wrong approach. You can't control what you feel; you can only control how you behave based on those feelings. If you think you should never feel anger, jealousy, frustration, or disgust at another person's thoughts, words, or deeds, you are setting yourself up for failure.

In his book *The Pursuit of Perfect*, Tal Ben-Shahar (2009) notes research demonstrating that trying to suppress negative emotions often intensifies them. Ben-Shahar (2009) uses the example of not thinking about a white bear to illustrate this principle:

> *In all likelihood, you could not stop thinking about a white bear for the last ten seconds. If you truly wanted to stop thinking of a white bear, you would be better off allowing yourself to think of one and then after a while the thought would naturally go away—just as every thought eventually does. The attempt to actively suppress a thought, to fight it and block it, keeps it fresh and intense. Similarly, emotions such as anxiety, anger, or envy intensify when we try to suppress them, when we try to fight them and block their natural flow. An Optimalist understands that and allows himself to experience painful emotions, knowing that by doing so these emotions are more likely to weaken and fade away. (p. 43)*

However, giving free rein to your emotions during a difficult conversation isn't a good idea either, especially if you haven't taken the time to analyze exactly what you feel and why. Think back to Jane's difficult conversation with her manager. She spoke with two other trusted individuals, in part to understand her dilemma, talk through other possible interpretations of the situation, and decide on a course of action. However, she also knew she needed to practice telling her story to ensure that she understood how she felt about it and had control of the behaviors her emotions might prompt during the difficult conversation.

To acknowledge and work with your emotions, Brown (2015) recommends writing or talking through the prompt, "The story I'm telling is . . ." Whether you choose to dialogue about your dilemma or write about it, think of the dilemma as a story and not as a hard-and-fast series of events. Why? Because at first, you work through only *your* viewpoint. As quickly as possible, you articulate what you think happened—your emotions, reasoning, beliefs, and actions. You won't edit. Brown (2015) calls this your *stormy first draft*. Don't judge yourself. Honestly express what you feel. This can help you decide whether or not to speak up.

Once you have that stormy first draft, open yourself up to the possibility that other people might see the situation differently. Ask yourself the following.

- "What are the facts? What assumptions have I made?"
- "What information am I missing? How can I get it?"
- "What other interpretations might there be, especially of others' thoughts, words, or deeds?"

Thinking through that last prompt opens you up to alternative perspectives, which is foundational to any difficult conversation. You might frame it as, "What would an objective bystander suggest as motives?" Note that this thought should come *after* you acknowledge your own emotions.

Now that you've moved away from your initial reaction, double-check your values and what is at stake by asking yourself the following.

- "What am I really feeling?"
- "What will matter ten minutes from now? Ten days from now? Ten years from now?"
- "Are there objective considerations I need to take into account? Might this situation set precedents? Do I need to establish any boundaries or clarify any expectations so this doesn't happen again?"

In this process, Brown (2015) emphasizes that you need to balance being generous with others and true to yourself with the principle of living BIG, which stands for *boundaries, integrity,* and *generosity.* "Living BIG is saying: 'Yes, I'm going to be generous in my assumptions and intentions while standing solidly in my integrity and being very clear about what's acceptable and what's not acceptable'" (Brown, 2015, p. 123).

Your Emotional Readiness

Once you've decided that you need to have a tough conversation, prepare yourself emotionally. Look back at the characteristics of people whom others perceive to have power (pages 124–125) to understand the demeanor you wish to display. In *Presence,* Cuddy (2015) cites research and women's stories that show the effectiveness of taking some time before an important meeting to stand tall, arms outstretched, and feel yourself expanding in the space around you. The body is continuously sending messages to the brain, and each person gets to control that content:

> Hundreds (maybe thousands) of studies have examined the body-mind connection, using many different methods—from breathing, to yoga, to lowering vocal pitch, to having people imagine themselves holding an expansive pose, to simply getting people to sit up straight. There are countless ways for us to expand our bodies. And whether the body-mind effect is operating through our vagal tone, our blood pressure, our hormones, or some other mechanism we haven't yet discovered, the outcome is clear: expanding our bodies changes the way we feel about ourselves, creating a virtuous cycle. (Cuddy, 2015, Location No. 3185)

Now that you're ready to speak up, let's look at how you might prepare to do so.

How to Speak Up

Speaking up—coming across as authentic while being assertive, as respectful while also engaging in confrontation, and as open-minded while also setting boundaries—is no easy feat. We frequently run sessions where people have the chance to practice these skills in low-stakes situations. Participants describe feeling as if they turn their brains inside out to find the right words and the right tone and to master listening without judgment when they are, in fact, taking a stand.

Conversations are not just about saying words and exchanging information. Conversations miss the mark because people avoid difficult conversations, argue, talk past each other, get stuck on being right, or fail to listen to what others really say. All conversations have significant neurochemical exchanges embedded in them, affecting how trusting or mistrustful your exchanges become. The neuroscience of conversational intelligence is grounded in the language of trust. Academic and business executive Judith E. Glaser's (2014) research concludes that great leaders and great cultures share something in common—*conversational intelligence*, the glue of truly effective dialogue.

Connecting with others in nonjudgmental ways exercises our conversational intelligence, activating neurotransmitters to bond and interact. Neurochemistry triggers our emotions, the way we make decisions, and the efficacy of our engagement with others. Importantly, our conversational intelligence can support our most challenging conversations. Following are processes for two of our favorite, most effective dialogue strategies for preparing for difficult conversations: (1) the STATE model and (2) the SCARF model. At the end of each strategy, you'll find a short Think About It scenario you can use for practice. We encourage you to find a partner and work through these scenarios together so you have experience with how these strategies work for you before you desperately need one of them.

The STATE Model

Kerry Patterson, Joseph Grenny, Ron McMillan, and Al Switzler (2012) developed a conversation tool called STATE My Path. The acronym STATE stands for five skills for navigating a difficult conversation. The model flows quite naturally once you've analyzed your stormy first draft. Here's how you use it.

1. **Share your facts:** Introduce the conversation by saying, "I trust you know that I value your opinion (or role) on this team (or staff). But on this issue, we hold different views. I'd like to share how I formed my position, and then, I hope to hear the same from you."

2. **Tell your story:** Share your personal experience with the issue, how you formed your position, and the impact you believe your interpretation or position will have. Avoid trying to persuade; the goal here is to explain why you believe what you believe.

3. **Ask for the other's paths:** Ask the person to share the facts and story that underlie his or her viewpoint.

4. **Talk tentatively:** Use phrases such as, "Could we explore . . . ?" "I'm wondering about . . . ," "Could you talk into that more?" "How else might that be interpreted?" or "Does that have any connections with my thoughts on . . . ?"

5. **Encourage testing:** Use phrases such as, "What might happen if . . . ?" or "What if we thought about or tried . . . ?"

 THINK ABOUT IT

How might you use the STATE model to respond in a situation similar to the following (in which someone asks you to take on responsibilities inappropriate to your role)?

As an instructional coach, you are eager to work with teachers individually and in groups and have laid out a pretty ambitious schedule to at least touch base with every teacher during grade-level and department meetings. You know you will have difficulty fitting them all into your schedule. Then your principal tells you that she wants you to work with small groups of students who are struggling and to regularly prepare and distribute all test-prep materials.

- Share your facts. ("Here's what you've said and done.")
- Tell your story. ("This is what I've begun to conclude.")
- Ask for your principal's path.

The SCARF Model

David Rock (2009), director of the NeuroLeadership Institute, developed the SCARF model, which has you look at the areas in which people might feel threatened and then adjust your approach to minimize those threats. Think through examples of resistance to instructional changes that you've seen. Might teachers have felt threatened in any of the SCARF model's following five areas (Rock, 2009)?

1. **Status:** To understand who may feel that their status is threatened by a change, ask yourself, "Whose ideas are being usurped or ignored? Who is being asked to take a lesser role? Or, whose decision-making authority is being undermined?" You might decrease threats to status by doing the following.

   ○ Seek people's input. Through active listening, you might gather gems of wisdom that will improve the effort as well as include them in it.

   ○ Provide opportunities for people to learn and improve, and recognize learning or improving when it happens.

2. **Certainty:** Uncertainty increases most people's anxiety and stress. Consider what you can add to or clarify in communication to lend certainty where you can, such as by doing one of the following.

   ○ If you are a big-picture thinker, realize that others often seek more details than you provide through your natural communication style (and if you aren't sure, think back to how many questions students had after you gave assignment instructions). Partner with a detail-oriented person who can guide you in providing what people want.

   ○ Script out what you know for sure about an upcoming change, when you hope to tell people the full details, and what you simply can't know until you all implement it. Even communicating certainty about what remains uncertain can help people cope better.

3. **Autonomy:** Again, Pink (2010) identifies *autonomy* as a key human motivator. Here, *power with*, emphasizing collaboration, goes a long way toward reducing threat and increasing collective efficacy. Consider the following strategies for increasing autonomy.

   ○ People can take many paths to reach the same goal. In what areas can you simply provide the goal and allow people to use their own methods to get there? Note that this only works well if you first make goals and expectations clear.

   ○ Say, "Here is my process. What would you like to change?" Frequently, people will say, "I guess I could try it your way once." This not only increases buy-in because you offered choice but frees them up to offer constructive suggestions based on hands-on experience.

4. **Relatedness:** To effectively lead, you need to create a sense of belonging—that family atmosphere that great leaders create where people know that others accept them. How can you reduce people's perception that you will exclude them? Remember from chapter 8 (page 131) the three key leadership cues that create a space of safety and belonging (Coyle, 2018) and use these questions to understand whether you are paying sufficient attention to relatedness.

   ○ First, do you invest energy in listening to the person in front of you while ensuring that others do not offer critiques or judgments?

   ○ Second, do you give individualized attention that makes each person feel unique and valued instead of like a problem to be solved or a nameless face in the crowd? And do you ensure that your direct reports do the same for those under their charge?

   ○ Third, do you make it clear that relationships, safety, and belonging are ongoing? When people feel safe, they can set aside worries about threats and concentrate on common goals.

   Keep in mind whether you are more task oriented or more people oriented—revisit the discussion in chapter 6 (page 99) about whether using the Thinking or Feeling function is more natural for you. Regularly ask yourself, "Do I give enough attention to the relationships we need to effectively move forward, and do I cultivate collective teacher efficacy?" The word *cultivate* relates to gardening, or to nurturing and growing things—an appropriate way to view the atmosphere you are creating and influencing as a leader.

5. **Fairness:** People are incredibly sensitive to whether things seem fair. Remember from chapter 6 (page 99) that people also have different definitions of what constitutes fairness, making a leader's job even more difficult. To decrease threats that result from perceptions of unfairness, do the following.

   ○ **Adjust policy, if necessary**—If you tend to see fairness as implementing policy consistently, talk through reasons to make exceptions with someone who thinks of fairness as adjusting policy to fit individual circumstances. And if the latter describes you, partner with someone who has the former view.

- ○ **Increase transparency**—This may mean disclosing the reasons you do or do not grant an exception, as appropriate, or clearly stating the finances that are driving a decision. Check out *Open Space Technology*, which presents Harrison Owen's (2008) masterful group facilitation technique of the same name that allows everyone to express their views on the topics most important to them. Note that it actually requires no technology but instead recreates an atmosphere similar to all the important conversations that take place around the coffee machine *after* a meeting ends.

 THINK ABOUT IT

How might you use the SCARF model in a situation similar to the following?

You are about to announce a new method for doing classroom walkthrough observations. Based on past experience, you worry that teachers may feel threatened by this. Analyze the potential threats they may now feel using the SCARF model, and consider how you might communicate about the classroom walkthroughs in ways that will decrease the threats they feel.

Next Steps in the Journey

Mastering tough conversations takes time and effort, but without them, true communication and trust cannot exist. When you let issues slide, they eventually erupt at the wrong place, at the wrong time, and in the wrong way. You increase your own autonomy and purpose by choosing how and when to address issues that are worth addressing.

> Take chances, make mistakes. That's how you grow. Pain nourishes your courage. You have to fail in order to practice being brave.
>
> —Mary Tyler Moore (1936–2017), American actor

Before you face your next inevitable hard conversation, make sure you have clarified how you'll know it's time to speak up by examining your values. Understand how to prepare using the tools we provide in this chapter. And make sure you're working on your hardiness. Educational leadership involves working with people as you collectively strive toward the audacious goal of helping every student succeed—and that means you will experience stress. Equip yourself to work through conflict with effective tools and personal hardiness to ensure you can step up to the fulfilling challenges ahead.

Step in for Further Reflection

The following activities provide you with valuable opportunities to reflect on the ideas, strategies, and concepts covered in this chapter. If you are approaching *Step In, Step Up* as a twelve-week journey, you can spread these out over several days.

You may complete them individually or with a group so you can share your thoughts and ideas. Keep a journal so you can revisit your thoughts as you travel this journey.

1. Think about past conflicts, bias incidents, or other issues that might have needed a difficult conversation. When did you avoid having those talks and were there consequences? If so, what happened? How might you use this chapter's information to set new guidelines for yourself as to when to speak up?

2. Reflect on your current goals, relationships, and responsibilities. While you might not need to have a difficult conversation right now, chances are, some issue might benefit from the STATE model or the SCARF model. For example, you can use the STATE model to gather input on an issue from someone whom you know holds a different viewpoint, even if you aren't in conflict. You can use the SCARF model to plan for something as simple as a coaching session or the introduction of a new snack policy.

3. If difficult conversations are a major growth area for you, commit to finding ways to practice consistently using the strategies in this chapter. Consider meeting regularly with a partner to practice having tough conversations. Or, read *Your Brain at Work* by Rock (2009) or *Crucial Conversations* by Patterson et al. (2012), the original sources for the SCARF and STATE models. Or, attend formal training in conflict resolution. Collaborative leadership depends on your ability to clear the air.

CHAPTER 11

ENCOURAGING MORE WOMEN TO LEAD

GUIDING QUESTIONS

- How have others supported your development as a leader? How might you pay that forward through inspiring, supporting, and encouraging other women to lead?

- For what purposes and in what ways might you partner with other women to take charge of your career and development?

In case you haven't noticed, women are changing things at a faster pace than ever before. Something shifted after the 2016 U.S. presidential election that started conversation and commentary rolling in a new direction. What happened? Women rediscovered that they could band together. In *Good and Mad*, Rebecca Traister (2018), an American author, points out the long trajectory of women's activism:

> *It was more than eighty years between the first 1830s meeting of abolitionists and suffragists and the passage of the Nineteenth Amendment, more than 130 years before the passage of the Voting Rights Act. That law was recently gutted by the Supreme Court, a body that in 2018 also defended states' rights to purge voter rolls, disproportionately targeting minority voters. Which means that the movement for full democratic enfranchisement in the United States is ongoing, two centuries hence. It's easy to feel defeated by this, but more worthwhile to instead feel inspired: to know that*

in resisting and dissenting today, we are playing our parts in a story with long, righteous, proud roots. (Location No. 43367)

More than seven million people worldwide participated in the first Women's March in January 2017 (Hartocollis & Alcindor, 2017). Women formed groups all over the United States to learn how to take political action. A record number of women have registered to run for public office (Traister, 2018). The OECD (2012, 2017) reports we mentioned in chapter 1 (page 9) and chapter 2 (page 33) have fueled a strong global movement in striving for gender parity, where activism for women's equality aims a bright spotlight on significant issues.

> **Women working together can and have changed the course of history. They will again if we choose because when women support women, everyone wins.**
>
> **—Jamila Rizvi,**
> Australian writer, presenter, and commentator

The Me Too movement established once and for all that when not just one woman, but two, and then a dozen, and then hundreds, and then even more join together, norms begin to change. Not one voice speaking for millions but millions speaking with one voice can finally bring about what should have been all along.

Sheryl Sandberg (2016), as she launched #TogetherWomenCan, pointed out the simple logic for banding together:

> *When women celebrate one another's accomplishments, we're all lifted up. I truly believe that together, women can level the playing field to go farther faster. The more we help one another, the more the notion of that "queen bee" will go out of style—like those 1980s leg warmers my girlfriends and I used to wear religiously. With our girlfriends, we are stronger than we are individually. And because of my girlfriends, I know I am never alone.*

Partnering for the leadership journey—whether you are just stepping onto the path, delving deeply into your development, in a role of positional power, or beginning to think about a legacy—is perhaps one of the biggest blessings you can experience. No need to go it alone—together is definitely better. Partnering makes the journey more enriching and much more enjoyable. With partners, you can have conversations about thoughts such as, "You mean I'm not the only one experiencing this?" to learn from each other's experiences, and encourage each other to try new experiences. Mentoring, coaching, sponsoring, joining support or accountability groups, engaging in professional learning, and advocating for other women and women's causes all help more women step into the leadership journey.

 WORDS FROM A LEADER

> Perhaps the most important high-impact capability that connects women leaders in education is the shared passion for substantive changes that address injustices that continue to be seen in education. Women must support, push, pull, and nudge each other to speak out about their incredible contribution to educational leadership through their unique ways of leading. Relentless passion is what it takes to make changes in bureaucracies and institutions to ensure that *all* students have the literacy and critical-thinking skills to improve their life chances. Women need to celebrate and replenish their passion by knowing who they are, what they stand for, and by recognizing and celebrating small wins they make. (Dr. Lyn Sharratt, Canadian teacher, principal, superintendent, and researcher, personal communication, April 12, 2018)

Our collective experience and observation emphasizes the relevance of and place for women-only professional learning as a stimulus for empowerment and confidence. Women report that by engaging in these opportunities, they learn to consider and forge their own paths. They also become more determined to find a way to lead a balanced life and give themselves permission to do so.

While women shouldn't have to choose between the roles of parent, partner, leader, or teacher, hearing how others have navigated these roles and what it means to tackle them simultaneously makes the journey seem possible. And as always, you'll find a solution, a pathway that works for you, while knowing that it will no doubt change—and that your response will differ depending on where you are in your career and in life. Although you'll learn from other women, you'll tie your path to your personal guiding framework, underpin it with your values, and align it with your role, the roles you seek, and the way you wish to show up in those roles. As one participant in Barbara's program wrote in her feedback, "I realized real leadership is not about your job title but *who* you are" (personal communication, in the form of written feedback, August 20, 2018).

No matter where you go, never lose sight of who you are. The strength, inspiration, and tenacity of courageous women all around the world are cause for celebration.

Their powerful stories, replete with passion, determination, and resilience, provide rich leadership lessons for all women. Wear the heels of other fabulous role models (or follow them in kicking off heels altogether!), find inspiration, and find how you can do the same.

Linda Douglas, principal of Ruyton Girls' School in Australia, claims, "Our inspiration often comes from hearing the bold stories of others . . . When we see what others are truly capable of, we start to contemplate our own boundaries, fears and dreams and take risks. The #TimeIsNow" (personal communication, April 16, 2018).

In this chapter, we will discuss strategic ways to build support structures for sustaining your leadership. Think about the women with whom you identify and have a natural rapport. Who encourages you to leverage your talents and seek opportunities? Who is key to building networks or finding new avenues for professional learning?

A More Systematic Leadership Talent Search

Surrounding yourself with a network of peers, mentors, trusted colleagues, and friends empowers you to support your and others' leadership and development aspirations. Through these moments and interactions, you may find hidden or reluctant leaders, those whom an organization's more formal talent search may not recognize as promising candidates. Kevin Lane, Alexia Larmaraud, and Emily Yueh (2017) argue that too few organizations systematically scan for hidden talent, suggesting that companies need to apply more rigor and better tools than they currently use because "sometimes these overlooked leaders remain invisible because of gender, racial, or other biases."

> Whenever women are honest about their struggles, they give other women a gift.
>
> **—Elizabeth Gilbert,**
> American author

Visibly committing to gender diversity in leadership requires organizations to crack the code on sponsorship. Like mentors, sponsors may help you to develop your leadership skills; more specifically they advocate for you and help you to advance. In their report *Unlocking the Full Potential of Women at Work*, Joanna Barsh and Lareina Yee (2012) find that sponsors can create opportunities for high-potential women and men:

> *While some executives make it to the top without sponsors, most gained new opportunities, active support, and advocacy from such relationships. Great sponsors believe in the talented women they help, open the door to growth opportunities, counsel them through valleys and peaks, and advocate for their advancement. (p. 9)*

THINK ABOUT IT

More and more amazing women are changing things and gathering together other women to change things even faster. What inspiration can you find in the following examples?

- A lifelong political activist and politician for the Cambodia National Rescue Party, Mu Sochua went into semi-exile from her country for eighteen years. When she returned in 1989, she was elected minister for women and ran a program that encouraged twelve thousand women to run for commune-level positions. Nine percent of these women won, and Sochua then worked with them to get elected at a district level, giving them bikes so they could commute between villages for their campaigning. She's influenced family violence laws, fought against corporate land grabs, and advocated for sex workers and people living with HIV (HuffPost, 2012). You can visit https://sochua.wordpress.com to read more about her.

- Watch the TED Talk titled *To Solve the World's Biggest Problems, Invest in Women and Girls* (Kanyoro, 2017). As CEO of the Global Fund for Women, Musimbi Kanyoro works to support women and their ideas so they can expand and grow. In her TED Talk, she explains the Maragoli language's concept of *isirika*—a pragmatic way of life that embraces the mutual responsibility to care for one another—something she sees women practicing all over the world. And, she calls for those who have more to give more to people working to improve their communities. "Imagine what it would look like . . . if you embraced isirika and made it your default," Kanyoro (2017) says. "What could we achieve for each other? What could we achieve for humanity?"

- Also check out Nadia Lopez's (2015) amazing story in the TED Talk *Why Open a School? To Close a Prison*. Students are the future, and they need to believe that themselves. That's why Lopez opened an academic oasis in Brownsville, Brooklyn, one of the most underserved and violent neighborhoods in New York. She believes in every student's brilliance and capabilities. In this short, energizing talk, Lopez, the founding principal of Mott Hall Bridges Academy, shares how she helps her scholars envision a brighter future for themselves and their families.

You can find more examples by searching for the "TED Talks by Strong Women Leaders" playlist (TED, n.d.; www.ted.com/playlists/486/ted_talks_by _strong_women_lead). Watch these videos with other women. What changes might women together bring about?

Networks and Learning Opportunities

Many women in education have benefited from women's networks, both formal and informal, within and beyond the education sector. We do not suggest that women's networks have more value than mixed-gender networks. They do, however, provide a different transformative space in which to learn, advocate, and grow. You may find having an informal, strong support network of women invaluable during a challenging time in your professional or personal life. Rest assured, while at times you may feel like the only one experiencing self-doubt or structural barriers holding you back, you are not alone, regardless of your career stage. Although you may have a large network in terms of access to a range of colleagues and opportunities, interacting with a smaller, more intimate group within the network, based on context and need, may prove invaluable. Determine what works best for you.

Professional networks can also provide you with stretch opportunities and expert or strategic advice. Also, they support you when things get tough and help you celebrate and plan for future career success. Reflect on how you might also do this with people in your network or on your team.

 THINK ABOUT IT

If, like Jane, you have a more introverted personality, a *support group* might seem antithetical to your needs. You might find that your ideal group is just two or three other women, rather than a large professional organization. A strategy that works for many introverts is to find one kindred spirit. Then, each one invites one other trusted soul. Voilà—you have a four-member support group that provides the deep conversations you prefer.

Or, if you discovered in chapter 6 (page 99) that you prefer Thinking over Feeling, support may seem like a waste of time. Reframe the group as an *accountability group*, where you gather to share goals, strategies, progress, and concerns.

Find a group structure that works for you—and it will be worth it. Name what you don't like about such gatherings, and then create the group that checks the boxes you need.

Learning from powerful examples and inspirational allies boosts your own and others' careers. Engaging in these networks can provide access to leadership experiences, such as avenues for investigating creative and flexible career options.

WORDS FROM A LEADER

My most important source of support as a female leader has been developing a personal network of other female leaders. I have learned to identify women I believe are strong leaders, and then I study them, striving to discover and understand the leadership characteristics, skills, patterns, and practices they employ that make them so remarkable. Sometimes, I study them from afar, reading about them or watching them and analyzing what I am observing. Sometimes, I am blessed to call them colleagues or acquaintances, so I'll offer to buy their lunch so I can explore their thought processes as they lead and invite their insights. Learning from the best has been invaluable to me on my own journey toward excellence. (Cassandra Erkens, American author and educational consultant, personal communication, April 16, 2018)

For example, Wendy (a pseudonym), whose experience provided a case study for one of Barbara's research colleagues who explored flexible options and co-principalship, worked as an Australian primary school's acting principal for a short period. As a part-time employee, she immensely enjoyed the role, and the experience highlighted what she missed when she had little to no access to more ongoing leadership roles. She and a colleague put forward the concept of co-principalship. While this required considerable investment and commitment, systemically and individually, the school developed structures that enabled its success. Undoubtedly, role clarity, personality, and communication are critical factors, and while co-principalship may not be a universal option, with the right people and at the right time, such shifts can have great success and highly benefit all involved.

Principals, teachers, and researchers express the value of participating in networks, joining relevant organizations and professional associations, and making professional connections beyond school as important aspects of professional learning that contribute to building a leader's social capital (Coleman, 2007). These connections have diverse benefits, including being exposed to new ideas and calls to action, informing practice, and enabling connectivity. You'll find numerous global examples of networks that focus on women in school leadership and provide relevant, practical opportunities for collegiality and growth, including the following.

- Women and Leadership Australia (2018) is the largest gender-focused leadership initiative in Australia and comprises a range of professional development programs, advisory services, networking channels, and ongoing research. Ideally positioned to respond to the ever-changing needs of contemporary female leaders and their organizations, Women and Leadership Australia (2018) regularly partners with diverse organizations, including those focused on women in school leadership, to help female leaders develop the skills they need to pursue career advancement.

- #WomenEd (2018) is a grassroots movement with chapters in Australia, the United Kingdom, and Canada. It connects women in school leadership with aspiring ones. With sponsorship support and a strong online and social media presence, members connect, collaborate, and empower one another.

- The vision of the National College for Teaching and Leadership's Women Leading in Education, South West Network (2018) team is to grow regional teacher equality networks throughout Great Britain, with a focus on leadership and gender (though not exclusively, as other factors, such as ethnicity and sexual orientation, could be addressed in the same way). Drawing membership from a range of backgrounds, it focuses on networks led by inspiring role models who have successful leadership track records and commit to overcoming leadership barriers for women and other groups that leadership underrepresents. It also recruits Women in Leadership Champions who act as mentors. They receive an intensive support program, which includes training in network facilitation skills, social media use, and regulations and laws surrounding equality.

- With a grant from the Bill and Melinda Gates Foundation, the American Association of School Administrators (2017) established the AASA Women in School Leadership Initiative in 2015 to help mitigate the impact of social barriers women face in reaching top leadership positions within school systems. The initiative facilitates building networks to advance women in leadership. It shares activities that help women prepare for leadership roles; gain insights into potential barriers and challenges; and prepare for the next career step. Through awards, consortium development, professional learning opportunities, and collaboration initiatives, it works to raise awareness across the United States to support aspiring women education leaders.

🔆 THINK ABOUT IT

What opportunities do you have to engage in and contribute to networks—formal or informal, virtual or face-to-face—that can nourish and support your leadership aspirations? If you aren't sure, ask other women.

Women in School Leadership Programs

Our collective work provides strong advocacy for women-only programs to inspire and support emerging and current school leaders. Well-documented projections about school leadership shortages and the need to manage succession planning in an increasingly complex educational environment require school systems to tap into the full pool of talent and expertise. New generations of potential school leaders have career aspirations that may lead them to work elsewhere and then return to education. Female potential school leaders may have a variety of reasons for exiting and re-entering the education workforce. A number of school leadership programs specifically target women, including via networks as previously evidenced, and address the issues and challenges that directly relate to women's role in school leadership and to their successful application for the principalship.

These programs demystify the principal role and give women opportunities to build confidence by engaging with and learning from others, networking with like-minded colleagues, and participating in activities specifically focused on women. You will gain significant benefits and empowerment from all these opportunities when you do the following.

- Listen to and learn from the experiences of female principals and those who hold other roles to which you aspire.

- Appreciate that others, from emerging to experienced leaders, have similar concerns and that you are not alone in your challenges.

- Build confidence to step forward into opportunities by identifying authentic, practical ideas that overcome self-doubt.

- Recognize and acknowledge your ability and potential.

- Focus on collaborative learning, reflection, and feedback.

- Discuss roles, reflect on (potentially unrealistic) expectations, and find answers to challenges and avenues for practice and growth.

More generally, encouragement and support significantly enhance career progression, increase the number of women in school leadership, and improve the quality of school leadership. In particular, sustained support from school and system leaders creates opportunities and instills confidence. By sharing insights and experiences, women gain the support they need to tap into their potential to develop and grow as teachers, leaders, experts, and influencers with impact. As we explored in chapter 8 (page 131), a safe place and caring relationships are key resources for the leadership journey. In our experience, anecdotally, these resources feature strongly in women leadership programs and enable women to learn how to build trust, find support, and experience interdependency.

Sharing your doubts, challenges, self-imposed limitations, and ambitions with others requires deep reflection and a willingness to expose your vulnerabilities. As someone who studies human connection, Brown (2010) has explored the power of vulnerability by showing vulnerability results in others trusting you. (If you haven't yet done so, check out the Think About It activity on page 122 based on her TED Talk.) You only need to look at the neuroscience of trust and Paul J. Zak's (2017) findings on the difference between high-trust and low-trust companies to appreciate the implications of high-trust relationships, where employees of high-trust companies have the following.

- 74 percent less chronic stress
- 14 percent less burnout
- 13 percent fewer sick days
- 76 percent more engagement
- 106 percent more energy
- 50 percent higher productivity

In other words, high-trust environments are also high-performance environments.

Mentors and Coaches

Privileging and investing in your development through building trusted relationships with mentors provides an intensely personalized avenue for growth. Mentoring and coaching conversations challenge the way you think about yourself, your work, and what you can achieve.

Many women indicate that their female and male mentors who believed in them were crucial to empowering them to open doors that they had previously not considered. Determine for yourself whether the gender of a mentor matters to you; we have both benefited from male and female mentors who could provide different avenues for enriching our experiences and insights over the course of our careers.

In launching Australia's Women United Mentoring program, Australia's minister for foreign affairs and mentor Julie Bishop shared her insights on mentoring and mentors' value: "They provide perspective, knowledge, experience and confidence. I am an avowed supporter of mentoring—sharing knowledge, drawing on their experience, challenging our thinking, helping navigating your career, giving us self-confidence and, belief in what can be achieved" (as cited in Shedden, 2018). This program, which gives women access to some of Australia's most inspiring women as mentors, aims to help the next generation of fierce female leaders and beyond to press for progress.

WORDS FROM A LEADER

People (men and women) aren't always comfortable with women who like themselves. Sometimes they smile a lot, talk loudly, wear clothes that make them feel great, have opinions, and live lives that challenge norms. I like being a woman and I like myself as a person. This positive sense of self is in no small part due to having had wonderful people (men and women) in my life: specific family members, honest and affirming friends, hugely supportive partners and important leadership mentors. (Josephine Wise, executive director of Independent Schools Queensland, Australia, personal communication, August 16, 2018)

Another form of mentoring is *sponsoring*. In the traditional sponsoring mentoring, people view the mentor as an expert who uses his or her power to open doors for the mentee. Developmental mentoring has a different focus. While the mentor usually has more experience, the key issue is developing with and learning from each other. Rizvi (2017) sees sponsors as people who advocate for you from above to get a particular job or promotion: "This means they actively help you to advance. A mentor, by contrast, actively helps you to help yourself to advance" (p. 282).

According to Lisa Catherine Ehrich and Megan Kimber (2015), mentoring programs and partnerships have the potential to benefit not only the mentee but also the mentor and the organization. "Whilst not a panacea for advancing women's leadership development, [mentoring] is one of a number of strategies that have a prominent place in supporting and encouraging women in their respective professional and personal endeavors" (p. 237).

In one of Barbara's 2017 women in school leadership programs, mentors and mentees affirmed the benefits of participating in the mentoring partnership, with the ripple effect reaching beyond the mentee and the partnership. Comments from mentor reflections included the following.

- "I can apply my learning to develop leaders at my school; my mentee's process of articulating her journey encouraged me to assist my middle leaders to do the same."

- "The partnership has assisted me to redefine my own leadership strengths, critically reflect on experiences in my leadership journey to pass on and develop another leader, further developing interpersonal skills, and reflect and rethink my practice."

- "I've really reflected on how much I can and should change my leadership style, depending on who I am working with."

Comments from mentees included the following.

- "It was so empowering to be able to seek advice and have conversations with a third party who is objective."

- "The process has been amazing—I have felt completely supported but challenged at the same time in a comfortable and reassuring way."

- "Confidence comes in knowing that there is a place for all kinds of women in leadership."

- "My courage and confidence in my own abilities and what I have to offer has grown so much."

The emphasis on learning, mutual accountability, and reciprocity sees the ripple effect of positive impact and growth beyond the mentoring partnership for both the mentor and mentee. And as the previous comments attest, for mentees, it instills the confidence to take the next step.

Coaching differs from mentoring in that most executive coaches view their role as helping leaders engage in reflective practices, tap their inner wisdom, identify their own growth edges, and hold themselves accountable for making progress toward self-selected goals. Note the origin of the word *coach*: a vehicle for taking valuable people from where they are to where they wish to go.

In many business organizations, being promoted to a higher-level management position comes with being assigned a coach. If you are stepping into a principalship for the first time, or a system position with significantly more responsibility, consider finding a coach if your organization doesn't provide one. You'll gain an outside, neutral pair of ears to listen to what you are experiencing and help you figure out how you can navigate your new leadership environment and role.

Readiness for the Leadership Job Search

Ready to join in on this critical journey? If you aren't in, you can't win. In an interview for *QBusiness*, Michelle Winzer shares her path to becoming chief executive of the Bank of Melbourne and describes how she overcame self-doubt and why discomfort is key to success (as cited in Galliott, 2018). Part of her process involved always being ready for an interview—tomorrow! While having no specific interview strategy, she keeps a book of herself and regularly updates it with example achievements she could share. She didn't anticipate that she would reach CEO level in a large banking corporation. Early in her career, though, people told her, "Don't limit yourself by a job role; always think what you can get out of each opportunity" (Galliott, 2018, p. 106). So, she took different opportunities throughout her career with the mindset of learning something new.

> Be bold, dig deep, and back yourself . . . The fact is that in the really big "fork-in-the-road" decisions, I stared into my fears and insecurities and pushed myself hard to get beyond them. I learned that, as challenging as it may be, it pays to be courageous and back yourself. I have been encouraged by others—sometimes strongly encouraged—to have a go. It has helped to be aware of the many people who will support and assist along the way.
>
> —Gail Kelly,
> first female CEO of one of
> Australia's big four banks

Look back to those limiting and high-flying beliefs in chapter 7 (page 115) that women often have. In addition to underestimating their ability, women may have a more deep-seated fear of rejection than men. This may hold them back from putting themselves forward and applying for a new position, or make them reticent to do so, because they are uncertain of the outcome. Women seem expert at knowing their limitations, but less so at recognizing their gifts, talents, and skills that make them valuable candidates for a position.

So how do you win the position you deserve? You may need to work with those women in your support or accountability group to help each other do the following.

- Recognize what each of you brings to the table.
- Crack the selection code before an interview.
- Avoid the pitfalls and mistakes that can thwart a career or leave ambitions unfulfilled.

This requires some preparation, planning, and insight into the most obvious and simple mistakes people make when seeking new positions, such as assuming they need more qualifications or failing to adequately connect personal strengths with job requirements. As Winzer shares, this preparation is just as much about always being ready for interviews (long-term planning) as it is about knowing how to effectively sell yourself in a highly competitive employee selection process (as cited in Galliott, 2018).

According to Jim Watterston (2018), an experienced school and system leader, you can make some simple changes to enhance your chances of finding the job you want, but there are also some deep-seated fundamental beliefs you should work on. Watterston (2018) points out the top five mistakes people make when applying for a job:

- *Not researching the position and comprehensively knowing and feeling compatible with the school or organization that you are seeking to join*

- *Not presenting your true self to the panel—trying too hard to be who you think they want rather than authentically presenting who you are and what you believe*

- *Not focusing the application and interview on a specific open position but instead simply identifying the qualities you possess*

- *Not preparing sufficiently, lacking confidence in positively presenting yourself*

- *Not treating the job selection process as the strategic and intense competition that it is (p. 11)*

Controlling every aspect of the job selection process ensures that you optimize your chances at every stage (determine why you want the job, apply for the job, compile your references, undergo the interview, and reflect on the interview). While not winning a position for which you feel well suited can demoralize you and sap your confidence, this process is informative and an opportunity for feedback and growth, whether or not you succeed.

 THINK ABOUT IT

Consider the advice about long-term planning, and how this links to defining your leadership aspirations. What are you doing to enhance your skills and maximize your chances of gaining the position you deserve? Are you being strategic in the way you take control of all stages of the job selection process? What's one action you can take now?

Next Steps in the Journey

Proactively and strategically seeking out peers, networks, mentors, and professional learning programs that support you, stretch you, and connect you to like-minded colleagues is an organic and mutually rewarding process. Stacie Hansel, the executive director who shared her advice in chapter 7 (page 115), perfectly captures this insight: "I think it wasn't until I was told by someone I looked up to that I was 'good enough' that I believed that I could . . . the power of great women empowering other great women to be even better" (personal communication, April 20, 2018).

Proactively seeking support and supporting others in their leadership journey is the gift that keeps on giving. It not only benefits you but also champions other women's success and talents.

Step in for Further Reflection

The following activities provide you with valuable opportunities to reflect on the ideas, strategies, and concepts covered in this chapter. If you are approaching *Step In, Step Up* as a twelve-week journey, you can spread these out over several days.

You may complete them individually or with a group so you can share your thoughts and ideas. Keep a journal so you can revisit your thoughts as you travel this journey.

1. Use the following quotes to stimulate discussion around what the future holds for women. For each quote (as cited in Weekes, 2007), consider whether it reminds you of any of your own experiences and what changes it might suggest. How might you help bring that change into existence?

   ○ "Because I am a woman, I must make unusual efforts to succeed. If I fail, no one will say, 'She doesn't have what it takes.' They will say, 'Women don't have what it takes.'"
   —Clare Boothe Luce, American journalist and politician (p. 8)

   ○ "I have never been especially impressed by the heroics of people who are convinced they are about to change the world. I am more awed by those who struggle to make one small difference after another."—Ellen Goodman, American journalist (p. 14)

   ○ "Would that there were an award for people who come to understand the concept of enough. Good enough. Successful enough. Thin enough. Rich enough. Socially responsible enough. When you have self-respect, you have enough."
   —Gail Sheehy, American social critic (p. 36)

- o "Feminist politics aims to end domination, to free us to be who we are—to live lives where we love justice, where we can live in peace. Feminism is for everybody."
  —bell hooks, African American activist and theorist (p. 121)

- o "Feminism has fought no wars. It has killed no opponents. It has set up no concentration camps, starved no enemies, practiced no cruelties. Its battles have been for education, for the vote, for better working conditions . . . for safety on the streets . . . for child care, for social welfare . . . for rape crisis centers, women's refuges, reforms in the law. [If someone says] 'Oh I'm not a feminist,' [I ask] 'Why? What's your problem?'"—Dale Spender, Australian sociolinguist and technology theorist (p. 122)

- o "There came a time when the risk to remain tight in the bud was more painful than the risk it took to blossom."
  —Anaïs Nin, French-American writer and diarist (p. 125)

- o "Many of our troubles in the world today arise from an over-emphasis of the masculine, and a neglect of the feminine. This modern world is an aggressive, hyperactive, competitive, masculine world, and it needs the woman's touch as never before."
  —Eva Burrows, Australian leader of Salvation Army
  (p. 139)

- o "Men are taught to apologize for their weaknesses, women for their strengths."—Lois Wyse, American writer (p. 140)

2. Join a women's group. Hopefully, we've now convinced you that gathering with other women for support in the leadership journey has great value. Which of the following suggestions might help you find the right group? Reflect on what might work best for you—and then move to action!

   - o Ask other women educators if they have found valuable networking or support groups. You may need to check out more than one or attend more than one group's session to find the right fit.

   - o If you aren't a member of a local education professional association, join one for a year. Attend just the main events if the commuting distance causes a problem, but make an effort at those events to find other women who also wish to form new connections. Arrange to meet virtually with those women via Skype (www.skype.com), Zoom (https://zoom.us), or another free web-conferencing service.

- If time is an issue, invite other women to form a walking support group. Walk and talk, perhaps following a fairly set agenda, such as discussing goals or communication strategies.

- Consider how professional development activities can provide opportunities to strategically link with other women who work in similar contexts or on similar themes. Annual state, provincial, or national conferences, for example, provide diverse connections that you can develop virtually or host at different locations throughout the year.

- Think about forming a group with colleagues who are at a similar stage of their career, determine where you have similar needs, and access others who can inform and support the group.

3. Pass it on—recognize and provide support for others. Even if you are at the beginning of the leadership journey, look for a way to pay it forward. Something as simple as inviting another woman to take this book's journey with you, or suggesting you both attend a professional development event, could give her just the catalyst she needs.

4. DNA—*do not assume*. While people often assume (correctly or incorrectly) what others may think of them, they also make assumptions about those they admire. You may think the people you admire know the positive impact they have and how their influence inspires and motivates actions in others, including yourself.

For example, Barbara sent a tweet to Margie Warrell, a best-selling author, speaker, media commentator, and international advocate for gender equality and women's empowerment. Barbara told Warrell how much she loved her blog and the practical advice in her enewsletter and thanked her for sharing her amazing insights and energizing encouragement. When thanking Barbara for the feedback, Warrell said she generally has no idea who reads her communications and often has to pull herself back from worrying that no one will.

Similarly, teachers often meet a student as an adult who shares how a discussion, an action, feedback received, or lessons learned was a turning point or inspiration in his or her life. Teachers feel privileged to receive these messages affirming how they had touched others' hearts.

Who do you admire? Have you told them that you do and, most important, why you do? Who might you write, call, or email today or this week? By supporting other women, we can collectively increase all of our power to become our best selves and, in turn, support the valuable contributions we will continue to make.

CRAFTING YOUR IDENTITY AS A FEMALE LEADER

GUIDING QUESTIONS

- What impact do you envision having as a woman in educational leadership?
- How will you know if you have become a more effective leader?

If you've followed our suggested plan for this leadership journey, you are now finishing up three months of learning and reflecting about who you are as a leader, what you might do, and how you might get there. In this rapidly changing world, where artificial intelligence is a reality, where connectedness to our humanness is challenged, and where ways of working in the future can only be imagined, we also need to reimagine our roles as educators and leaders. In this final chapter, you'll have a chance to polish your leadership philosophy, identify a few key next steps, and ensure that you've put in place the support for your journey. Before we jump in, though, let's get clear about one very important aspect of leadership.

Realizing That It Isn't, and It Is, All About You

Hopefully, you've thought hard about your views on power as you've worked through these pages and you feel excited about having *power to*. As cited in the introduction, Jeane Kirkpatrick, the first female U.S. ambassador to the United Nations, puts it well:

"Power . . . is not an end in itself, but is an instrument that must be used toward an end" (as cited in Weekes, 2007, p. 255).

We believe that while each woman in educational leadership hopes to have *power to* influence in unique ways, we all share a common goal: as instructional leaders, we want to create enabling conditions that clearly and intentionally support the development of teachers' capacity to create a positive impact on student learning.

This definition of instructional leadership includes the following three elements.

1. **Creating enabling conditions:** In chapter 8 (page 131), we suggested EQ as a model for ensuring you have the skills and capacity to create an environment where collective teacher efficacy can thrive, to motivate others around a common purpose, to establish an emotionally safe environment, and to provide individual coaching and support.

2. **Clearly and intentionally supporting the development of teachers' capacity:** What responsibilities might you have for creating effective individual and group professional development opportunities? In chapter 4 (page 67), we discussed the collaborative nature of school leaders' work—the *power with* that fosters collaboration and shared leadership to increase effectiveness. Are you ready to differentiate, plan strategically, and use the platinum rule to meet teachers where they are and take them where they want to go?

   In emphasizing the importance of diagnosis before prescription, the question is, What are we developing people to do? The answer to this question affects the nature of how we develop them. In chapter 5 (page 83) and chapter 6 (page 99), you looked at your development and strengths in order to reflect on your natural style and where you might need to adjust. What did you learn about your growth edges as your increase your capacity to support others' growth?

3. **Creating a positive impact on student learning:** Of course, energizing your moral purpose is the real reason for engaging in this work. Do you have a clear understanding of how existing education norms and practices affect students? Are students learning? Are they learning both content and how to use the content? Are they making progress? Are they engaged, building belief in their efficacy as they make progress? As the world changes, the best thing you can do is teach students how to learn, for they *must* become lifelong learners to keep up with changes in the skills and

knowledge the world requires. That means that they need to see learning as enjoyable and purposeful, as well as know how to learn effectively.

Together, these three elements make up a tall order, don't they? That makes it essential to partner *power to* with *power with*. Creating teams, coalitions, partnerships, and champions is core to an effective school leadership journey.

But rather than become overwhelmed, take a deep breath, and remember that you will only truly gain all these skills if you begin doing the work of leadership. If you aspire to a noble purpose, plan for using your strengths, seek support and learning for the tasks ahead, remain open to wisdom and feedback, *and* balance caring for yourself and for others, how far from success can you stray? Good things will happen.

Dealing With Leadership's Inevitable Stress

Key to success, as we have emphasized, is readying yourself for the inevitable stress of striving toward goals and working with people. Shirzad Chamine, founder of the Coaches Training Institute (a powerhouse executive-coaching organization), developed the Saboteur Assessment (www.positiveintelligence.com/assessments) that can help you learn how to best describe your defense mechanisms, or mental models, you've developed for dealing with difficulties that may be self-sabotaging. The ten *saboteurs* include (1) stickler, (2) pleaser, (3) hyper-vigilant, (4) restless, (5) controller, (6) avoider, (7) hyper-achiever, (8) victim, (9) hyper-rational, and (10) judge, the *master saboteur* that we all have. We've found this saboteur framework helpful for avoiding discouragement and navigating your limiting beliefs.

Jane, for example, knows that one of her top saboteurs is *controller*. Planning and commitment are actually core strengths, but when she feels stressed, she tries to control everything, including things she can't control. She's named this saboteur Eunice after the very controlling fiancée Madeline Kahn plays in the movie *What's Up, Doc?* and has gotten adept at telling Eunice to simmer down.

Barbara says her mantra, "Let go," when her *hyper-achiever* saboteur rears its head through an overemphasis on doing something well and tells her, "If it's worth doing, it's worth doing well." For example, this saboteur makes her constantly go back and forth to change a presentation even moments before the presentation begins.

Using Chamine's (n.d.) vocabulary for these cycles of unhelpful behaviors helps you recognize the behaviors and refocus much more quickly. Chamine (n.d.) claims that disappointment over a setback or mistake is only useful for about ten seconds, until you become curious about how to learn from it. Whenever you find yourself feeling negative for more than those ten seconds, try this:

1. *Pause. Ask yourself if you've already heard the message, and if there is any value in staying in the reaction.*
2. *Chuckle to your Saboteur and say, "I've got it and I'm on it. Now get out of my way!"*

Take your hand off the hot stove of life's challenges. You'll see how much easier life instantly becomes. (Shirzad Chamine, personal communication, May 11, 2018)

If you haven't completed the stress exercise in chapter 10 (see page 169), take the time to do so now. Take the Saboteur Assessment at www.positiveintelligence.com /assessments and add the information from the Saboteur Assessment report you receive. Remember that stress, properly addressed, has an upside. And you can't escape stress if you want to have relationships with others and pursue worthwhile goals, two key realities of leadership.

Determining Your Leadership Impact

Several times in these pages, we have asked you to think about who you are and want to be as a leader. In coaching, we often employ 360-degree feedback tools—surveys that a leader's supervisor, peers, direct reports, community members, and sometimes family complete—to add objectivity to this process. The surveys provide invaluable insights as to how others perceive the individual's leadership style.

You can use a similar, less formal process to form a more complete picture of your leadership identity and ways you might wish to shift or polish it. Women's leadership speaker Jo Miller (2018) suggests you ask yourself:

What am I currently known for at work? How do others perceive me, and what skills, or areas of expertise, do they associate with me? What impression immediately comes to mind when co-workers hear my name? And what do others say about me when I'm not in the room? Ask a trusted colleague, manager, or mentor for feedback. Let them know you're working on building self-awareness and that you'd like their assistance in understanding how you're perceived at work. Questions to ask include . . .

- *What three words would you use to describe me?*
- *What strengths, weaknesses, or expertise do you and others closely associate with me?*
- *How am I currently perceived by other members of our team?*

Take this information, and revisit the leadership philosophy you've created for yourself. Does anything suggest changes? A goal or two? A strength or quality you lacked awareness of? Remember, the best way to lead is in the way you are naturally wired to lead. What might you do to ensure your skills shine as brightly as they can?

Beware, though, to identify what is *good enough* because perfection isn't possible. You are not perfect and never will be. Revisit the perfectionist-optimalist exercise in table 2.1 (pages 42–43). What is good enough as a parent, professional, partner, or leader?

Limiting Your Leadership Goals

With an eye to your *power to* hopes, your development as an instructional leader (including your collaborative skills, coaching and professional development skills, and knowledge of effective and engaging instruction), your strengths, and your leadership philosophy—in sum, everything we've discussed—what two or three goals might form the next phase of your leadership journey?

Two or three goals are plenty; people simply aren't built to focus on more than two or three things at a time. And, as mentioned previously, *priority* originally had no plural form. You had only one. As you pick and choose, considering the reflection exercises from each chapter, use this prompt to narrow down the possibilities: "What two or three things will make it easier for me to have *power to* in the areas I hope to influence?"

If you find five or six crucial goals, fine. Rank and record them. But set aside all but the first three for now. You have years to develop as a leader. Learning never stops. Remember, learning is the work. When you determine you've made progress on your most important goals, you may find that your list has shifted. It's taking the journey that counts, not crafting the full destination right now.

Once you've identified your top two or three goals, the next step is ensuring that you reach them—and that involves going beyond SMART goals, using the power of *why* and *how*.

Beyond SMART Goals

Perhaps you've learned about the SMART acronym for setting strategic and specific, measurable, attainable, results-oriented, and time-bound goals (Conzemius & O'Neill, 2014). Supposedly, such goals motivate people and lead to higher performance. Many schools use the SMART goal framework to set goals and action steps based on student assessment data. However, this framework has dangers and downsides.

Maxim Sytch (2015) points out four key limitations to SMART goals. Consider the following points to center the limitations in an educational context.

1. In many cases, people meet specific goals but do not align them with the true overarching purpose. Look back at chapter 6's discussion of reading instruction as an example (page 99).

2. People are four times more likely to lie about performance when they receive specific goals and worry that they may not reach them (Sytch, 2015). Thus, there is wisdom in plans that tolerate failing to meet SMART goals. Think *good enough*.

3. Conflict may exist among discrete goals. As you ponder your goals, do any sit in tension with others, such as more reflection time and more networking, for example?

4. Having specific goals can limit learning and creativity. This is particularly dangerous in complex environments without clear pathways to success.

Where have you seen strategic goals for education reform limit teacher or administrator learning and creativity? As you work with your goals, you may find that some demand *not* being specific and time bound—after all, will you ever arrive as the perfect collaborative leader? If you employ a quantitative measurement as suggested in literature on SMART goals (Conzemius & O'Neill, 2014), what qualitative factors might you overlook?

With this tension between needing understandable goals and ensuring that the goals themselves don't result in unintended consequences, let's focus on turning your goals into a flexible plan.

The Why *for Each Goal*

Goals are no doubt important, but as you've seen, just because a goal is SMART doesn't mean it's worth pursuing. However, you'll still find the acronym useful in evaluating how you state your goal by working through the following five-step process.

1. Articulate your greater purpose, and make sure every goal links back to this. This is the *why* of goal setting. People who state why they pursue a goal will far more likely reach it. It changes how you feel about the difficulties involved in reaching that goal.

2. Use the acronym *SMART* to evaluate how clearly you state the goal. In other words, the acronym works best as a check on the goal's clarity and wording rather than on the quality.

3. Step back and consider, "Is this goal the right size?" SMART goals often motivate people to choose easy tasks that they can finish, rather than make sure they choose the right tasks. However, greater purposes generally come from dreaming big and thus involve goals that stretch you; those purposes are worthy of effort.

4. Do a reality check. The A for *attainable* in SMART is still crucial. A great goal walks that fine line between audacious and impossible—the latter crushes motivation. You can accomplish this by creating solid action steps. "Within psychology, these smaller ambitions are known as 'proximal goals,' and repeated studies have shown that breaking a big ambition into proximal goals makes the large objective more likely to occur" (Duhigg, 2016, p. 105).

5. Finally, figure out the answer to, "How will I know I am making progress?" Get creative—again, many leadership goals will have a qualitative *measurable* aspect, yet having a clear way to measure progress is key to success. The following are examples from leaders who created qualitative ways to know if they are making progress.

   ○ "Might a trusted colleague give me feedback on my listening skills in meetings?"

   ○ "What changes in teacher behavior might I see as I work toward creating an atmosphere where collective teacher efficacy flourishes?"

   ○ "This week, did I pause before making important decisions to ensure I considered both objective and subjective criteria?"

   ○ "How does my spouse view my handling of work-life balance this week?"

And, as you set these goals, take to heart ensuring that they are realistic. Joan Leegant (2017) describes a crucial, additional way in which women often sabotage their chances of success. First identified in 1969 by researcher Matina Horner, *fear of success* differs from fear of failure and affects women more than men. She claims that fear of success particularly seems to affect young, often well-educated women who are likely to succeed. Fear of success assumes one is capable but fears the consequences of those capabilities. This fear might include a husband, boyfriend, or father who is threatened by your competence, or that your competence might appear unladylike in some way.

Or, you might fear the guilt of not spending enough time with your family. Leegant (2107) continues:

> So Fear of Success, the theory goes, conveniently comes along to shoot you in the foot. It undermines you from pursuing your goals, thus rescuing you from anxiety and the consequences you're worried about. To the untrained eye, your behavior may look like Fear of Failure—you don't apply yourself, you're riddled with doubt and second-guessing, you procrastinate or blow off requirements or, in the case of one study, get pregnant just when your success is about to peak—but it has nothing to do with the terror of failure and all to do with the terror of succeeding. (p. 247)

Marking your success can, of course, help you overcome fear of failure. You can make avoiding fear of success a goal in its own right.

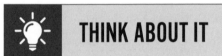

THINK ABOUT IT

If Leegant's description of fear of success sounds familiar, what goals might you set to overcome these fears?

Balancing Work and Life

And finally, we circle back to one of our big reasons for focusing on women in educational leadership separately from men: we dream that someday, gender won't play a role in the difficult, personal decisions around balancing two careers, relocating, or sharing parenting responsibilities. Other factors, such as talent identification, targeted support and opportunities to build leadership capacity, and flexible and responsive workplaces, would consistently play a bigger role.

Further, that perfectionist-optimalist dichotomy we covered in chapter 2 (page 33) needs to play into how you view your success in maintaining balance. Erin Skinner Cochran (2018), who served as vice president of communications for former Secretary of State Madeleine Albright, has written about what she learned from working for the secretary. She states that women should stop thinking it's possible to manage their careers and family life at the same pace and focus. Their focus on one or the other ebbs and flows, and that's a good thing. She continues:

This brings me to the most important lesson I wished I'd known when I first had kids: There's no such thing as balance, only priorities of the moment. The parents I know who seem most content, and the most high-functioning, are those who have their priorities figured out. They focus on two, maybe three, things (i.e. family, job, health), and let the rest of the chips fall where they may. It's those of us who seek the great job, quality time with our kids, a full social calendar, fitness, and travel who are inevitably disappointed. (Cochran, 2018)

In other words, be kind to yourself. You are as important as your goals, and you can only reach your goals if you remember to take care of yourself.

Next Steps in the Journey

You've stepped in, reaching the end and the beginning of the journey. As we said at the start, none of us ever fully arrive as leaders. We will always have more to learn, new people to understand, new challenges. Hopefully, though, you now have a journal filled with information, ideas, and inspiration to equip you to step up in confidence.

And at least two or three female leaders for mutual support.

And aspirations for having *power to* as you step in and step up. Be bold and strategic. Your next big move is ensuring that you continue to take the time for reflection on this crucial and fulfilling endeavor to make a difference in the lives of students.

> **Step into your power. Because behind every successful woman is herself.**
>
> **—Margie Warrell,** Australian best-selling author, women's advocate, and sought-after international speaker

Step in for Further Reflection

The following activities provide you with valuable opportunities to reflect on the ideas, strategies, and concepts covered in this chapter. If you are approaching *Step In, Step Up* as a twelve-week journey, you can spread these out over several days.

You may complete them individually or with a group so you can share your thoughts and ideas. Keep a journal so you can revisit your thoughts as you travel this journey.

1. If you've reached this point without identifying other women who can support you in this leadership journey, pause now to do so by answering the following questions. Who might fill one or more than one of the following roles? Where might you need a group's support?

- Who nurtures you and lets you know you are competent and full of potential?

- With whom can you process mistakes and worries with a focus on development? We call these *gripe and grow partners*.

- Do you need colleagues for specific workplace or environment changes that must happen now? Think of the movements around #MeToo, #PressforProgress, and #TimeIsNow and how the power of many can shift culture.

- Who challenges you to become the best version of you and provides you with inspiration and, of course, celebration?

- Who do you admire? Who would you like to seek out and learn from?

2. Write a fictional letter from a student or teacher, letting you know of your impact. What would you want the student or teacher to say about how you have influenced his or her school or work experience?

3. Courage is indispensable for creating what you want most—in work, love, and life—and change what you don't like. As Margie Warrell (2017) advises, this means rising above your instinctive desire to play it safe. Think about how you might show courage. Do you do the following?

- Not let what others think pilot your life

- Take the proverbial road less traveled and do what's right over what's easy

- Pursue big goals even when they daunt you

- Say no and risk disappointing people

- Have the tough conversations you'd rather avoid

- Say sorry, forgive yourself, or forgive another

4. Do you have a favorite leadership slogan? How about you craft your own? Figure 12.1 offers several example slogans. What resonates, and what would you change? What might summarize your leadership philosophy?

As a leader I have discovered the importance of purpose in my life. Purpose has given me strength in the face of challenges. It has converted barriers into opportunities and problems into possibilities. Purpose has supported me by transforming my labor into a labor of love. I have learned that relationships are everything and that building relationships is the heart and soul of building community.

—D. Trinidad Hunt, personal communication, April 19, 2018

The creed I live by:
Excellence can be achieved if you—
- Care more than others think is wise.
- Risk more than others think is safe.
- Dream more than others think is practical.
- Expect more than others think is possible.

—Joellen Killion, senior advisor, Learning Forward, personal communication, April 19, 2018

You have to look at leadership through the eyes of the followers and you have to live the message. What I have learned is that people become motivated when you guide them to the source of their own power and when you make heroes out of employees who personify what you see in the organization.

—Anita Roddick, founder, The Body Shop (as cited in Institute of People Management, 2017)

Never doubt that a small group of thoughtful, concerned citizens can change the world. Indeed it is the only thing that ever has.

—Margaret Mead (as cited in Weekes, 2007, p. 16)

Figure 12.1: Leadership slogans.

A FINAL NOTE

From being introduced through a mutual colleague in 2015, to sharing the stage as keynote speakers at a 2016 Women in School Leadership conference in Brisbane, Australia, to agreeing to write this book together in 2017, we've thoroughly enjoyed our collaboration. What a delight we've found it to meld our collective expertise, research, strategies, and networks of colleagues and contributors with each other—but more important, with you. We hope this book stands as a vivid example of how working with other women creates a different and transformative space for learning. When women work with other women, great things can happen.

The contents of this book grew out of conversations we had with women at the Brisbane conference and in other leadership development forums that followed. The conference delegates talked of lack of support and lack of resources for undertaking the leadership journey—and our ideas began to germinate for a practical guide that would engage, encourage, and support current and future women leaders.

Before you leave these pages, answer the following questions, and reflect on whether you feel ready for your next step or you wish to again explore some reflection exercises.

- Do you feel grounded in the *why* of women in school leadership— why education needs women leaders, why gender still matters, and why understanding your strengths, core values, and priorities are key to success?

- Have you spotted any limiting beliefs and developed strategies for setting them aside?

- Are you aware of potential barriers in your system? Do you feel prepared to navigate them, most likely with the help of other women?

- Have you identified the *how*—how to thrive as the leader you are meant to become?

- Which practical tools for developing EQ—approaching hard conversations, improving communication, obtaining work-life balance, mentoring others or finding support, and more—will you be using?

- And finally, do you have a clear picture of who you might become and what you might influence if you pursue *power to*, as this ambition provides crucial motivation for the journey?

While we hope that each woman who navigates these pages finds the inspiration, information, and support she needs for her leadership journey, we have a bigger vision.

We want narratives of women in leadership to become commonplace.

We want a web search for *school leader* or *principal* to return a mix of positive images that feature people of all genders and ethnicities, various ages, and other markers of diversity, reflecting a culture that includes everyone.

We want young women and men to naturally ponder a career path to the top in education, whether they eventually feel called to step up to leadership or to remain in vital teaching roles—and for more men to see the latter as a natural, excellent choice.

When we open books, go to conferences, hear from researchers, and see political panels on television, we want powerful and empowering women from diverse areas in our global community to bombard us with their perspectives, their voices heard equally to men's. We want these events to happen so often that they wouldn't even warrant a remark; people would find them as expected and as natural as could be. No one would blink at finding nine women on the U.S. Supreme Court, an all-female conference speaker lineup, or a woman at the top of her field while also raising a family.

Take a moment to celebrate your identity as a leader—an intrinsic, unique part of you. You've worked hard to step into leadership and step up to the challenges ahead.

We wish you well in the leadership journey. And as you navigate your own complex course, may the helpful winds of collaboration, courage, purpose, and a passionate desire to help students grow, all be at your back.

REFERENCES AND RESOURCES

Abrams, J. (2009). *Having hard conversations.* Thousand Oaks, CA: Corwin Press.

Abrams, J. (2016). *Hard conversations unpacked: The whos, the whens, and the what-ifs.* Thousand Oaks, CA: Corwin Press.

Abrams, J. (in press). *Swimming in the deep end: Four foundational skills for leading successful school initiatives.* Bloomington, IN: Solution Tree Press.

Abramson, A. (2018, January 2). The number of women in the Senate will hit an all-time high of 22. *Fortune.* Accessed at http://fortune.com/2018/01/02/tina-smith-al-franken -women-senate on December 18, 2018.

Adamson, M. (2017). Postfeminism, neoliberalism and a 'successfully' balanced femininity in celebrity CEO autobiographies. *Gender, Work and Organization, 24*(3), 314–327.

Albert, E. (2017). The snarling girl: Notes on ambition. In R. Romm (Ed.), *Double bind: Women on ambition* (pp. 193–212). New York: Liveright.

Albright, M. (2016, February 12). Madeleine Albright: My undiplomatic moment. *New York Times.* Accessed at www.nytimes.com/2016/02/13/opinion/madeleine-albright-my -undiplomatic-moment.html on October 17, 2018.

Alcott, L. M. (2018). *Little women* (150th anniversary illustrated ed.). New York: Little, Brown. (Original work published 1868)

Always. (2014, June 26). *Always #LikeAGirl* [Video file]. Accessed at www.youtube.com /watch?v=XjJQBjWYDTs on October 23, 2018.

American Association of School Administrators. (2015). *The study of the American superintendent: 2015 mid-decade update summary of findings.* Accessed at www.aasa.org /uploadedFiles/Policy_and_Advocacy/files/AASA%20Mid-Decade%20Summary%20 of%20Findings.pdf on March 24, 2018.

American Association of School Administrators. (2017). *AASA women in school leadership initiative.* Accessed at www.aasa.org/WomenInSchoolLeadership.aspx on December 7, 2018.

The Atlantic. (2017, August 9). *'Why do men assume they're so great?'* [Video file]. Accessed at www.youtube.com/watch?v=aiC3mu5jWmY on October 28, 2018.

Australian Bureau of Statistics. (2018). *Schools, Australia, 2017*. Accessed at www.abs.gov.au /ausstats/abs@.nsf/mf/4221.0 on December 7, 2018.

Australian Human Rights Commission. (2009, May 11). *After 30 years, PML finally in: A great first step* [Press release]. Accessed at www.hreoc.gov.au/about/media/media _releases/2009/33_09.html on January 12, 2010.

Australian Institute for Teaching and School Leadership. (2016, August). *What do we know about early career teacher attrition rates in Australia?* Melbourne: Author. Accessed at www.aitsl.edu.au/docs/default-source/research-evidence/spotlight/spotlight---attrition .pdf?sfvrsn=40d1ed3c_0 on April 21, 2018.

Barsh, J., & Yee, L. (2012). *Unlocking the full potential of women at work*. New York: McKinsey. Accessed at www.mckinsey.com/business-functions/organization/our-insights /unlocking-the-full-potential-of-women-at-work on March 29, 2018.

Beard, M. (2017). *Women and power: A manifesto*. London: Profile.

Bennet, A. (2010). *The shadows of type: Psychological type through seven levels of development*. Whitchurch, England: Lulu.

Bennis, W. (2003). *On becoming a leader*. New York: Addison-Wesley.

Ben-Shahar, T. (2009). *The pursuit of perfect: How to stop chasing perfection and start living a richer, happier life*. New York: McGraw-Hill.

Berger, J. G. (2012). *Changing on the job: Developing leaders for a complex world*. Stanford, CA: Stanford University Press.

Berry, J. (2016). *Making the leap: Moving from deputy to head*. Williston, VT: Crown House.

Berry, J. (2017, January 24). Becoming a headteacher: Four things future leaders need to know. *Guardian*. Accessed at www.theguardian.com/teacher-network/2017/jan/24 /becoming-a-headteacher-what-future-leaders-need-to-know on February 15, 2018.

Bischel, R. (2016). *A fix for gender-bias in animal research could help humans*. Accessed at www.npr.org/sections/health-shots/2016/02/10/464697905/a-fix-for-gender-bias-in -animal-research-could-help-humans on January 10, 2019.

Blackmore, J. (2006). Redesigning schools and leadership: Exciting opportunities and entrenched barriers for women. *Redress, 15*(1), 2–9.

Brown, B. (2010, June). *Brené Brown: The power of vulnerability* [Video file]. Accessed at www .ted.com/talks/brene_brown_on_vulnerability on October 17, 2018.

Brown, B. (2015). *Rising strong: The reckoning. The rumble. The revolution*. New York: Spiegel & Grau.

Bryk, A. S., & Schneider, B. (2002). *Trust in schools: A core resource for improvement*. New York: Russell Sage Foundation.

Burke, T. (2018) *#MeToo Founder Tarana Burke on the rigorous work that still lies ahead*. Accessed at https://variety.com/2018/biz/features/tarana-burke-metoo-one-year -later-1202954797 on December 16, 2018.

Burnison, G. (2018). *The drive to achieve*. Accessed at www.kornferry.com/institute/the-drive -to-achieve on November 25, 2018.

Caldwell, F. (2018, February 11). *Meet the women who run Queensland*. Accessed at www.brisbanetimes.com.au/queensland-election-2017/meet-the-women-who-run -queensland-20180208-p4yzr2.html on December 19, 2018.

Carnevale, A. P., Smith, N., & Gulish, A. (2018, February 27). *Women can't win: Despite making educational gains and pursuing high-wage majors, women still earn less than men*. Accessed at https://cew.georgetown.edu/GenderWageGap on March 25, 2018.

Case, S. S., & Oetama-Paul, A. J. (2015). Brain biology and gendered discourse. *Applied Psychology, 64*(2), 338–378.

Case Western Reserve University. (2012, October 30). Empathy represses analytic thought, and vice versa: Brain physiology limits simultaneous use of both networks. *ScienceDaily*. Accessed at www.sciencedaily.com/releases/2012/10/121030161416.htm on November 12, 2012.

Catalyst. (2007). *The double-bind dilemma for women in leadership: Damned if you do, doomed if you don't*. New York: Author.

Center for Applications of Psychological Type. (2003). *Estimated frequencies of the types in the United States population*. Accessed at www.capt.org/products/examples/20025HO .pdf on January 10, 2019.

Chambers, N. (2018, January 21). *Thousands of kids were asked to draw their ideal job—with surprising results*. Accessed at www.weforum.org/agenda/2018/01/kids-draw-their-future -jobs-careers on October 1, 2018.

Chamine, S. (n.d.). *Positive intelligence*. Accessed at www.positiveintelligence.com on January 12, 2019.

Chiaet, J. (2013). Novel finding: Reading literary fiction improves empathy. *Scientific American*. Accessed at www.scientificamerican.com/article/novel-finding-reading -literary-fiction-improves-empathy on December 6, 2018.

Clance, P. R., & Imes, S. A. (1978). The impostor phenomenon in high achieving women: Dynamics and therapeutic intervention. *Psychotherapy Theory, Research and Practice, 15*(3), 241–247.

Cochran, E. S. (2018, February 22). What Madeleine Albright taught me about work-life balance. *Washington Post*. Accessed at www.washingtonpost.com/news/parenting/wp/2018/02/22/what-madeleine-albright-taught-me-about-career-choices on February 26, 2018.

Coghlan, C. (2018, April 10). This female founder aims to narrow gender pay gap by sharing salary data. *Forbes*. Accessed at www.forbes.com/sites/clairecoghlan/2018/04/10/this-female-founder-aims-to-narrow-gender-pay-gap-by-sharing-salary-data on April 10, 2018.

Coleman, M. (2007). Heading on up: Women and leadership [Transcript]. *Tomorrow's leaders today*. Nottingham, England: National College for Leadership of Schools and Children's Services.

Conzemius, A. E., & O'Neill, J. (2014). *The handbook for SMART school teams: Revitalizing best practices for collaboration* (2nd ed.). Bloomington, IN: Solution Tree Press.

Cooper, S. (2001). *King of shadows*. New York: Aladdin.

Covey, S. M. R. (2012). *The speed of trust: The one thing that changes everything*. New York: Simon & Schuster.

Coyle, D. (2018). *The culture code: The secrets of highly successful groups*. New York: Bantam Books.

Crowther, F., & Boyne, K. (2016). *Energising teaching: The power of your unique pedagogical gift*. Camberwell, Victoria, Australia: ACER Press.

Csikszentmihalyi, M. (1997). *Finding flow: The psychology of engagement with everyday life*. New York: Basic Books.

Cuddy, A. (2012, June). *Amy Cuddy: Your body language may shape who you are* [Video file]. Accessed at www.ted.com/talks/amy_cuddy_your_body_language_shapes_who_you_are?language=en on October 16, 2018.

Cuddy, A. (2015). *Presence: Bringing your boldest self to your biggest challenges* [Kindle ed.]. New York: Little, Brown.

Dennett, C. (2018, March 20). Be kinder to yourself. Research shows it could make you healthier. *Washington Post*. Accessed at www.washingtonpost.com/lifestyle/wellness/want-to-be-healthier-try-a-little-tenderness/2018/03/19/c079567a-262b-11e8-874b-d517e912f125_story.html?utm_term=.71d640e31b92 on March 26, 2018.

Denworth, L. (2017). Is there a "female" brain? *Scientific American, 317*(3), 38–43.

Department for Education. (2017, June 22). *School workforce in England: November 2016*. London: Author. Accessed at www.gov.uk/government/uploads/system/uploads/attachment_data/file/620825/SFR25_2017_MainText.pdf on March 24, 2018.

DeWitt, P. M. (2017). *Collaborative leadership: Six influences that matter most.* Thousand Oaks, CA: Corwin Press.

Dickinson, R. (2017, June 8). *The power to include: A practice based approach to advancing gender equality at the top* [Blog post]. Accessed at www.powertopersuade.org.au/blog /the-power-to-include-advancing-gender-equality-higher-education/7/6/2017 on April 15, 2018.

Duhigg, C. (2016). *Smarter, faster, better: The secrets of being productive in life and business.* New York: Random House.

Edge, K. (2014). A review of the empirical generations at work research: Implications for school leaders and future research. *School Leadership and Management, 34*(2), 136–155.

Edge, K., Descours, K., & Frayman, K. (2016). Generation X school leaders as agents of care: Leader and teacher perspectives from Toronto, New York City and London. In K. Leithwood, J. Sun, & K. Pollock (Eds.), *How school leaders contribute to student success: The four paths framework* (pp. 175–202). Cham, Switzerland: Springer.

Education and Employers. (2016, August 11). *Redraw the balance* [Video file]. Accessed at www.inspiringthefuture.org/redraw-the-balance on October 23, 2018.

Ehrich, L. C., & Kimber, M. (2015). The purpose and place of mentoring for women managers in organisations: An Australian perspective. In M. L. Connerley & J. Wu (Eds.), *Handbook of well-being of working women* (pp. 225–241). Dordrecht, Netherlands: Springer.

Erma Bombeck Quotes. (n.d.). *BrainyQuote.* Accessed at https://brainyquote.com/quotes /erma_bombeck_164141 on February 28, 2019.

Federal Communications Commission. (n.d.). *The dangers of distracted driving.* Accessed at www.fcc.gov/consumers/guides/dangers-texting-while-driving on November 25, 2018.

Filipovic, J. (2012). *Justice Ginsburg's distant dream of an all-female Supreme Court.* Accessed at www.theguardian.com/commentisfree/2012/nov/30/justice-ginsburg-all-female -supreme-court on November 19, 2018.

Foley, K. E. (2017, November 7). Female scientists make medicine better for all genders. *Quartz.* Accessed at https://qz.com/1121339/female-scientists-make-medicine-better -for-all-genders on November 7, 2017.

Ford, H. (1947). Filler item. *Reader's Digest, 51*(9), 64.

Franklin Covey. (2018). *Habit 7: Sharpen the saw.* Accessed at www.franklincovey.com/the -7-habits/habit-7.html on December 28, 2018.

Fraser, A. (2011). *The third space: Using life's little transitions to find balance and happiness.* North Sydney, New South Wales, Australia: Penguin Random House.

Fraser, A. (2012, July 9). *Dr. Adam Fraser explains the third space* [Video file]. Accessed at www.youtube.com/watch?v=dpk_dssZXqs on September 4, 2018.

Freeman, H. (2013, July 3). Ellen Page: 'Why are people so reluctant to say they're feminists?' *Guardian*. Accessed at www.theguardian.com/film/2013/jul/03/ellen-page-interview -the-east on April 21, 2018.

Fullan, M. (2011, April). *Choosing the wrong drivers for whole system reform* (Seminar Series Paper No. 204). East Melbourne, Victoria, Australia: Centre for Strategic Education.

Galliott, K. (2018, March). QBusiness: View from the top. *Qantas Spirit of Australia Magazine*, 105–107.

Gallup. (2016). *2016 Gallup student poll snapshot report*. Accessed at http://news.gallup.com /reports/210995/6.aspx on March 21, 2018.

Garrett-Staib, J., & Burkman, A. (2015). Leadership practices of Texas female superintendents. *Advancing Women in Leadership, 35*, 160–165.

Gerzema, J., & D'Antonio, M. (2013). *The Athena doctrine: How women (and the men who think like them) will rule the future*. San Francisco: Jossey-Bass.

Gilbert, E. (2015). Review of the book *Work strife balance*, by M. Freedman. Accessed at www.panmacmillan.com.au/9781760553241 on January 15, 2019.

Gino, F., Wilmuth, C. A., & Brooks, A. W. (2015). Compared to men, women view professional advancement as equally attainable, but less desirable. *Proceedings of the National Academy of Sciences, 112*(40), 12354–12359. Accessed at www.pnas.org /content/112/40/12354.full.pdf on August 31, 2018.

Glaser, J. E. (2014). *Conversational intelligence: How great leaders build trust and get extraordinary results*. New York: Bibliomotion.

Goldstein, E. (2013, May 29). *Stressing out? S.T.O.P.* Accessed at www.mindful.org/stressing -out-stop on April 23, 2018.

Goleman, D. (1998). *Working with emotional intelligence*. New York: Bantam Books.

Goman, C. K. (2016, March 31). Is your communication style dictated by your gender? *Forbes*. Accessed at www.forbes.com/sites/carolkinseygoman/2016/03/31/is-your -communication-style-dictated-by-your-gender on February 12, 2018.

Gordon, S. (2018) Julia Gillard on resilience after misogyny. *Financial Times*. Accessed at www.ft.com/content/6c08ca36-7b70-11e8-af48-190d103e32a4 on January 13, 2019.

Gray, J. (1993). *Men are from Mars, women are from Venus: A practical guide for improving communication and getting what you want in your relationships*. New York: HarperCollins.

Grogan, M., & Shakeshaft, C. (2011). *Women and educational leadership*. San Francisco: Jossey-Bass.

Guillen, L. (2018, March 26). Is the confidence gap between men and women a myth? *Harvard Business Review.* Accessed at https://hbr.org/2018/03/is-the-confidence-gap -between-men-and-women-a-myth on April 21, 2018.

Gujral, H. K., Gupta, A., & Aneja, M. (2012). Emotional intelligence: An important determinant of well-being and employee behaviour: A study on young professionals. *International Journal of Management, IT and Engineering, 2*(8), 322–339.

Hartocollis, A., & Alcindor, Y. (2017). Women's March highlights as huge crowds protest Trump: "We're not going away." *New York Times.* Accessed at www.nytimes .com/2017/01/21/us/womens-march.html on December 7, 2018.

Heick, T. (2017, December 10). *Want to change education? You'd better have these 6 things.* Accessed at www.teachthought.com/the-future-of-learning/seem-like-great-ideas -education on August 31, 2018.

Helal, M., & Coelli, M. (2016, June). *How principals affect schools* (Melbourne Institute Working Paper No. 18/16). Melbourne, Victoria, Australia: Melbourne Institute of Applied Economic and Social Research, University of Melbourne. Accessed at https:// melbourneinstitute.unimelb.edu.au/downloads/working-paper-series/wp2016n18.pdf on August 31, 2018.

Helgesen, S., & Goldsmith, M. (2018). *How women rise: Break the 12 habits holding you back from your next raise, promotion, or job.* New York: Hachette Books.

Helgesen, S., & Johnson, J. (2010). *The female vision: Women's real power at work.* Oakland, CA: Berrett-Koehler.

Hoffman, E. (Ed.). (2003). *The wisdom of Carl Jung.* New York: Citadel Press.

Holder, M. (2017, October 11). *7 key findings from the OECD report: The pursuit of gender equality—An uphill battle* [Blog post]. Accessed at www.criterionconferences.com/blog /professional-development/7-key-findings-oecd-report-pursuit-gender-equality-uphill -battle on September 3, 2018.

Holland, J. (2017). Ambitchin'. In R. Romm (Ed.), *Double bind: Women on ambition* (pp. 213–224). New York: Liveright.

Huffpost. (2012). *Global Ambassadors Program: Empowering women leaders around the globe.* Accessed at www.huffpost.com/entry/global-ambassadors-program_b_1681201 on February 26, 2019.

HuffPost. (2015a, December 21). *48 things men hear in a lifetime (that are bad for everyone)* [Video file]. Accessed at www.youtube.com/watch?v=jk8YmtEJvDc on October 23, 2018.

HuffPost. (2015b, December 9). *48 things women hear in a lifetime (that men just don't)* [Video file]. Accessed at www.youtube.com/watch?v=9yMFw_vWboE on October 23, 2018

Hughes, V. (2013). *The orphanage problem.* Accessed at www.nationalgeographic.com/science /phenomena/2013/07/31/the-orphanage-problem on January 10, 2019.

Hunt, D. T. (2013). *Wisdom's way: The art of the true leader.* Kaneohe, HI: Elan Enterprises.

Institute of People Management. (2017, May 23). *What does leadership mean to you? 12 quotes from those who lead.* Accessed at www.ipm.co.za/2017/05/23/what-does-leadership -mean-to-you on April 10, 2018.

Isaac, A. (2016, March 10). Julia Gillard: "The world is talking about girls' education." *Guardian.* Accessed at www.theguardian.com/global-development-professionals -network/2016/mar/10/julia-gillard-the-world-is-talking-about-girls-education on April 12, 2018.

Jack, A. I., Dawson, A. J., Begany, K. L., Leckie. R. L., Barry, K. P., Ciccia, A. H., et al. (2013). MRI reveals reciprocal inhibition between social and physical cognitive domains. *Neuroimage, 66,* 385–401.

Jackson, D. (2017, November 4). *School leadership without fear (part 1)* [Blog post]. Accessed at https://davidjackson7.wordpress.com/2017/11/04/school-leadership-without-fear -part-1 on August 31, 2018.

Joel, D., & McCarthy, M. M. (2017). Incorporating sex as a biological variable in neuropsychiatric research: Where are we now and where should we be? *Neuropsychopharmacology, 42*(2), 379–385.

Johnson, B. (2016). *Looking at this election through a polarity lens.* Unpublished article.

Jordan, M. (2018, November 8). Record number of women heading to Congress. *Washington Post.* Accessed at www.washingtonpost.com/politics/record-number-of-women-appear -headed-for-congress/2018/11/06/76a9e60a-e1eb-11e8-8f5f-a55347f48762_story.html on December 18, 2018.

Jung, C. G. (1971). Psychological types. In G. Adler & R. F. C. Hull (Eds.), *Collected works of C.G. Jung* (Vol. 6). Princeton, N.J.: Princeton University Press. (Original work published 1921)

Kanyoro, M. (2017, November). *Musimbi Kanyoro: To solve the world's biggest problems, invest in women and girls* [Video file]. Accessed at www.ted.com/talks/musimbi_kanyoro_to _solve_the_world_s_biggest_problems_invest_in_women_and_girls on October 17, 2018.

Kay, K., & Shipman, C. (2014, May). The confidence gap. *Atlantic.* Accessed at www .theatlantic.com/magazine/archive/2014/05/the-confidence-gap/359815 on January 31, 2018.

Kegan, R. (1994). *In over our heads: The mental demands of modern life.* Cambridge, MA: Harvard University Press.

Kegan, R., & Lahey, L. L. (2009). *Immunity to change: How to overcome it and unlock the potential in yourself and your organization.* Cambridge, MA: Harvard Business Review Press.

Kelly, G. (2017). *Live, lead, learn: My stories of life and leadership.* Melbourne, Victoria, Australia: Penguin Random House.

Kise, J. A. G. (2014). *Unleashing the positive power of differences: Polarity thinking in our schools.* Thousand Oaks, CA: Corwin Press.

Kise, J. A. G. (in press). *Holistic leadership, thriving schools: Twelve lessons to balance priorities and serve the whole student.* Bloomington, IN: Solution Tree Press.

Korn Ferry. (2016, March 31). *Korn Ferry Hay Group global study finds employee engagement at critically low levels.* Accessed at www.kornferry.com/press/korn-ferry-hay-group-global -study-finds-employee-engagement-at-critically-low-levels on April 21, 2018.

Kouzes, J. M., & Posner, B. Z. (2010). *The truth about leadership: The no-fads, heart-of-the-matter facts you need to know.* San Francisco: Jossey-Bass.

Krawcheck, S. (2017). *Own it: The power of women at work.* New York: Crown Business.

Krivkovich, A., Robinson, K., Starikova, I., Valentino, R., & Yee, L. (2017, October). *Women in the workplace 2017.* New York: McKinsey. Accessed at www.mckinsey.com/featured -insights/gender-equality/women-in-the-workplace-2017 on September 3, 2018.

Lane, K., Larmaraud, A., & Yueh, E. (2017, January). Finding hidden leaders. *McKinsey Quarterly.* Accessed at www.mckinsey.com/business-functions/organization/our-insights /finding-hidden-leaders on March 29, 2018.

Leegant, J. (2017). Ambition: The Cliffie notes. In R. Romm (Ed.), *Double bind: Women on ambition* (pp. 240–252). New York: Liveright.

Leithwood, K. (2012). *The Ontario leadership framework with a discussion of the research foundations.* Toronto: Institute for Educational Leadership.

Leithwood, K. (2017). The Ontario leadership framework: Successful school leadership practices and personal leadership resources. In K. Leithwood, J. Sun, & K. Pollock (Eds.), *How school leaders contribute to student success: The Four Paths framework* (Studies in Educational Leadership series, Vol. 23, pp. 31–43). Cham, Switzerland: Springer.

Leithwood, K., Louis, K. S., Anderson, S., & Wahlstrom, K. (2004). *How leadership influences student learning.* Minneapolis, MN: Center for Applied Research and Educational Improvement, University of Minnesota.

Leithwood, K., & Riehl, C. (2005). What do we already know about educational leadership? In W. A. Firestone & C. Riehl (Eds.), *A new agenda for research in educational leadership* (pp. 12–27). New York: Teachers College Press.

Lieberman, M. D. (2013). *Social: Why our brains are wired to connect.* New York: Crown.

Loehr, J., & Schwartz, T. (2003). *The power of full engagement: Managing energy, not time, is the key to high performance and personal renewal.* New York: Free Press.

Lopez, N. (2015, November). *Nadia Lopez: Why open a school? To close a prison* [Video file]. Accessed at www.ted.com/talks/nadia_lopez_why_open_a_school_to_close_a_prison on October 17, 2018.

Louis, K. S., Leithwood, K., Wahlstrom, K., & Anderson, S. E. (2010, July). *Learning from leadership: Investigating the links to improved student learning* (Final report of research to the Wallace Foundation). St. Paul, MN: Center for Applied Research and Educational Improvement, University of Minnesota.

Lyman, L. L., Strachan, J., & Lazaridou, A. (2012). *Shaping social justice leadership: Insights of women educators worldwide.* Plymouth, United Kingdom: Rowman & Littlefield Education.

Mansfield, K. C., Welton, A., Lee, P.-L., & Young, M. D. (2010). The lived experiences of female educational leadership doctoral students. *Journal of Educational Administration, 48*(6), 727–740.

Mark, G., Gudith, D., & Klocke, U. (2008). The cost of interrupted work: More speed and stress. In M. Czerwinski, A. Lund, & D. Tan (Eds.), *CHI '08 proceedings of the SIGCHI Conference on Human Factors in Computing Systems* (pp. 107–110). New York: Association for Computing Machinery.

Markow, D., & Pieters, A. (2012, March). *The MetLife survey of the American teacher: Teachers, parents and the economy.* New York: MetLife. Accessed at www.metlife.com/assets/cao/contributions/foundation/american-teacher/MetLife-Teacher-Survey-2011.pdf on August 31, 2018.

Maslow, A. H. (1943). A theory of human motivation. *Psychological Review, 50*(4), 370–396.

Maunder, M., & Warren, E. (2008). *Is there still a glass ceiling?* West Sussex, England: National Association of Headteachers.

Maxwell, J. C. (2014). *The 15 invaluable laws of growth: Live them and reach your potential.* New York: Little, Brown.

Maxwell, J. C. (2018). *Developing the leader within you 2.0.* San Francisco: HarperCollins Leadership.

McGonigal, K. (2012). *The willpower instinct: How self-control works, why it matters, and what you can do to get more of it.* New York: Penguin.

McGonigal, K. (2015). *The upside of stress: Why stress is good for you, and how to get good at it.* New York: Penguin Random House.

McKenzie, P., Weldon, P., Rowley, G., Murphy, M., & McMillan, J. (2014, April). *Staff in Australia's schools 2013: Main report on the survey*. Canberra, Australian Capital Territory: Australian Council for Educational Research.

McKeown, G. (2014). *Essentialism: The disciplined pursuit of less*. New York: Random House.

Mears, B. (2009, June 16). Justice Ginsburg ready to welcome Sotomayor. *CNN Politics*. Accessed at www.cnn.com/2009/POLITICS/06/16/sotomayor.ginsburg/index.html on April 18, 2018.

Medina, J. (2014). *Brain rules: 12 principles for surviving and thriving at work, home, and school* (Updated and expanded ed.). Seattle, WA: Pear Press.

Miller, D. (2009). *The book whisperer: Awakening the inner reader in every child* [Kindle ed.]. San Francisco: Wiley.

Miller, G. A. (1994). The magical number seven, plus or minus two: Some limits on our capacity for processing information. *Psychological Review, 101*(2), 343–52.

Miller, J. (2018). Is it time to rebrand yourself at work? *Be Leaderly*. Accessed at https://beleaderly.com/time-rebrand-yourself-work on September 3, 2018.

MindMatters. (2016). *School staff: Your wellbeing matters!* Accessed at www.mindmatters.edu.au/about-mindmatters/news/article/2016/10/04/school-staff---your-wellbeing-matters on December 7, 2018.

Moir, S., Hattie, J., & Jansen, C. (2014). Teacher perspectives of 'effective' leadership in schools. *Australian Educational Leader, 36*(4), 36–40.

Mulford, B. (2008). *The leadership challenge: Improving learning in schools*. Camberwell, Victoria: Australian Council for Educational Research.

Mullainathan, S., & Shafir, E. (2013). *Scarcity: The new science of having less and how it defines our lives*. New York: Holt.

Myers, I. B., McCaulley, M., Quenk, N., & Hammer, A. (1998). *MBTI® manual: A guide to the development and use of the Myers-Briggs Type Indicator®* (3rd ed.). Palo Alto, CA: Consulting Psychologists Press.

Nardi, D. (2011). *Neuroscience of personality: Brain savvy insights for all types of people*. Los Angeles: Radiance House.

National Association for Gifted Children. (n.d.). *Resources for administrators*. Accessed at www.nagc.org/resources-publications/resources-administrators on March 6, 2017.

National Center for Education Evaluation and Regional Assistance. (2008). *Reading first impact study final report*. Accessed at https://ies.ed.gov/ncee/pubs/20094038/index.asp on December 9, 2018.

National Center for Education Statistics. (n.d.a). *Fast facts*. Accessed at https://nces.ed.gov /fastfacts/display.asp?id=84 on December 7, 2018.

National Center for Education Statistics. (n.d.b). *NAEP National Indian Education Study: Summary of results.* Accessed at http://nces.ed.gov/nationsreportcard/nies/nies_2011 /national_sum.aspx on September 3, 2018.

National Center for Education Statistics. (n.d.c). *National assessment of educational progress.* Accessed at https://nces.ed.gov/nationsreportcard on December 21, 2018.

National Center for Education Statistics. (2016). *Trends in public and private school principal demographics and qualifications: 1987–88 to 2011–12.* Accessed at https://nces.ed.gov /pubs2016/2016189.pdf on November 19, 2018.

National Center for Education Statistics. (2017). *Highlights from the condition of education 2017.* Accessed at https://nces.ed.gov/pubs2017/2017144_Highlights.pdf on March 21, 2018.

National College for Leadership of Schools and Children's Services. (2010). *10 strong claims about successful school leadership.* Nottingham, England: Author.

National Sleep Foundation. (2018). *Napping.* Accessed at www.sleepfoundation.org/sleep -topics/napping on December 9, 2018.

The Nation's Report Card. (2018). *2015 mathematics and reading at grade 12.* Accessed at www.nationsreportcard.gov/reading_math_g12_2015 on November 19, 2018.

Obama, M. (2012, September 4). *Michelle Obama's convention speech* [Transcript]. Accessed at www.npr.org/2012/09/04/160578836/transcript-michelle-obamas-convention-speech on August 9, 2018.

Omotosho, K. (2017, March 20). *Adichie's 10 new quotes on feminism that will inspire you.* Accessed at www.pulse.ng/books/chimamanda-ngozi-adichies-10-new-quotes-on -feminism-that-will-inspire-you-id6397309.html on July 7, 2018.

Organisation for Economic Co-operation and Development. (2012). *Closing the gender gap: Act now.* Paris: Author.

Organisation for Economic Co-operation and Development. (2017). *The pursuit of gender equality: An uphill battle.* Paris: Author. Accessed at http://dx.doi.org/10.1787 /9789264281318-en on September 3, 2018.

Owen, H. (2008). *Open space technology: A user's guide* (3rd ed.). San Francisco: Berrett-Koehler.

OWN. (2016, March 20). *Daniel Goleman on the three kinds of empathy* [Video file]. Accessed at www.youtube.com/watch?v=2PSfT8GLB4M on April 4, 2018.

Palmieri, J. (2018). *Dear Madam President: An open letter to the women who will run the world.* New York: Grand Central.

Pan Macmillan Australia. (2015). *Work strife balance: Mia Freedman.* Accessed at www .panmacmillan.com.au/9781925479935 on April 10, 2018.

Pang, A. S.-K. (2016). *Rest: Why you get more done when you work less.* New York: Basic Books.

Patterson, K., Grenny, J., McMillan, R., & Switzler, A. (2005). *Crucial confrontations: Tools for resolving broken promises, violated expectations, and bad behavior.* New York: McGraw-Hill.

Patterson, K., Grenny, J., McMillan, R., & Switzler, A. (2012). *Crucial conversations: Tools for talking when stakes are high* (2nd ed.). New York: McGraw-Hill.

Pearl, D. (2017, March 15). 'Prosecco and cupcakes with chambers crew': Inside the notorious RBG's 84th birthday celebration. *People.* Accessed at https://people.com /politics/happy-birthday-ruth-bader-ginsburg-see-how-fans-wished-the-notorious-rbg -a-happy-84th-and-read-her-best-quotes on March 1, 2019.

Pfafman, T. M., & McEwan, B. (2014). Polite women at work: Negotiating professional identity through strategic assertiveness. *Women's Studies in Communication, 37*(2), 202–219.

Pink, D. H. (2010). *Drive: The surprising truth about what motivates us.* New York: Riverhead Books.

Plan International. (2017, October). *The dream gap: Australian girls' views on gender equality.* Southbank, Victoria, Australia: Author. Accessed at https://isuu.com/planaustralia/docs /the_dream_gap_final_small/1?ff&e=1049359/54133461 on February 27, 2019.

Pollack, K. (2017). *Healthy schools, healthy principals.* EdCan Network, Canada. Accessed at www.edcan.ca/articles/healthy-principals-healthy-schools on December 14, 2018.

Ratey, J. J. (2013). *Spark: The revolutionary new science of exercise and the brain.* New York: Little, Brown.

Riley, P. (2017). *Principal health and wellbeing survey.* Victoria, Australia: Institute for Positive Psychology and Education.

Rizvi, J. (2017). *Not just lucky: Why women do the work but don't take the credit.* North Sydney, New South Wales, Australia: Penguin Random House.

Robinson, K. K., Shakeshaft, C., Newcomb, W. S., & Grogan, M. (2017). Necessary but not sufficient: The continuing inequality between men and women in educational leadership—Findings from the AASA mid-decade survey. *Frontiers in Education, 2*(12), 1–12.

Rock, D. (2009). *Your brain at work: Strategies for overcoming distraction, regaining focus, and working smarter all day long.* New York: HarperCollins.

Romm, R. (Ed.). (2017). *Double bind: Women on ambition.* New York: Liveright.

Roosevelt, E. (n.d.). *Famous leadership quotes.* Accessed at https://leadership-central.com/famous-leadership-quotes.html on December 16, 2018.

Sandberg, S. (2013). *Lean in: Women, work, and the will to lead.* New York: Knopf.

Sandberg, S. (2016, October 18). Sheryl Sandberg on the secret career weapon you're not using. *Cosmopolitan.* Accessed at www.cosmopolitan.com/career/a6109592/sheryl-sandberg-secret-career-weapon on October 16, 2018.

Schaubhut, N. A., & Thompson, R. C. (2008). *MBTI® type tables for occupations.* Mountain View, CA: Consulting Psychologists Press.

Schein, V. (2007). Women in management: Reflections and projections. *Women in Management Review, 22*(1), 6–18.

Schwartz, T. (2010). *The way we're working isn't working: The four forgotten needs that energize great performance.* New York: Free Press.

Shedden, M. (2018, March 7). *Exclusive: 'I never forget those who stand by me with things get tough.'* Accessed at www.whimn.com.au/talk/people/i-never-forget-those-who-stand-by-me-when-things-get-tough/news-story/0be6a470129a0673ae96ba4ea5cfeecb on March 18, 2018.

Sinek, S. (2009, September). *Simon Sinek: How great leaders inspire action* [Video file]. Accessed at www.ted.com/talks/simon_sinek_how_great_leaders_inspire_action on October 17, 2018.

Skakon, J., Nielsen, K., Borg, V., & Guzman, J. (2010). Are leaders' well-being, behaviours and style associated with the affective well-being of their employees? A systematic review of three decades of research. *Work and Stress, 24*(2), 107–139.

Smart, A. (2013). *Auto-pilot: The art and science of doing nothing.* New York: OR Books.

Sparks, S. D. (2012). New literacy research infuses Common Core. *Education Week Spotlight on Literacy and the Common Core, 32*(12), 6–9.

Spiller, K. (2017). *Women in leadership* (National chair's report). Canberra, Australian Capital Territory: Association of Heads of Independent Schools of Australia.

Stoll, L., Harris, A., & Handscomb, G. (2012, Autumn). *Great professional development which leads to great pedagogy: Nine claims from research.* Nottingham, England: National College for School Leadership.

Subban, P. (2016). *Australian students are becoming increasingly disengaged at school, here's why.* Accessed at https://theconversation.com/australian-students-are-becoming-increasingly-disengaged-at-school-heres-why-51570 on April 17, 2018.

Suliman, A. (2017, October 9). Going to school? Unlikely if you're a girl in South Sudan, report says. *Reuters*. Accessed at www.reuters.com/article/us-women-education/going -to-school-unlikely-if-youre-a-girl-in-south-sudan-report-says-idUSKBN1CF01S on December 12, 2017.

Sun, J., & Leithwood, K. (2015). Leadership effects on student learning mediated by teacher emotions. *Societies, 5*(3), 566–582.

Swan, P. (2017, March 6). Why women make the best stock traders. *The Conversation*. Accessed at https://theconversation.com/why-women-make-the-best-stock-traders -74081 on March 21, 2018.

Sytch, M. (2015). *Limitations of SMART goals: Inspiring and motivating individuals* [Video file]. Accessed at www.coursera.org/lecture/motivate-people-teams/02-04-limitations-of -smart-goals-2g69s on September 3, 2018.

Tarica, E. (2010, September 13). Women and the matter of principals. *Sydney Morning Herald*. Accessed at www.smh.com.au/education/women-and-the-matter-of-principals -20100910-154tq.html on October 12, 2017.

TED. (n.d.). *TED Talks by strong women leaders* [Video playlist]. Accessed at www.ted.com /playlists/486/ted_talks_by_strong_women_lead on October 17, 2018.

The Telegraph. (2017, January 26). *'You can't be brave if you've only had wonderful things happen to you': Mary Tyler Moore's best quotes* [Photo gallery]. Accessed at www.telegraph .co.uk/women/life/cant-brave-had-wonderful-things-happen-mary-tyler-moores-best /take-chances-make-mistakes-grow-pain-nourishes-courage-have on April 15, 2018.

Terkel, A. (2017, March 24). Room full of men decides fate of women's health care. *HuffPost*. Accessed at www.huffingtonpost.com.au/entry/room-men-maternity-coverage _us_58d416e6e4b02d33b749b713 on December 19, 2018.

Thorpe, A. (2016). *Women and leadership: A thematic review of literature from the education sector*. London: Susanna Wesley Foundation.

Traister, R. (2018). *Good and mad: The revolutionary power of women's anger.* [Kindle iOS version]. New York: Simon & Schuster.

United Nations. (2013, July 12). *Malala Yousafzai addresses United Nations youth assembly* [Video file]. Accessed at www.youtube.com/watch?v=3rNhZu3ttIU on August 31, 2018.

University of Washington Center for Educational Leadership. (n.d.). *4DTM Instructional leadership growth continuum*. Accessed at http://info.k-12leadership.org/4d-instructional -leadership-growth-continuum?_ga=2.135100341.501272525.1544763441 -1417192525.1534994084 on December 14, 2018.

Unterhalter, E. (2007). *Gender, schooling and global social justice*. London: Routledge.

U.S. Bureau of Labor Statistics. (2015). *American time use survey: Charts by topic—Household activities* [Chart]. Accessed at www.bls.gov/TUS/CHARTS/HOUSEHOLD.HTM on October 13, 2017.

Useem, J. (2017). Power causes brain damage. *Atlantic.* Accessed at www.theatlantic.com /magazine/archive/2017/07/power-causes-brain-damage/528711 on February 10, 2018.

Vartanian, O., Bristol, A. S., & Kaufman, J. (2013). *Neuroscience of creativity.* Boston: MIT Press.

Vukovic, R. (2016, March 31). *Why female leaders remain an underutilised national resource.* Accessed at https://au.educationhq.com/news/34352/why-female-leaders-remain-an -underutilised-national-resource on November 14, 2017.

Walker, M. (2017). *Why we sleep: Unlocking the power of sleep and dreams.* New York: Scribner.

Warrell, M. (2015, December 5). *Prepare your kids for success: Teach them how to fail* [Blog post]. Accessed at www.forbes.com/sites/margiewarrell/2015/12/05/prepare-your-kids -for-success-teach-them-how-to-fail on December 27, 2018.

Warrell, M. (2016, January 20). *For women to rise, we must close 'the confidence gap'* [Blog post]. Accessed at https://margiewarrell.com/forbes-columns/women-rise-must-close -confidence-gap on February 15, 2018.

Warrell, M. (2017, March 20). *Do you need to dial up your courage?* [Blog post]. Accessed at www.linkedin.com/pulse/do-you-need-dial-up-your-courage-margie-warrell on November 15, 2017.

Warrell, M. (2018a, April 6). *Live bravely* [Enewsletter]. Singapore: Author.

Warrell, M. (2018b, April 3). *Why women need to stop talking themselves down* [Blog post]. Accessed at www.forbes.com/sites/margiewarrell/2018/04/03/women-how-to-use -power-language-to-stand-out-grow-presence-and-get-ahead on April 20, 2018.

Watkins, M. D. (2013). *The first 90 days: Proven strategies for getting up to speed faster and smarter.* Boston: Harvard Business Review Press.

Watterston, B. (2010). Why a focus on women? In J. Watterston & B. Watterston (Eds.), *Women in school leadership: Journeys to success* (pp. 11–29). Melbourne, Victoria, Australia: Centre for Strategic Education.

Watterston, B. (2015, March). *Environmental scan: Principal preparation programs.* Melbourne, Victoria: Australian Institute for Teaching and School Leadership.

Watterston, J. (2017, November 20). *Winning the position you deserve.* Presentation for the Women in School Leadership Program, Queensland Educational Leadership Institute, Brisbane, Queensland, Australia.

Watterston, J. (2018). *Winning the position you deserve: Creating and gaining the competitive edge.* Unpublished manuscript.

Watterston, J., & Watterston, B. (Eds.). (2010). *Women in school leadership: Journeys to success.* Melbourne, Victoria, Australia: Centre for Strategic Education.

Weber, C. (2013). *Conversational capacity: The secret to building successful teams that perform when the pressure is on.* New York: McGraw-Hill.

Weekes, K. (2007). *"Women know everything!" 3,241 quips, quotes, and brilliant remarks.* Philadelphia: Quirk Books.

Weite, A. K. (2013). *Leadership and emotional intelligence: The keys to driving ROI and organizational performance.* White River Junction, VT: Human Capital Institute.

West-Burnham, J. (2011). *Leading through trust.* Accessed at www.johnwest-burnham.co.uk /index.php/leading-through-trust on September 3, 2018.

Wheatley, M. J. (2006). *Leadership and the new science: Discovering order in a chaotic world* (3rd ed.). San Francisco: Berrett-Koehler.

Wilcox, G. (n.d.). *The feeling wheel.* Accessed at https://med.emory.edu/excel/documents /Feeling%20Wheel.pdf on November 30, 2018.

Winfrey, O. (2014). *What I know for sure.* New York: Flatiron Books.

Wise, P. (2018, March 19). *Are women leaders different from men?* Accessed at www.linkedin .com/pulse/women-leaders-different-from-men-phyllis-wise on March 23, 2018.

Wise, R. A. (1996). Addictive drugs and brain stimulation reward. *Annual Review of Neuroscience, 19,* 319–40.

Wolf, M. (2018). *Reader, come home: The reading brain in the digital world.* New York: Harper.

Women and Leadership Australia. (2018). *About.* Accessed at www.wla.edu.au/about.html on December 16, 2018.

Women Leading in Education, South West Network. (2018). *Home.* Accessed at www .womenleadingineducation-sw.org.uk on December 16, 2018.

WomenEd. (2018). *#WomenEd.* Accessed at www.womened.org on December 16, 2018.

Zak, P. J. (2017). *Trust factor: The science of creating high-performance companies.* New York: Amacom.

Zeisler, A. (2016). *We were feminists once: From riot grrrl to CoverGirl®, the buying and selling of a political movement.* New York: PublicAffairs.

Zomorodi, M. (2017). *Bored and brilliant: How spacing out can unlock your most productive and creative self.* New York: St. Martin's Press.

INDEX

Holistic Leadership, Thriving Schools
Jane A. G. Kise
Build a school where students flourish academically while getting their needs met socially, physically, and emotionally. With this practical guide, school leaders will discover a toolkit of strategies for navigating competing priorities and uniting their school communities around one common purpose: supporting the whole child.
BKF821

Swimming in the Deep End
Jennifer Abrams
Acquire the knowledge and resources necessary to lead successful change initiatives in schools. In *Swimming in the Deep End*, author Jennifer Abrams dives deep into the four foundational skills required of effective leadership and provides ample guidance for cultivating each.
BKF830

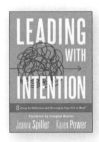

Leading With Intention
Jeanne Spiller and Karen Power
Designed as a guide and reflective tool, *Leading With Intention* will help focus your invaluable everyday work as a school leader. Discover actionable steps for creating a highly effective school community in which staff collaborate, make evidence-based decisions, and believe students are the top priority.
BKF829

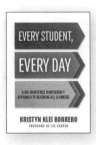

Every Student, Every Day
Kristyn Klei Borrero
No-Nonsense Nurturers® are educators who build life-altering relationships with students and hold themselves and their students accountable for achievement. *Every Student, Every Day* details the lessons, mindsets, beliefs, and strategies these high-performing teachers use daily to support the needs of every student.
BKF843

Solution Tree | Press
a division of
Solution Tree

Visit SolutionTree.com or call 800.733.6786 to order.

Wait! Your professional development journey doesn't have to end with the last pages of this book.

We realize improving student learning doesn't happen overnight. And your school or district shouldn't be left to puzzle out all the details of this process alone.

No matter where you are on the journey, we're committed to helping you get to the next stage.

Take advantage of everything from **custom workshops** to **keynote presentations** and **interactive web and video conferencing**. We can even help you develop an action plan tailored to fit your specific needs.

Let's get the conversation started.

Call 888.763.9045 today.

SolutionTree.com